Ulster and Scotland: history, language and identity, 1600–2000

ULSTER AND SCOTLAND

General editors
Professor John Wilson and Dr William Kelly
A series published by Four Courts Press
in association with the
Institute of Ulster Scots Studies
University of Ulster

1   William Kelly & John R. Young (eds), *Ulster and Scotland, 1600–2000:
history language and identity*

Ulster and Scotland, 1600–2000

History, Language and Identity

William Kelly & John R. Young

EDITORS

FOUR COURTS PRESS

Set in 10.5 on 12.5 Ehrhardt for
FOUR COURTS PRESS LTD
7 Malpas Street, Dublin 8, Ireland
e-mail: info@four-courts-press.ie
http://www.four-courts-press.ie
and in North America
FOUR COURTS PRESS
c/o ISBS, 920 N.E. 58th Avenue, Suite 300, Portland, OR 97213.

ISBN 1–85182–808–7

Printed in Ireland by
ßetaprint Ltd, Dublin.

Contents

Preface

This book is the first in a series of publications on Ulster and Scotland. The aim of this new series is to promote quality research in the field of studies related to the history, heritage and culture of Ulster and Scotland and specifically the role of the Scots in Ulster from the Early Modern period onwards. There is a particular research emphasis on those people who became known as the Ulster Scots and on their diaspora.

The series is specifically designed to be open-ended in terms of disciplinary focus. It does not proclaim a new subject but rather hopes to harness the intellectual energies of scholars in different disciplines in a co-operative engagement, sharing expertise and learning in the promotion of research of the highest quality.

This first volume in the series arose from a conference at the University of Ulster's Magee Campus on the theme of 'Common Ground, Ulster and Scotland: History, Language and Identity, 1600–2000'. The conference was organized to provide a forum for scholars to examine the often fraught, but always intriguing, relationship between Ulster and Scotland from the Early Modern period to the present day. The book draws on the most recent research to locate the study of the comparative history of Ulster and Scotland within modern historiography. By bringing together a diverse range of distinguished historians and commentators from Britain and Ireland, the United States and New Zealand, this volume contributes significantly to our understanding of historical and contemporary links between Ulster and Scotland.

By examining a shared history and heritage it also contributes to the contemporary debate on issues of diversity, language and identity, regionally and nationally. By including studies on the impact of the Ulster Scots diaspora it underlines the relevance of the shared history of Ulster and Scotland internationally.

The book is in three sections. In section one, History and Heritage, John Young provides an essential context by outlining the tortured politics of Scottish-Irish relations in the Early Modern period. Graham Walker elaborates on these relationships by analyzing how the relationships between Ulster and Scotland have often been used politically to foster a sense of a British, as opposed to Irish, identity in Ulster. In the final article of this section Máirtín Ó Catháin reverses the perspective and by considering political linkages between radical republican groups in Derry and Glasgow in the nineteenth and twentieth centuries.

Section two explores an issue that many would argue has only recently come into historiographical prominence – emigration and a 'Scottish empire' and the role of Scots from Ulster in that diaspora. Professor Jock Philips details an often hidden migration in his article on 'Emigration to New Zealand from Scotland and Ulster.' Paddy Fitzgerald analyzes socio-economic and political factors that prompted, initially, migration to Ulster and eventually the massive migration from Ulster to the American colonies. The vast geographical scale of Scots migration and their impact in Europe is revealed by Steve Murdoch in his article on Scottish and Irish interaction in Scandinavia in the seventeenth century. Kerby Miller discusses the important role of emigrants in the formation of an elitist political mentalité after the American Revolution in 'The New England and federalist origins of "Scotch-Irish" ethnicity.'

The final section of the book, Language, Literature and Culture, contributes to the contemporary debate on language by providing an historical context for discussion. Michael Montgomery surveys the relations between written and spoken Ulster Scots over the past four centuries and argues that its loss of distinctiveness in writing (and its 'merger with English') is unrelated to the maintenance of distinctiveness in speech. Richard Finlay elucidates the similarities and differences with the language 'issues' in Scotland and Ulster in 'The politics of language: Scots, Gaelic and anglicization'. By examining Gaelic texts from Ireland and Scotland, Alan Titley presents a comparison of aspects of native autobiography in Irish and Scottish Gaelic reminding us all of the rich diversity of languages shared between Ulster and Scotland.

The editors would like to thank all those who made this volume possible. Funding for the conference was provided by the Ulster-Scots Agency through the Institute of Ulster Scots Studies at the University of Ulster. Generous grants were also provided by Derry City Council through the office of the late Dermot Francis and by Mr Liam Ronayne, Donegal County Librarian. It goes without saying of course that the staff at Four Courts Press deserve our fullest thanks.

I. HISTORY AND HERITAGE

Scotland and Ulster in the seventeenth century: the movement of peoples over the North Channel

JOHN R. YOUNG

> This long devyded Ile, he joined in One,
> And made this Britaine, orbe, one Albion:
> In him, surceased, the Irish warres, and THEY,
> By him, wer taught, a Sovaraigne, to obey:
> And for to setle, that Estate the better,
> Made large plantations, thousands came his debtor,
> Of late, my second Scotia he erected,
> And colonies t' America directed.
> What gift, or grace did Nature e're adorne,
> To which my mighty monarch was not borne.[1]

Such were the poetic comments of the famous seventeenth-century Scottish poet and traveller, William Lithgow, written in 1625 as part of a eulogy to James VI & I after his death. *Scotland's Tears in his Countreyes Behalf*, commented on the growing Scottish presence in Ulster, and celebrated the expansion of British territory. There had been close ties between the two areas over the centuries, but the nature and intensity of Scottish contacts with Ulster changed dramatically with James VI's political, military, ideological and cultural efforts to smash traditional ties between Scottish and Irish Gaeldom as part of a 'frontier policy' first attempted in Scotland pre-1603 and thereafter continued as part of a wider British agenda following the Union of the crowns and the Anglo-Scottish dynastic union of 1603. A cultural ideological agenda seeking the imposition of 'civility' and the eradication of 'barbarity', articulated in James VI's *Basilikon Doron* of 1599, and directed towards the Gaels of Scotland, was transposed on to the island of Ireland by a British monarch. Ireland was to be 'civilized' through a policy of Plantation, following the successful end of the Irish wars of the late sixteenth and early seventeenth centuries and the Flight of the Earls in 1607.[2]

---

1 W. Lithgow, 'Scotland's tears in his countreyes behalf, 1625', 6, in J. Maidment (ed.), *The poetical remains of William Lithgow, the Scottish traveller 1618–1660* (Edinburgh, 1863). 2 A.I. Macinnes, *Clanship, commerce and the house of Stuart, 1603–1788* (East Linton, 1996), pp. 56–81; M. Lynch, 'James VI and the Highland problem', in J. Goodare & M. Lynch (eds), *The reign of James VI* (East Linton, 2000), pp. 208–27; P. Lenihan (ed.), *Conquest and resistance: war in*

The Plantation of Ulster has obviously played a central role in Irish history in general and the early modern period in particular. Scottish migration to Ulster did not begin with the Plantation, nor was it was exclusively Lowland and Protestant based, but it marked the first wave of substantial large-scale migrations throughout the seventeenth century. The nature and impact of the Plantation has been well-documented by scholars such as Nicholas Canny, Michael Perceval-Maxwell, Raymond Gillespie and Philip Robinson.[3] Exact migration figures are difficult to document and more local case studies need to be undertaken charting migration trends over the North Channel, but by the time of the 1641 Rebellion, it has been estimated, there were between 20,000 and 30,000 Scots in Ulster. Contemporaries, such as William Petty, estimated that around 72,000 'new Scots' had settled in Ireland by 1672, although modern-day estimates state that *c.*10,000 Scots migrated to Ulster between the Restoration of 1660 and the outbreak of the Revolution of 1688. Petty's overestimate may reflect a psychological effect, common in modern society, of a feeling or perception of a country or region being swamped by new migrants. During the 1690s, a period of severe economic and demographic crisis for the Scottish economy, a further 40,000–70,000 Scots migrated, and it has also been estimated that 60,000–100,000 Scots migrated to Ulster over the fifty-year period of 1650–1700.[4] What is less clear is the level of permanent settlement of these migrants and to what extent there were significant levels of return migration. As this article indicates, return migration took place during several crisis points such as post-1641 and 1688 when the Scottish homeland was faced with the social problem of refugees and victims of warfare. Nevertheless, as Jean Agnew's work on the Belfast merchant community of the later seventeenth century has demonstrated, there was a generational aspect to the different Scottish migrations.[5] In turn, this raises several questions which are worthy of further scholarly exploration. To what extent did these migrants first and foremost think of themselves as Scots and Scottish? After a Scottish migrant family or community had been settled for several generations, did they cease to think of themselves as Scots and begin to regard themselves as Ulster-Scots and/or British? Moreover, how were they regarded on the Scottish mainland in terms of their identity? What I am suggesting here is that numbers alone do not

seventeenth-century Ireland (Leiden, 2001); J. Goodare, *State and society in Early Modern Scotland* (Oxford, 1999), pp. 254–85. 3 N. Canny, *Making Ireland British, 1580–1650* (Oxford, 2001); M. Perceval-Maxwell, *The Scottish migration to Ulster in the reign of James I* (London, 1973); R. Gillespie, *Colonial Ulster: the settlement of East Ulster, 1600–1641* (Cork, 1985); P. Robinson, *The Plantation of Ulster: British settlement in an Irish landscape, 1600–1670* (Dublin, 1984). 4 J.R. Young, 'The Scottish response to the Siege of Londonderry, 1689–90', in W. Kelly (ed.), *The sieges of Derry* (Dublin, 2001), p. 53. 5 J. Agnew, *Belfast merchant families in the seventeenth century* (Dublin, 1996), pp. 207–58.

provide the sole indicator in attempting to assess the impact of the Scots in Ulster in terms of migration and settlement over several generations. The geographic aspect of migration is also important in terms of the areas of Scotland where migrants predominantly came from. Accordingly, there is an important regional Scottish dimension as opposed to a purely national Scottish dimension, particularly in terms of links between south-west Scotland and Ulster. From the Scottish perspective, therefore, a national-regional model is important. Scottish national institutions, located in Edinburgh, such as the Scottish parliament, the Scottish privy council and the General Assembly of the Church of Scotland (when it existed in the seventeenth century) were important with regard to the articulation of national political, military, economic and religious policies (as explored below), but there was also an important regional impact on areas such as Ayrshire and the south-west, with regard to communities and individuals.

These issues require further research, but this article aims to raise some pointers and issues in terms of the use of descriptive language and ethnic identity, especially with regard to some case studies of the 1640s and the 1690s. Collectively, these are areas of research being pursued through the scholarly activities of the Institute of Ulster Scots Studies at the University of Ulster and the Glasgow-Strathclyde School of Scottish Studies.

NON-CONFORMING PRESBYTERIANISM AND RELIGIOUS LINKS BETWEEN SCOTLAND AND ULSTER IN THE 1620s AND 1630s

The bonds of Presbyterianism formed an important link over the North Channel and important individuals can be identified for the 1620s and 1630s who were later active in the Covenanting movement. The Five Articles of Perth of 1618 were theologically and politically controversial in the post-Reformation Church of Scotland under James VI, arousing hostility in the 1617 General Assembly and only approved through astute political management of the 1618 General Assembly and the 1621 Scottish parliament. Presbyterians who refused to acknowledge the Articles were known as 'non-conformists'.[6]

David Stevenson has identified a 'radical party' in the Church of Scotland in the 1630s. Several of the ministers belonging to this group had links with Ulster going back to the 1620s. Radical Scottish ministers often fled to Ulster in the 1620s to avoid adhering to the controversial Five Articles of Perth. Robert Blair, John Livingstone and John McLellan were important figures

---

6 P.H.R. Mackay, 'The reception given to the Five Articles of Perth', *Records of the Scottish Church History Society*, 19 (1975–7), 185–201; J. Goodare, 'The Scottish parliament of 1621', *Historical Journal*, 38 (1995), 29–51; G. Donaldson, *Scotland: James V–James VII* (Edinburgh, various editions), pp. 208–11.

in this respect. They were part of a wider radical group from south-west Scotland which included Samuel Rutherford, minister of Anwoth in Kirkcudbrightshire, and David Dickson, minister of Irvine. Dickson played a leading role in the supplications and petitions against the 1637 Prayer Book. In terms of the Ulster link, Blair, Livingstone and McLellan had been driven out of Scotland to Ulster by religious persecution. They worked among the Scots settlers in Ulster and often returned to Scotland on an intermittent basis where they preached and met with sympathizers, before sneaking back over the North Channel before the Scottish bishops could take any action against them. Blair became minister of Bangor in 1622, Livingstone became minister of Killinchy in 1630 and McLellan was worked as a schoolmaster. Complaints from the Scottish bishops about the activities of Blair and Livingstone led Charles I to instruct the Irish bishops to take action. Livingstone and Blair were suspended in 1631 and they were later deposed from their ministries in Ulster in 1634–5. Despite this, both Livingstone and Blair continued to preach in private, and both visited Edinburgh where they were closely linked to individuals involved in 'radical' religious behaviour.

Religious links between Scotland and Ulster also took on an Atlantic context in the mid-1630s. Persecution on both sides of the North Channel led to the decision of Robert Blair to emigrate to New England in 1634–5. Based on the example of many English Puritans, Blair and other associates in Ulster proposed the emigration idea to John McLellan, John Livingstone and John Stewart, provost of Ayr. All agreed to take part, but a key role in the plan was played by John Livingstone. Early in 1634 Livingstone was chosen as one of the two men to go to Massachusetts to meet with the governor and council there, but bad weather thwarted the journey and they were forced to return to Ulster after reaching no further than England. Despite this initial setback, Livingstone was in correspondence with John Winthrop, the governor of Massachusetts, by July 1634, discussing issues relating to religion and land. By September 1634 it had been decided that these emigrants from the north of Ireland should have land on the Merrimac river. Later in January 1635 Blair and Livingstone met John Winthrop junior in Antrim. Livingstone suggested that Winthrop junior should also go to Scotland to meet with John Stewart in Ayr, David Dickson in Irvine and a James Murray in Edinburgh. It appears that Winthrop did proceed to Scotland after leaving Ulster, although little is known of his activities there. Continued correspondence from Massachusetts encouraged the development of the project. Blair, Livingstone and their friends built a ship at Belfast and set sail in autumn 1636, but bad weather again wrecked the project, almost sinking their ship, and they were forced to return to Ireland.

The failure of the New England venture did not mark the end of links between Scotland and Ulster in relation to Blair, Livingstone and McLellan.

Blair and Livingstone were forced out of Ulster after the failure of the New England project when their arrest was ordered. They fled to Scotland where they were helped by David Dickson. Livingstone also went to Edinburgh, became involved in conventicling there and returned to Irvine in March 1637 where he publicly preached and led the worship in private meetings. With the increased persecution of Scots in Ulster, many Scottish settlers returned home and Livingstone preached to them in public and in private. Blair was also involved in public and private preaching in the west of Scotland. Blair, Livingstone and McLellan were each appointed as ministers of Scottish parishes in Scotland in 1638–9. Livingstone and McLellan were appointed as ministers of Stranraer and Kirkcudbright in south-west Scotland in 1638 and Blair was appointed as minister of St Andrews in Fife in 1639. Other leading figures with whom they had been associated enjoyed career progression at this time. Samuel Rutherford was appointed as professor of Divinity at the University of St Andrews in 1639 and David Dickson was appointed as professor of Divinity at the University of Glasgow in 1640.[7]

SCOTLAND, ULSTER AND THE FIRST WAR OF THE THREE KINGDOMS, 1637–51

With the growth of the Covenanting movement in Scotland by the late 1630s and the outbreak of the First Bishops' War in 1639, the Scots in Ulster were regarded as an 'enemy within' by Thomas Wentworth, first earl of Strafford, lord deputy of Ireland. In the early years of the Plantation, Scottish Presbyterian ministers had been accepted into the established church in Ireland and there had been a practical theological accommodation adopted towards them, especially on the issue of ordination. This position changed in 1634, however, when the Irish Convocation, convened by Wentworth, adopted a hard-line stance of conformity. Those Scottish Presbyterian ministers who refused to conform were to be ejected from their livings.[8] The outbreak of the First Bishops' War in 1639 between Charles I and the Scottish Covenanters resulted in a further hard-line stance on Wentworth's part, with the issue of the notorious 'Black Oath'. After May 1639, Scots living in Ulster were obliged to take an oath of loyalty and allegiance to the king and the established church. In essence, the Scots in Ulster were being forced to abjure the 1638 National Covenant. In the aftermath of the 1639 Pacification of

---

7 D. Stevenson, 'Conventicles in the Kirk, 1619–37: the emergence of a Radical party', in D. Stevenson (ed.), *Union, revolution and religion in seventeenth-century Scotland* (Aldershot, 1997), pp. 97–114. See also D. Stevenson, *The Scottish revolution, 1637–1644: the triumph of the Covenanters* (Newton Abbot, 1973).   8 P. Kilroy, 'Radical religion in Ireland, 1641–1660', in J. Ohlmeyer (ed.), *Ireland from independence to occupation, 1641–1660* (Cambridge, 1995), p. 203.

Berwick, increased legal action was taken against people who refused to take the Black Oath. In September 1639, for example, Henry and Mary Stewart were brought before the court of Castle Chamber for refusing to take the oath. They had not taken the National Covenant, but still they refused to abjure it. As their trial proceeded, the case was converted from refusing the Black Oath to a charge of rebellion. As a result of this, both were fined £3000 sterling and imprisoned for life.[9] In Wentworth's eyes, the Scots in Ulster were dangerous subversives and Wentworth had stationed *c.*1,500 troops in Ulster by 1639 to keep a watchful eye over them.[10]

Raymond Gillespie's research on East Ulster has noted the impact of the 'Black Oath' in that area. The army and local volunteers were used to enforce the oath and this involved the quartering of soldiers on tenants during a year of poor harvests. Many tenants and labourers fled to Scotland and this had a negative effect on the local East Ulster economy. Tenants on the lands of Sir Edward Chichester in Carrickfergus fled to Scotland with their cattle, sheep and food to the detriment of the local area. In parts of County Down labour shortages as a result of people escaping to Scotland meant that the 1640 harvest could not be collected. A proclamation was issued in 1639 forbidding Scots in Ireland returning to Scotland. Gillespie notes that it was significant that this was issued at harvest time. Popular protest and rioting against the Black Oath was also linked to the quartering of troops and poor harvests in the late 1630s.[11] Gillespie's East Ulster case study therefore indicates an example of return migration to Scotland due to religious persecution.

The growth and nature of the three-kingdom political, military and religious conflict is well-known. Attempts by Charles I to use an Irish Catholic military force to suppress the Covenanters in 1639 had to be abandoned, the 1641 Ulster Rebellion resulted in Scottish military intervention in Ulster in 1642 (with an accompanying Presbyterian ministerial presence which has been historically controversial in the attempt to explain the growth of Presbyterianism in seventeenth-century Ulster) and the 1643 Solemn League and Covenant sought to impose a Presbyterian church structure on England and Ireland. For the Scottish Covenanters, military intervention in the British struggle came at the price of a Presbyterian England and Ireland and, for some Covenanters in 1644, the extension of the Solemn League and Covenant into a European Protestant defence league with the Dutch and the Swedes in the context of the religious struggles of the Thirty Years War. Likewise, the intervention and military successes of the Irish brigades on Scottish soil as part of the Montrose rebellion against the Covenanters has attracted much attention.[12] In terms of migration, however, a relatively unexplored area has

9 M. Bennett, *The Civil Wars in Britain and Ireland, 1638–1651* (Oxford, 1997), p. 37. 10 A. Hughes, *The causes of the English Civil War* (London, 1992), p. 48. 11 Gillespie, *Colonial Ulster*, pp. 81–3. 12 J.R. Young, 'The Scottish parliament and European diplomacy, 1641–1647:

Church of Scotland in a 'bottom up' approach from individual parishes to
sbyteries. Two organizational divisions were created for the collection of
sbyteries' contributions and the collections were to be forwarded to named
rchants in each of the two divisions. Later on 25 February the privy coun-
set up a committee to advise on the answers to be given to petitions given
for a proportion of the collections 'for the poore people of Ireland'.[18] The
nisters of the Church of Scotland in Edinburgh were also to advise on this.
he council proceeded to deal with the crisis in south-west Scotland on 28
bruary. The presbyteries of Ayr and Irvine were to receive priority. George
ttie, an Edinburgh merchant, was instructed to deliver £4,000 out of the
lections already made to John Kennedy in Ayr and John Ross in Irvine.
he money was to be distributed by a local committee made of some (unspec-
d) members of the two presbyteries and the local magistrates in Ayr and
vine.[19] Despite these administrative initiatives, there were problems through-
t March and April in the implementation of these structures and the avoid-
ce of corrupt activities.[20]

Information exists concerning the actual numbers of refugees in south-
st Scotland. On 9 June 1642 the privy council estimated that without ade-
ate voluntary contributions then 'the multitudes of these poore people
sideing in the presbyteries of Air and Irwing, being above foure thousand
rsons, are lyke to starve'.[21] Therefore, it was estimated that there were over
000 refugees in the presbyteries of Ayr and Irvine in south-west Scotland.
ased on the estimated figures of the numbers of Scots in Ulster at the time
the 1641 Rebellion, 4,000 refugees amounts to a percentage figure of
tween 13 per cent and 20 per cent for the numbers of refugees compared
the Scottish population in Ulster (based on a population of 20,000–30,000
ople). Sampling of local presbytery and kirk session records indicates that
fugees were not restricted to south-west Scotland, albeit it would appear
at they were concentrated there. Local presbytery and kirk session records
rovide evidence of money being raised for refugees and named refugees
ceiving financial aid. Refugees from Ireland can be traced as far north as
lgin in the north-east of Scotland, as indicated by the kirk session records of
lgin. The first direct reference to the Irish troubles appeared on Sunday 28
ovember 1641 when it was intimated that a fast should be held in Elgin
pon the following Sunday 'for the troubles of Ireland'.[22] Several months
ter, on 27 February 1642, an intimation for the Irish contribution was read
ut and 'the contribution for the distressed that cam out of Irland' was to be
ollected. Individual refugees received money from the local Irish contribution
etween 31 January 1643 and 3 May 1644 (the last recorded date of payment

8 Ibid.   19 Ibid., pp. 209–10.   20 Ibid., pp. 227, 231, 237, 255, 264.   21 Ibid., p. 267.   22
V. Cramond (ed.), *The records of Elgin, 1234–1800* (Aberdeen, 1908), p. 241.

been the return of Scottish migrants in the aftermath of tl
and the response of the Covenanting administration of Sco
and humanitarian aid problem.[13]

RETURN MIGRATION AND THE 1641 ULSTER RI
REFUGEES AND LOCAL CASE STUDIES

In terms of the migratory links between Scotland and Ulst
demographic feature of the early 1640s was the movement
Ulster to Scotland in the aftermath of the 1641 Ulster rebellic
can be defined as 'victims of warfare' or refugees. The prob
was first discussed by the Scottish privy council on 1 Febr
council stated that due to 'the crueltie of the rebells in Irelan
of his Majesties good subjects and our countrey men thair a
to flee out of Ireland to those parts in the west countrey q
best occasion of landing'.[14] This clearly suggests that refugees
ing in to the west coast of Scotland in the months after the
result of this, 'the multitude of whiche poore people is becon
thair necessities and wants so pressing' that the western pari
refugees had landed simply could not cope. Parish funds for
the poor had been exhausted as had informal collections in th
light of this growing financial and human crisis, it was becom
to help the refugees 'who in that regarde are lyke to be in w
heere, quhair they looked for succour and refreshment, in so fa
having escaped the sword of the enemie, by famine they will m
if they be not tymouslie supplied'.[16] The privy council accordin
'the cause for which they suffer, being loyaltie and religion, v
ful motives with all good subjects and true hairted christians lil
tribut of thair best meanes for the refreshment and comfort of s
tian soules, especiallie being our owne countrey men'.[17] Fina
therefore to be raised through the institutional structures and n

the Palatine, the Dutch Republic and Sweden', in S. Murdoch (ed.), *Scotlan
Years War, 1618–1648* (Leiden, 2001), pp. 77–106; M. Perceval Maxwell, 'Irela
1638–1648', in J. Morrill (ed.), *The Scottish National Covenant in its British cor
(Edinburgh, 1990), pp. 193–211; Bennett, *The Civil Wars in Britain and Irelana
Highland warrior: Alasdair MacColla and the Civil Wars* (Edinburgh, 1980); J. t
War and Restoration in the three Stuart kingdoms: the career of Randal MacDoı
Antrim, 1609–1683* (Cambridge, 1993); J. Kenyon & J. Ohlmeyer (eds), *The Ci
itary history of England, Scotland and Ireland, 1638–1660* (Oxford, 1998).   13
Ireland British, pp. 561–3.   14 *Register of the privy council of Scotland* [hereafter
series, vi, 1638–1643, ed. P. Hume Brown (Edinburgh, 1906), pp. 189–90.   1
16 Ibid.   17 Ibid.

to a refugee from Ireland). These refugees fall into three main categories; ministers who had fled from Ireland, the widows or families of ministers who had been killed in the 1641 Rebellion and victims of the rebellion who were now left with dependents.[23] The synod of Lothian and Tweeddale dealt with 35 cases of Irish refugees between 4 November 1641 and 8 November 1649. These cases were concentrated in 1644 and the categories of refugees were similar to those in Elgin. Ministers or ministers' widows with or without dependents constituted the majority of cases considered, along with the widows of soldiers killed in military action and widows whose husbands had been killed by the Irish rebels. Supplications for financial aid told tales of murder, mutilation, loss of goods and property and robbery.[24]

Voluntary contributions and financial aid was not restricted to the social issue of refugees and returning migrants as victims of warfare. Voluntary contributions were also to be raised to help finance the Scottish military presence in Ulster, as the Covenanting army there was severely under-financed. On 28 February 1643 the privy council issued an appeal to ensure the maintenance of the Scottish army in Ireland. Tripartite meetings between the privy council and two parliamentary interval committees which had been appointed at the end of the 1641 parliament, the Conservators of the Peace and the Commissioners of the Common Burdens and Brotherly Assistance, took place on 3 and 4 March 1643 respectively. In response to the appeal of 28 February, 14 individual sums were contributed on 3 March for maintaining the Covenanting army in Ireland. In addition, a decision was taken on 4 March to borrow £20,000 sterling (£240,000 Scots) to support the Scottish decisions there.[25]

Financial accounts provided by the Edinburgh merchant, John Jossie, give details of the sums of money provided by privy councillors and members of the Common Burdens-Brotherly Assistance Commission, as well as contributions from a wider social spectrum. These latter contributions, based on Jossie's accounts, came from the sheriffdoms of Fife, Lothian, Linlithgow and the citizens of Edinburgh. In Edinburgh, many of the contributions came from merchants, such as one Thomas Young who contributed £200, but specific trades and occupations of artisans were often identified. James Wright, a hatmaker in Edinburgh, advanced £333 6s. 8d. Scots and 'Nicoll Eving', a fishmonger, advanced £66 13s. 4d. Ministers of the Church of Scotland are also listed in the contributions, such as Andrew Ramsay, Robert Douglas, Patrick Gillespie and William Bennett. Each of these ministers contributed £666 13s. 4d. Women, especially widows, were active among the citizenry of Edinburgh in forwarding contributions. Eleven of the 94 individual contributions (12 per cent) listed in Jossie's accounts for Edinburgh in 1643 came

23 Ibid., pp. 244–9.   24 J. Kirk (ed.), *The records of the synod of Lothian and Tweeddale: 1589–96, 1640–1649* (Edinburgh, 1977), pp. 121–301.   25 J.R. Young, *The Scottish parliament, 1639–1661: a political and constitutional analysis* (Edinburgh, 1996), p. 59.

from women. Ten of these women were listed as widows and one was listed
as a daughter. In the sherriffdom of Lothian, Lady Carnegie contributed £666
13s. 4d. and in the sherrifdom of Linlithgow, a minister named Robert
Melville contributed the same amount on behalf of his daughter. Ministers
formed a significant group of contributors in the sheriffdom of Lothian.
George Leslie, minister at Holyrood Abbey, contributed £333 6s. 8d. and an
identical sum was forwarded by James Sharp, minister at Leith. This was the
famous Sharp who was later closely involved in the re-introduction of episcopacy in Scotland as part of the Restoration settlement. As archbishop of St
Andrews, Sharp was later assassinated by Covenanters on 3 May 1679.[26]

RESTORATION TRENDS AND THE MOVEMENT OF PEOPLE

The Restoration Scottish administration of Charles II and James VII (post-
1685) faced a combination of uprising (with the 1666 Pentland Rising and the
1679 Covenanting Rising) and external invasion (the abortive Argyll rebellion
of 1685) against its authority. Restoration Scotland was noted for elements of
Presbyterian non-conformity and religious dissent and the emergence of radical, hard-line Cameronian ideology by the 1680s. State suppression of these
forms of dissent was brutal and remains a controversial, yet not fully
researched, area of seventeenth-century Scottish history.[27] The movement of
Covenanters over the North Channel was an identifiable feature of this period.
For the respective Stuart administrations, a London-Edinburgh-Dublin axis
often co-ordinated strategic security measures and attempted to monitor the
activities of rebels and dissenters. With the outbreak of the 1679 Covenanting
rebellion in Scotland, for example, the Scottish privy council wrote to John
Maitland, first duke of Lauderdale, on 6 June proposing that military forces be
sent to Scotland from England or Ireland to help quell the rebellion. This was
in response to advice from George Livingston, third earl of Linlithgow, commander of crown forces in Scotland, that increased troop numbers should be
sent to Scotland 'before the enemy is engaged'.[28] Linlithgow's call for more
troops was due to a perceived increase in the number of 'rebels'. In the aftermath of the failed rebellion, many Covenanters appear to have fled to Ireland
as a safe haven. Correspondence from the privy council to Lauderdale on 31
July noted that 'a great many of the rebells are taken in severall places in

26 *RPCS*, vii, 1638–1643, pp. 83–92.   27 I.B. Cowan, *The Scottish Covenanters, 1660–1688*
(London, 1976); J. Buckroyd, *Church and state in Scotland, 1660–1681* (Edinburgh, 1980); C.S.
Terry, *The Pentland Rising and Rullion Green* (Glasgow, 1905); J.R. Elder, *The Highland host
of 1678* (Glasgow, 1914).   28 *RPCS*, vi, 1678–80, pp. 218–19. The council wrote again to
Lauderdale on 13 June reporting thanking the king for his resolution to help the council by
sending forces from England and Ireland (ibid., pp. 235–6).

Ireland'.[29] Charles II had ordered that they were to be returned to Scotland as prisoners and that sufficient notice be given to the privy council in order that enough guards could be made available when they landed in order to bring the prisoners to secure prisons. The privy council had decided that the prisoners 'may be most securly landed' at Greenock, Newport (Port Glasgow in modern-day Scotland) and Glasgow. Accordingly, the council wanted Lauderdale to inform those who had custody of the prisoners in Ireland that the prisoners be 'landed' at the above-named locations on the west coast of Scotland.[30] From a different perspective, on 29 June a petition was subscribed by 15 Presbyterian ministers in the 'North of Ireland' and addressed to Charles II. The petition professed loyalty to the king and referred to the 'wicked conspiracies and treasonable attempts of enemies, alsweill at hom as abroad'.[31] Thus, these 15 Presbyterian ministers in Ulster were effectively condemning the Scottish rebellion.

One of the murderers of James Sharp, archbishop of St Andrews (murdered at Magus Moor near St Andrews on 3 May 1679) took refuge in Ireland. James Russell in Kettle fled to Ireland as he and the other murderers were hunted down in Scotland. On 4 May the council offered a large reward for their capture, and on 26 June it issued a proclamation prohibiting the lieges from harbouring rebels (Russell was specifically named), as well as issuing another proclamation ordering the arrest of Sharp's murderers.[32] Russell was later apprehended in Ireland by one Simon Johnston in 1680. The council informed Lauderdale of this development on 7 October 1680 and requested that an order be issued for sending Russell back to Scotland, under a secure guard, for trial. Johnston had also provided the council with a list of 'some persons he informes to be in Ireland who are accesorie to the said murder [Sharp's murder] or the late rebellion [1679 rebellion]'.[33] Thus, the council wanted a warrant issued for the arrest of these people in order that they could be sent back to Scotland. Despite these developments, only two of Sharp's murderers, David Hackston of Rathillet and Andrew Guillan, were ever punished for the murder (Hackston and Guillan were executed in 1680 and 1683 respectively).[34]

Contemporary pamphlets noted the influx of Covenanters into Ireland in the aftermath of the failed 1679 rising. The author of *The Conduct of Dissenters* noted this trend between the Covenanting defeat at Bothwell Bridge in 1679 and the Revolution. Thus, 'in the interval between the defeat of the Presbyterians in Scotland they increased and multiplied by a numerous conflux of their brethren from Scotland'.[35] These comments were concerned with

---

29 Ibid., pp. 295–6. 30 Ibid. 31 Ibid., pp. 655–7. 32 Ibid., pp. 322–5; Cowan, *The Scottish Covenanters*, 95. 33 *RPCS*, vi, 1678–80, p. 559. 34 Cowan, *The Scottish Covenanters*, p. 95. 35 Quoted in J.C. Beckett, *Protestant dissent in Ireland, 1687–1780* (London, 1946), p. 23.

the growth of Presbyterianism in Ireland during these years, which was attributed to Scottish influence. The author further argued that 'numbers of meet-
ing-houses were built, and they were connived at in the exercise of their ecclesiastical jurisdiction, however contrary to law'.[36]

The accession of James VII and II in 1685 resulted in the failed Argyll
and Monmouth rebellions in Scotland and England, respectively. Strategic
security was obviously an important consideration for James VII's Scottish
administration and there were fears that Archibald Campbell, ninth earl of
Argyll, might attempt a landing in the north of Ireland. Perceived subversive
activities in the north of Ireland were to be closely monitored. James VII and
II, Robert Spencer, third earl of Sunderland, Arthur Forbes, first earl of
Granard and Michael Boyle, archbishop of Armagh, primate and lord chancellor of Ireland, and the lords justices of Ireland were all closely involved in
monitoring 'subversives' in the north of Ireland, attempting to prevent liai-
son with the disaffected in Scotland and keeping a watchful eye of Argyll's
manoeuvres in Scotland.[37] On 30 May 1685, for example, Sunderland
informed the lord justices of Ireland that King James approved of 'the orders
given for preserving the quiet of Ireland, preventing ill designs and hinder-
ing correspondence with the rebels in Scotland'.[38] Frigates were also ordered
to 'cruise in the channel' between Scotland and Ireland for coastal security.[39]
In addition, Henry Hyde, second earl of Clarendon, lord lieutenant of Ireland,
later informed Secretary of State Sunderland from Dublin Castle that he had
information of 'several rebels, who run to and again from Scotland into the
north of this kingdom'.[40] Accordingly, he had employed one Cormack O'Neill,
a justice of the peace in County Antrim, with other justices of the peace,
'who are active good men to watch those parts'.[41]

THE COLONIAL NORTH AMERICAN HERITAGE OF COVENANTING PERSECUTION IN SCOTLAND

It appears that the collective memory of Covenanting persecution in
Restoration Scotland was carried over to Ulster by Scottish migrants and

36 Ibid.   37 *Calendar of state papers domestic series* [hereafter *CSPD*], James II, i,
February–December 1685, ed. E.K. Timings (London, 1960), pp. 145, 148–9, 152–3, 155, 173–6,
184–7, 251–2, 273; *Historical notices of Scottish affairs, selected from the manuscripts of Sir John
Lauder of Fountainhall, Bart., one of the Senators of the College of Justice*, 2 vols (Edinburgh,
1848), ii, p. 630. 38 *CSPD*, Feb.–Dec.1685, pp. 173–4. 39 Ibid. 40 S.W. Singer (ed.), *The
correspondence of Henry Hyde, earl of Clarendon and of his brother Laurence Hyde, earl of Rochester;
with the diary of Lord Clarendon from 1687 to 1690, containing minute particulars of the events
attending the Revolution: and the diary of Lord Rochester during his embassy to Poland in 1676*
(London, 1828), 2 vols, i, p. 269. 41 Ibid.

thereafter carried into north America by migrants, of Scottish descent, from Ulster. George Fraser Black, author of *Scotland's Mark on America*, which was published in New York in 1921, made this case. Black stated that:

> The mountaineers of Tennessee and Kentucky are largely the descendants of these same Ulster Scots, and their origin is conclusively shown by the phrase used by mothers to their unruly children – 'if you don't behave, Clavers will get you'.[42]

Black was referring to the descendants of the 'Ulster Scots' living in the United States who had maintained an interest in their ethnic origins, insisting that they were of Scottish and not Irish origin. The bogey-man figure of 'Clavers' was none other than John Graham of Claverhouse, a controversial figure in terms of Scottish identity. The schism in the perception of the Scottish past is reflected in the interpretation of Claverhouse. As a romantic hero, he has often been referred to as 'Bonnie Dundee', and celebrated as such in Scottish literature and popular folk songs as the romantic hero fighting for the cause of the House of Stewart against the usurper William of Orange in the First Jacobite Rising in Scotland. As Viscount Dundee, he was killed in action at the battle of Killiecrankie in Perthshire on 27 July 1689, where Jacobite forces routed a Williamite army. Thus emerged the figure of the heroic Jacobite military man, fighting for King James, yet tragically killed in battle, thereby depriving the Jacobite cause in Scotland of an outstanding military commander. From a different perspective of the Scottish past, however, Graham of Claverhouse was known as 'Bloody Clavers', the hardline persecutor of Covenanters in south-west Scotland and an agent of Stewart absolutism and tyranny.[43] It is this latter image belonging to the Covenanting tradition which was transplanted from Scotland to colonial north America through the Ulster migrations. The phrase 'Clavers will get you' in Tennessee and Kentucky was therefore ultimately derived from south-west Scotland in the Restoration period, carried over into Ulster by Scottish migrants and thereafter into Tennessee and Kentucky via Ulster Scots settlement. From a contemporary perspective, this phrase 'Clavers will get you' is still used by mothers towards their children in modern day south-west Scotland.

---

42 G.F Black, *Scotland's mark on America* (New York, 1921), p. 12.   43 For Claverhouse, see C.S. Terry, *John Graham of Claverhouse, viscount of Dundee, 1648–1689* (London, 1905) and A.M. Scott, *Bonnie Dundee: John Graham of Claverhouse* (Edinburgh, 1989). In terms of Scottish literature, see, for example, Sir Walter Scott, *Old Mortality* (various editions). On the First Jacobite Rising, see P. Hopkins, *Glencoe and the end of the Highland War* (Edinburgh, 1998 edition).

SCOTLAND, ULSTER AND THE SECOND WAR OF THE
THREE KINGDOMS, 1688–91

In common with the experience of the 1640s, the outbreak of the Williamite war in Ireland resulted in the return migration from Ulster to Scotland of Scottish migrants or migrants of Scottish descent. Given the experience of the Wars of the Covenant and the military successes attributed to the Irish brigades under Alasdair MacColla for the short-term success of the Montrose rebellion in 1644–5, a fundamental element of the strategic outlook of the fragile and newly-established Williamite regime in Scotland was to avoid and prevent a military invasion from Ireland. This became a more acute and pressing issue in the summer of 1689 with the outbreak of the First Jacobite Rising. The nightmare scenario for the strategic security of the Williamite regime was the potentially lethal combination of the domestic internal threat of a Jacobite rising and the external threat of a military invasion from Ireland. Thus, measures were taken for the defence of the south-west of Scotland, intelligence reports collected information on Franco-Irish naval activities and the unauthorized movement of people between Scotland and Ireland was to be curtailed. Fundamentally, Ireland and not Scotland was to be the main theatre of war and measures were taken to provide troops and supplies, but the main conflict was to be kept out of Scotland. By 1690 and the development of the military conflict in Ireland, a logistical structure was drawn up for the supply and provisioning of Danish troops landing on the east coast of Scotland and thereafter transferred over to the west before being shipped out to the field of war in Ireland. When news of Williamite victories in Ireland reached Edinburgh in 1690, state-sponsored celebrations were initiated, such as the lighting of bonfires and the firing of the guns of Edinburgh, Stirling and Dumbarton castles. From a religious perspective, the newly-established General Assembly of the Church of Scotland (the first in Scotland since 1653) called for the natives of Ireland to be converted to what it referred to as the truth.[44]

The outbreak of the war in Ireland resurrected fears of a repeat of the 1641 Ulster Rebellion. In 1689–90 returning migrants and victims of warfare brought back tales of persecution and atrocities to Scotland. In contrast to the 1640s, more information on this theme is available in the records of the period. Individual tales can be identified and they did have an impact on the policy-making process and increased fears in Edinburgh over perceived Irish barbarity. One (unidentified) refugee informed the 1689 Convention on 28 May of the murder of four elderly gentlemen and twelve women, five of whom were pregnant, in Killheagh. The refugee informed the Convention

---

[44] These issues are discussed in Young, 'The Scottish response to the Siege of Londonderry', in Kelly (ed.), *The sieges of Derry*, pp. 53–74.

that 'the Irish have been barbarously cruel there' and the pregnant women were killed because 'they bred heretics'.[45] It should be stressed, of course, that the historical accuracy of these stories cannot be verified. Different types of returning migrants can be identified as forming victims of warfare and not all of those who fled from the war in Ireland into Scotland were necessarily Scottish. Affluent merchants from Belfast and other important trading centres in the north of Ireland constitute one of these groups. Belfast merchants appear to have been the dominant element here. Jean Agnew has comprehensively shown the extent of Scottish penetration and dominance within the Belfast merchant community. Out of 32 Belfast merchant families studied by Agnew, no less than 22 (69 per cent) were of Scottish origin. This definition of Scottish origin included direct immigrants from Scotland as well as descendants of Scottish families who had already settled in Ulster.[46]

THE ANTRIM SYNODS OF ULSTER AND THE POST-1690 CHURCH OF SCOTLAND

The Antrim synods of the 1690s took a close interest in Scottish affairs. This was often based on individual ministers who fled to Scotland and who remained there to the detriment of their flock left behind in Ulster. The synod attempted to deal with the problem of non-returning ministers at various stages in the 1690s. On 30 September 1691 the synod noted that 'several of our Br^n are yet in Scotl^d, and diverse of them continue there, notwithstanding they have been written for to return'.[47] This delay in returning was resented by the synod as provision had been made for their subsistence in Ulster. The synod stated that it would use 'all means that may be effectual to bring them to a sense of their duty' and each presbytery was to signify this to their respective brethern.[48] It would appear that Presbyterian ministers from the other side of the North Channel who had been forced to temporarily relocate to Scotland as a result of the Williamite war in Ireland were now reluctant to return home. This reluctance was perhaps reinforced by attitudes within Scotland. On 11 July 1690 the Scottish privy council had passed legislation in favour of Presbyterian ministers. This act was not primarily concerned with Presbyterian ministers from Ireland, but it did mention their situation. A general principle was established concerning Presbyterian ministers who had fled from Ireland and had since taken up the ministry of vacant parishes in Scotland. Several unidentified presbyteries in the west of Scotland

45 E.W.M. Balfour-Melville (ed.), *An account of the proceedings of the Estates of Scotland 1689-90*, 2 vols (Edinburgh, 1954–55), i, p. 107. See Young, 'The Scottish response to the Siege of Londonderry 1689–90', pp. 61–3, for more on this theme. **46** Agnew, *Belfast merchant families*, p. 10. **47** *Records of the General Synod of Ulster, 1691–1820* (Belfast, 1890), i, p. 5. **48** Ibid.

were described as having 'unfixed ministers (for the most part fledd out of Ireland)'.[49] As per the terms of the legislation of 11 July 1690, these ministers were allowed to take up vacant stipends of those parishes where they were now based, although they had to be approved by the local presbytery 'upon productione of certificats testifieing their service'.[50]

From the perspective of the Antrim synod, the problem does not seem to have been solved and it was further discussed in the 1692. Many brethern were still in Scotland, despite the fact that 'several of their parishes are able to maintain them and desirous to have them'[51] Thus, every meeting was instructed to 'authoritatively call them to return to their respective Charges'.[52] Yet it would appear that the synod was fearful of taking on the authority of the General Assembly of the Church of Scotland in the cases of individual ministers whom the General Assembly wanted to remain in Scotland. On 5 June 1694 the synod considered a letter from the Scottish General Assembly regarding the case of one Mr John Hamilton of Comber in County Down. The General Assembly's letter, presented by one Lieutenant Hall, requested that Hamilton be 'loosed' from Comber and allowed to settle in the city of Edinburgh, the Scottish capital. The synod was also faced with a rival supplication from Comber itself. Presented by James Murray and John Wallace, the supplication argued that the synod 'may renew their positive orders to Mr John Hamilton to return to his charge'.[53] After 'long and serious debate', by a majority of votes it was decided that Hamilton 'be at the desire of the General Assembly loos'd from Comber and continu'd at Edinburgh'.[54] From Hamilton's perspective, Edinburgh offered a more lucrative post than Comber, but the synod had been unwilling to stand up to the General Assembly. The 1694 synod also considered a supplication from 'Dunmurry', presented by a Thomas Mulligan. This related to Mr Alexander Glass of 'Dunmurry' who was still in Scotland. The supplication therefore argued that 'either some effectual course may be taken to bring over Mr Alex.ʳ Glass to them, or that the relation 'twixt him and them may be loos'd, that so they may be provided otherwise'.[55] The 'Glass case' led to a general principle being established by the synod, having approved an overture from the committee to prepare overtures for the synod. This overture dealt with 'ministers who are now in Scotland, and have been appointed by the Synod to return to their charge'.[56] Presbyteries were instructed to write to such ministers and were to inform them that 'their so staying in Scotland is very offensive both to ministers and people'. If they did not return from Scotland then they were to be 'lookt

49 *RPCS*, xv, 1690, pp. 315–17. The problem of Irish Presbyterian ministers in Scotland had already been noted in 1689. See the 'Memorial of the Irish presbyterian ministers' in Sir W. Fraser, *The Melvilles, earls of Melville, and the Leslies, earls of Leven*, 3 vols (Edinburgh, 1890), iii, p. 199. 50 *RPCS*, xv, 1690, p. 316. 51 *Records of the General Synod of Ulster*, p. 9. 52 Ibid. 53 Ibid., p. 13. 54 Ibid. 55 Ibid. 56 Ibid.

upon as scandalous persons, and be dealt with as such'. They were to be informed in writing of their 'scandalous' status.[57]

The Antrim synods of the 1690s played close attention to the proceedings of the General Assembly in Scotland as well as to the demographic crisis known as 'The Lean Years', which hit the Scottish economy in the mid-to-late 1690s. On 2 June 1697 the Antrim synod decided that 'some particular Minister be appointed ... to overlook the Acts of the General Assembly of the Church of Scotland'. This minister was to 'consider' and 'draw out what may be applicable to us in this Church'.[58] Mr Alexander Hutcheson was appointed for this task and at the following synod held on 1 June 1698 he reported back with his findings. Hutcheson 'drew out some of the Acts of the General Assembly of the Church of Scotland, which he judged applicable to this Church'.[59] These were thankfully received by the synod who proceeded to remit them to the brethren for revision and consideration.[60] Earlier in the 1690s, Mr Hugh Wilson from the presbytery of Stranraer in south-west Scotland had attended the 1692 synod.[61] The Lean Years of the 1690s, without doubt, represented the most significant demographic crisis of the seventeenth century for Scotland's society and economy. As Paddy Fitzgerald shows in his article, this was also a significant migratory period for the flow of human traffic from Scotland to Ulster. Ian Whyte has argued that contemporary estimates claimed that over 50,000 people migrated to Ireland between 1689 and 1700. Whyte argues that this represented *c.*5 per cent of the Scottish population at that time.[62] The famine of the 1690s has been described as 'the last time when large numbers of people died of starvation and, as a result, it had a striking impact on folk memory'.[63] Most areas of Scotland here hit by a series of three or four harvest failures between 1695 and 1698 (there were also problems before this) and 'it is likely that Scotland's population was cut by around 13 per cent'.[64] A variety of terms such as 'the seven ill years, 'King William's dear years' and the 'black years of King William' were used to describe these horrific events.[65] As late as 1977, the authors of the influential *Scottish Population History* stated that 'even now oral tradition has not entirely

---

57 Ibid. Ironically, the meeting went on to note the case of one Mr Hugh Kirkpatrick who had been previously ordered to return from Scotland, but had not yet done so. He was still in Scotland and he had written to the synod requesting that the synod 'loose' him from 'Bellmony', despite the fact that the people of Bellmony were 'all reddy for receiving Mr Kirkpatrick' (ibid.). In common with John Hamilton, Scotland was a more attractive option for Hugh Kirkpatrick. 58 *Records of the General Synod of Ulster*, p. 22. 59 Ibid., p. 30. 'Alexander Hutchisoun' is one of the 15 names of the Presbyterian ministers who subscribed the petition of 29 June 1679 which professed loyalty to Charles II in the wake of the 1679 Rising in Scotland (*RPCS*, 1678–80, pp. 655–7). 60 *Records of the General Synod of Ulster*, p. 30. 61 Ibid., p. 7. 62 I.D. Whyte, *Scotland before the Industrial Revolution: an economic & social history, c.1050–c.1750* (London, 1995), p. 120. 63 Ibid., p. 124. 64 Ibid. 65 M. Flinn (ed.), *Scottish population history from the seventeenth century to the 1930s* (Cambridge, 1977), p. 164.

forgotten them: we have heard it related that when skeletons were uncovered
by council workmen near the foreshore at a village on the Moray Firth they
were immediately identified by local people as the victims of King William's
ill years who had died after trying to live on shellfish just above the reach of
high tides'.[66] Andrew Fletcher of Saltoun commented on the impact of the
demographic crises in his pamphlet *An Account of a Conversation concerning a
Right Regulation of Governments for the Common Good of Mankind, in a Letter
to the Marquiss of Montrose, the Earls of Rothes, Roxburg and Haddington from
London the first of December 1703.*[67] Published in 1704 during the crisis in
Anglo-Scottish relations, Saltoun's letter stated that 'the number of our people'
had been 'very much diminished by the late famine; by extraordinary levies
of soldiers; and chiefly by ill government, which having given no encouragement to industry of any kind, *has necessitated great numbers of men to abandon
the country and settle themselves in other nations, especially in Ireland*'.[68] The collective combination of these problems, in Saltoun's eyes, had led to emigration with Ireland the key destination. Harvest failure, famine and the demographic crisis in Scotland attracted the attention of the Antrim synods in the
late 1690s. Harvest failure was one of the issues mentioned by the Antrim
synod on 1 June 1698 in its call for a fast and humiliation. The synod mentioned the 'unseasonableness of the Weather in seed time & Harvest these
Years last Past, the *Scarcity of Victualls in Scotland*, the sad persecution of the
Protestants in France, with many sins abounding among ourselves'.[69]
Collectively, these formed the grounds for the fast and humiliation, which was
to be held by the several congregations on 2 August 1698 to 'deprecate the
Lord's anger with the Evidences & Effects thereof, and wrestle with Him for
a Blessing to ourselves and others, particularly for a seasonable Harvest'.[70]

In common with the Church of Scotland, spiritual concern was shown by
the Antrim synods for the Huguenot diaspora following their expulsion from
France by Louis XIV in 1685. Evidence also exists of the Antrim synod having
concern for the welfare and safety of individual migrants who had recently
crossed the North Channel from Scotland as part of the large 1690s migration. On 1 June 1698 Alexander Small in the parish of Finvoy informed the
synod of a recent migrant who had gone missing. Jean McGee was described
as 'a Girll about 11 or 12 Years of Age'.[71] She had recently arrived from
Scotland and had 'landed safely some Place in the County of Antrim, but
cannot now be heard of'.[72] Alexander Small was married to her mother, one
Mary Dickie. The synod was asked to look out for the girl in their parishes.
If anyone heard of her welfare and whereabouts then he was to inform one
Allan Dunlop in Ballymoney who would send her on to Alexander Small.[73]

66 Ibid.   67 This is printed in Andrew Fletcher, *Political works*, ed. J. Robertson (Cambridge,
1997), pp. 175–215.   68 Ibid., p. 192.   69 *Records of the General Synod of Ulster*, p. 31.   70
Ibid.   71 Ibid., p. 32.   72 Ibid.   73 Ibid. Unfortunately, the synod records do not indicate if

THE MOVEMENT OF PEOPLE ACROSS THE NORTH CHANNEL IN THE SEVENTEENTH CENTURY: THE USE OF LANGUAGE AND ETHNIC DESCRIPTIONS

An important issue identified at the outset of this article was that of how Scottish migrants in Ulster were perceived in Scotland in terms of their identity. Return migration post-1641 and 1688–90 of refugees back to Scotland provides an opportunity to analyze different types of Scottish records to investigate how these refugees were being described by different types of Scottish institutions and in different historical sources. Such sources include the records of the General Assembly and the Scottish parliament, but a key church source is that of kirk session and presbytery records as it was at this local level that money was being raised for and later distributed to refugees. What follows is by no means an exhaustive study, but rather a sample which indicates a range of different descriptions.

Elgin kirk session in the north-east of Scotland is one such source. The privy council records for 1642 indicated that the refugee problem was focused on the south-west, but the Elgin records indicated that refugees had penetrated a considerable distance to the north-east of Scotland. On 10 September 1643 Elgin kirk session dealt with cases of 'distressed Irishes'.[74] Thus, one Elizabeth Cumning, wife of Robert Smith, received £4 out of the local 'Irish contributione'.[75] The session also dealt with the case of Margaret 'Sime', who was left with two or three bairns as her husband had been killed by the 'Irish rebells'.[76] Interestingly, Elgin kirk session records describe Margaret Sime as 'ane uther Scottis Irish gentlewoman'.[77] The description of gentlewoman suggests some level of social status, but the description of her as Scots-Irish suggests Scottish descent. Later, on 6 October the kirk session made further financial provisions for the 'distressed people come from Ireland'.[78] Similar language was used by the presbytery of Kirkcaldy in Fife. At a meeting at Dysart on 13 July 1642, the brethern concluded to 'collect for the distressed people of Irland'.[79] As an example of this, Nicholas Black, 'ane Irish minister', was to be supported by a decision of the presbytery on 25 January 1643.[80]

This linguistic dimension also extended into the field of Covenanting European diplomacy. On 10 May 1644 the Committee of Estates, the most important parliamentary interval committee of the Scottish parliament, sitting in Edinburgh issued formal instructions for one Thomas Cunningham as part of a diplomatic mission to the United Provinces. This was part of an attempt to extend the 1643 Solemn League and Covenant into a Protestant

---

Jean McGee was ever found or what happened to her.   **74** *Records of Elgin*, p. 245.   **75** Ibid.,pp. 245–6.   **76** Ibid., p. 246.   **77** Ibid.   **78** Ibid.   **79** W. Stevenson (ed.), *The Presbyterie Booke of Kirkcaldie being the record of the proceedings of that presbytery from the 15th day of April 1630 to the 14th day of September 1653* (Kirkcaldy, 1900), p. 236.   **80** Ibid., p. 246.

defence league in Europe involving the Dutch and later the Swedes.[81] Cunningham's instructions also dealt with the war in Ireland. Cunningham was instructed to thank the States General of the United Provinces and 'such particular incorporations and persons as had hand' in the provision of charitable supplies which had been sent to 'the Protestants in Ireland and the Scots army there'. Cunningham was also instructed to press the United Provinces to consider the 'treacherous and bloodie attempts and conspiracies of the enemies of God' who were working for the 'subversion of the true religion' and that such kingdoms and states that professe the same' would 'not only joyne with the kingdoms of Scotland, England and Ireland in this Solemne League and Covenant for opposing poperie and prelacie and establishing the true religion, but also invite all other Christian princes to doe the lyke'. In order to pursue the 'better furtherance of this great work', Cunningham was instructed to press the Dutch to 'continue their begune charitie to *the distressed British in Ireland* and Scots army who are hazarding their lyves for defence of the true Protestant religion and whom wee are confident they will be as carefull to supply with victuall, ammunition, money and other necessaries as the Pope, Spanjard and other popish powers are in supplying the rebels and assisting them in their bloodie designes'.[82]

Legislation of the 1689 Convention of Estates dealt with return migration and victims of warfare. On 18 April the Convention legislated in favour of 'the *British* Protestants comed from Ireland'.[83] Later, on 29 April the Convention passed an Act for the Voluntary Contribution to the *Irish* and *French* Protestants.[84] This latter enactment therefore made no legislative distinction between French Huguenots and Irish Protestants, whereas the former act dealt specifically with British Protestants. Perhaps this use of the word 'British' embraced a perceived wider group of Protestants from Ireland and was not restricted to Scots. Further ethnic descriptions can be detected during the revolutionary period, this time in a military context. One Arthur Upton esquire petitioned King William *c.*1690 to have a commission to 'raise a regiment of foot of the *Irish Protestants* there'.[85] Upton had earlier raised two troops of horse for the Williamite cause in Ireland and had fought for that cause there before being 'broken by Irish rebels'.[86] The 1689 Convention had ordered that Upton should be allowed to raise a regiment of foot in Scotland. Upton appears to have come to Scotland as a victim of warfare, although he may not necessarily have been of Scottish origin. In military terms, Upton clearly wanted to raise troops in Scotland to participate in the ongoing military campaign in Ireland. What is interesting from an ethnic perspective is the language used in

---

81 Young, 'The Scottish parliament and European diplomacy, 1641–1647', pp. 77–106. 82 E.J. Courthope (ed.), *The journal of Thomas Cuningham of Campvere, 1640–1654* (Edinburgh, 1928), pp. 86–7. 83 *APS*, ix, 1689–95, p. 49. 84 Ibid., p. 78. 85 Fraser, *The Melvilles*, iii, p. 217. 86 Ibid.

the formal endorsement of his petition. This read 'Indorsed: Esquire Uptun petitione desiring warrant to raise a regiment of *Scots Irisihes* in Scotland'.[87] This would appear to relate directly to returning migrants in Scotland.

The term Scots-Irish was later used in 1698 by Andrew Fletcher of Saltoun, who later emerged as a vocal patriotic opponent to the 1707 Act of Union and who was closely associated with the articulation of a reform programme of constitutional nationalism in the early eighteenth century. In 1698 Fletcher wrote *Two Discourses concerning the Affairs of Scotland*.[88] These represented Saltoun's views and opinions about the growing Scottish political and demographic crisis under King William. In the first discourse Saltoun reflected bitterly on Scottish participation in the Nine Years War (1688–97), which had recently ended. For Saltoun, this was a 'long and tedious war, which has cost this nation much blood'.[89] For Saltoun, the negative impact of Scottish participation in William's European warfare was as much human as economic. Thus, Saltoun asserted that 'in the loss of our people, which is an expence of blood and riches too, we have paid a treble proportion'.[90] He went on to list figures of 7,000–8,000 Scots in the English fleet and 2,000–3,000 in the Dutch fleet, as well as twenty battalions of foot and six squadrons of dragoons 'here' (meaning Scotland) and in Flanders. What is of greater interest, however, in the context of this article, was that Saltoun went on to make an ethnic link between Scotland and Ulster. Saltoun therefore stated that he was 'credibly informed' that 'every fifth man in the English forces was *either of this nation, or Scots-Irish, who are a people of the same blood with us*'.[91] For Saltoun, then, one-fifth of the English forces were either Scottish or Scots-Irish and these people belonged to the same ethnic group.

Evidence of perceived identity on the part of the Scottish communities on the other side of the North Channel can also be found. On 6 August 1642 a petition was presented to the General Assembly of the Church of Scotland, at St Andrews, asking that ministers be sent from Scotland for their spiritual welfare. This petition was entitled 'The humble Petition of the most part of the *Scottish Nation* in the North of Ireland, in their own names, and in name of the rest of the Protestants there'.[92] It is clear, therefore, that a diversity of lin-

---

87 Ibid.   88 See Andrew Fletcher, *Political works*, pp. 33–81.   89 Ibid., p. 42.   90 Ibid.   91 Ibid.   92 T. Pitcairn (ed.), *Acts of the General Assembly of the Church of Scotland, 1638–1842* (Edinburgh, 1843), pp. 69–71. A similar petition was presented to the 1643 General Assembly at Edinburgh on 5 August, but on this occasion the petition was called 'The humble petition of the distressed Christians in the North of Ireland' and no specific mention was made of Scots. The 1643 petition was presented by William Mackenna, a Belfast merchant, and Sir Robert Adair of Kinhilt (ibid., pp. 74–5). The Adair family held land in Ireland (Ballymena) and Scotland (Wigtownshire). Adair was one of the members of parliament for Wigtownshire in the Covenanting parliament of 1639–41 [M. Young (ed.), *The parliaments of Scotland: burgh and shire commissioners*, i (Edinburgh, 1992), p. 4]. Mackenna presented a similar petition to the 1644 General Assembly at Edinburgh (*Acts of the General Assembly*, pp. 97–8).

guistic descriptions was in operation throughout the period; distressed Irish, Irish, Scots-Irish, Scottish Nation, Irish Protestants, British Protestants.

CONCLUSION

The seventeenth century marked a clear acceleration in migratory trends between Scotland and Ulster over the North Channel. The Scottish presence in Ulster had important implications for the history of the island of Ireland during this period. Building on the substantial migrations from Scotland in the 1690s, the presence of an 'Ulster-Scots'/Scots-Irish community in eighteenth century Ulster thereafter took on a colonial dimension with the Scots-Irish migrations to colonial north America. As has been well-documented, the Scots-Irish as an ethnic group played a crucial role in the political and military struggle for American independence against British rule. The Scots, however, played more of a mixed role in the revolutionary struggle as both despised British loyalists (many of whom were Scottish Highlanders who had suffered at the hands of the British state in Scotland) and as enthusiastic patriots.[93] This eighteenth-century dimension offers future research opportunities along ethnic and geographic lines in a colonial context. The Scots-Irish with their origins in Ulster, traced back primarily to south-west Scotland, as patriots, yet many Scots in the 'ethnic homeland' were loyalists and many Scottish loyalists in America were Gaels. From the perspective of twentieth-first century Scottish history, this poses intriguing questions, which may be uncomfortable for many. Further research into the relationship between the Scots and the Scots-Irish in America and the exposure of such research findings to a Scottish audience which is largely unaware of these issues should provide fruitful, if controversial, contemporary debate. That audience needs to become more fully aware of the long-term impact of the 'second Scotia' on the history of its country. From the wider perspective of the history of the Scotch-Irish in an American context and the use of the term Scotch-Irish as a historical badge or label, this article has shown that 'Scots-Irish' was being used in Scotland in the seventeenth century. With that in mind, it could perhaps be suggested that 'Scotch-Irish' was less of a historical invention of language and identity than a continuation of an existing seventeenth-century Scottish description and awareness, albeit not an exclusive one. This may also provide an area of further debate and research for modern day scholars.

93 For the most recent synthesis, see T.M. Devine, *Scotland's empire, 1600–1815* (London, 2003), pp. 140–87.

Ulster unionism and the Scottish dimension

GRAHAM WALKER

I

The Scottish dimension to Ulster unionism receives relatively slight attention in the scholarly literature concerning the movement's historical development. Yet I hope to show, in this chapter, that Scotland's relationship to
Ulster was invoked strikingly by unionists for the political purpose of coun-
tering the Irish home rule threat of the late nineteenth and early twentieth
centuries; and that images of Ulster-Scottish ties and bonds have, in very
recent times, been re-conjured by unionists in order to bolster their position
in an age of 'identity politics'. However, I will also indicate that, substantial
as the connections were/are between Scotland and Ulster, it has never been
a straightforward tactic for Ulster unionists to use, or, indeed, benefit from.
I want, therefore, to offer some observations on this theme in both a historical and a contemporary context.

II

In the period of the Irish home rule bills, Ulster Protestants held, to varying
degrees, depending on different contexts, Irish and Ulster allegiances.[1]
Attachments to the Union, the Empire and the British crown were considered
paramount, although an Irish identification was often proclaimed proudly.
However, the nationalist appropriation of Irishness in the political struggles of
the era and the association of Irish identity with Catholicism and Gaelic culture increasingly called into question the compatibility of Britishness and
Irishness, and made life difficult for those who only felt secure in their Irishness
when it was complemented – as they saw it – by Britishness. This reflected
the fear that home rule would break, or at least impair, the British link.

It was against such a background that the cultivation of a distinctive *Ulster*
identity was driven as a cultural project to serve political ends. Ulster
Protestants in effect felt that their protestations of loyalty to the Union, as

1 See I. McBride, 'Ulster and the British problem', in R. English and G. Walker (eds), *Unionism
in modern Ireland: new perspectives on politics and culture* (Basingstoke, 1996).

Irishmen, were not enough in the political battle against Irish nationalism. To
the 'civic' strain of argument against any change to their British citizenship,
was added the decidedly 'ethnic' one of an Ulster Protestant distinctiveness
with its own rights of self-determination.[2] Ulster Protestants thus cast around
for what distinguished them culturally from the Catholic Irish: religion came
easiest to hand given the extent to which Protestant denominational conflict
had waned and pan-Protestant rivalry with Catholicism had increased during
the nineteenth century;[3] and there was also the suitability, as will be made
clear, of significant Scottish aspects of their history and heritage.

Ulster Unionism proceeded to meet the nationalist challenge on its own
ground, and to attempt thereby to controvert the unitary vision and narrative
of Irish nationalism. In this sense, unionism was about *disruption*: disruption
of a homogenous view of Irish nationality. As Unionism developed into a mass
movement in the heavily Protestant counties of Ulster, a distinctive Ulster
Protestant identity was promoted and popularized out of the raw materials
which had long existed with such potential: that is, the historical narratives
and folktales, the poems and songs, the customs and rituals.[4] Cultural activities and historical inquiry of the kind which fuelled the development of an
Irish nationalist consciousness in general, and the Gaelic Revival in particular,
were used by the countervailing force of Ulster unionism in the same era.

Perhaps most arresting in this respect was the proliferation of texts devoted
to establishing both the historical antecedence of the 'Ulster Scots' and the
assumed destiny towards which this group drove. These were classic 'Whig'
histories of the kind produced by nationalists elsewhere at the time.[5] Central to
what was arguably an ethnic or ethno-national, identity fashioned in defiance
of Irish nationalist assumptions was the notion of the Ulster Scots as a distinctive people – a pioneering people with a glorious history in Ireland, the British
Empire and North America. (where they were known as 'Scotch-Irish'). Thus,
from the late 1880s we see a steady outpouring of works such as John Harrison,
The Scot in Ulster (1888); W.T. Latimer, *The Ulster Scot: His Faith and Fortune*
(1899); J. Heron, *The Ulster Scot* (1900); C. Hanna, *The Scotch Irish* (1902); and
J.B. Woodburn, *The Ulster Scot: His History and Religion* (1914).

The Reverend J.B. Woodburn's text, appearing just at the height of the
controversy over the third Home Rule bill, might be regarded as the apogee
of this whole Ulster–Scot enterprise. In the manner of his literary predeces-

2 See P. Bew, *Ideology and the Irish question* (Oxford, 1994) pp. 22–3; also discussion in G.
Walker, 'Thomas Sinclair: Presbyterian Liberal Unionist', in English and Walker (eds), *Unionism
in modern Ireland*; also the seminal study by J. Todd, 'Two traditions in Unionist political culture', *Irish Political Studies*, 2 (1987), 1–26.   3 See F. Wright, *Two lands on one soil: Ulster politics before Home Rule* (Dublin, 1996), passim.   4 I. McBride, *The Siege of Derry in Ulster
Protestant mythology* (Dublin, 1997), p. 80.   5 See C. Calhoun, *Nationalism* (Buckingham, 1997),
chapter 3.

sors, Woodburn's was an essentialist reading of the identity of Ulster. Presbyterianism was promoted as the decisive force shaping the personality of the Province, and the actual denominational divisions and intra-Presbyterian struggles of Ulster's Protestant history were largely elided in order to construct a coherent 'passion play' which would answer the Irish Catholic story with the Ulster Scot epic: the same dramatic themes of sacrifice, suffering and heroic struggle were fore-grounded.[6]

Woodburn's book was rapturously received by the Unionist press in Ulster and, if reviews are any guide, also made an impact across the water in Scotland. The *Aberdeen Daily Journal*, for example, commented in relation to it: 'Clearly it will be no easy matter to coerce the Covenanters, the descendants of those "grim, stern people" who conquered the wilderness, and bore a great part in seizing American Independence.'[7] *Glasgow Herald's* review, however, hinted at a more ambiguous Scottish response to Ulster when it remarked on the book's portrayal of episodes in Presbyterian history 'largely forgotten on this side of the Irish channel'.[8] Indeed, in the same month as Woodburn's book appeared, the Belfast Presbyterian newspaper, *The Witness*, expressed disappointment that many Scottish Presbyterians 'put their politics before their Presbyterianism' over the issue of Irish Home Rule,[9] a reference to the entrenched Radical/Liberal and anti-Tory political stance of many Scottish Presbyterians, particularly those in the Free Church which had broken away from the Established Church of Scotland in 1843. Ulster Presbyterian unionists, many of them from a Liberal political background, made impassioned 'Kith and Kin' appeals to their Scottish counterparts, particularly during the crisis of 1911–14,[10] and played up issues such as the Catholic Church's educational designs, and the Catholic *Ne Temere* decree on mixed marriages, in an effort to exploit the anti-Catholic sentiment which in Scotland was culturally strong although not as politically focussed.

6 See, for example, the treatment of the 1641 massacres of Protestants in Woodburn, *The Ulster Scot*, chapters 9 and 10. This episode enabled ethno-historians like Woodburn to stress the themes of Presbyterian sacrifice in particular, and the aid given by a Scottish Presbyterian army. See also Thomas Sinclair's speech at the 1912 Presbyterian Anti-Home Rule Convention: G. Walker, 'The Irish Presbyterian Anti-Home Rule Convention of 1912', *Studies* 86:341 (spring 1997), 71–7; according to the census figures of 1911, the Protestant denominational breakdown in Ulster (nine counties) was as follows: Presbyterian 421, 410; Anglican 366, 773; Methodist 48, 816. P. Buckland, *Ulster Unionism and the origins of Northern Ireland, 1886–1922* (Dublin, 1973), p. xx. 7 Quoted in *The Witness*, 29 May 1914. 8 Ibid. 9 Ibid. 10 See, for example, the sentiments of Samuel Brown of Castledawson expressed at an Orange Order meeting in Scotland. Brown said they were all citizens of 'the great British Empire', but that he was also a great 'Ulster Scot': "his forebears on both sides were Scotch people so that in coming home to Scotland he as coming home to his own people, to the Kith and Kin of his forbears and he was proud to be in grand old Scotland to address his people as an 'Ulster Scot'". Brown added that he and many like him were 'looking to Scotland in a very real sense to come to their help in their extremity if necessary'. *Belfast Weekly News*, 9 January 1913.

Ulster unionists had a limited amount of success with such propaganda exercises. They got the backing of many church ministers and congregations particularly in the urban West of Scotland, but were less able to make inroads in rural and small town Scotland, where Liberal voting was an act of faith and often tied up with land questions. However, the endorsement of prominent Scottish political figures such as Lord Rosebery and the novelist John Buchan helped them significantly. Buchan, in a speech in 1912, referred to the Ulstermen as 'a race comprised of men of our own blood and our own creed', before proceeding to argue: 'If Home Rule Ireland is a nation, how on earth can you deny the name to the Ulster Protestants? Indeed, they have a far higher title to it. They are one blood and one creed; they have such a history behind them as any nation might be proud of'.[11] Buchan's point illustrated the extent to which, by the time of the third Home Rule bill, the case against Irish home rule had come to be put much more in terms of Ulster distinctiveness and an Ulster right to self determination. Moreover, Ulster's stand was being defended increasingly in a nationalist idiom, and with the historicist justifications and a cultural gloss of a peculiarly Presbyterian, and Scottish, kind.

The Scottish Presbyterian dimension to the Ulster Protestant story lent itself readily to the political defiance required to defeat home rule; indeed also to the rebellious posturing against the British Liberal government. It provided the stuff of ethno-nationalism to rival its Irish Catholic counterpart. At a Presbyterian Anti-Home Rule convention in 1912, organized by former Liberals turned Unionists such as Thomas Sinclair, another leading Presbyterian layman, T.G. Houston, proclaimed that Ulster's stand had been misunderstood in Britain, that it was not a manifestation of the 'jingo spirit' but of the 'martyr spirit'.[12] In his pamphlet, *Ulster's Appeal* (1913), Houston summed up very well the prevailing Presbyterian self-image of the time – the 'backbone of Ulster' he asserted, before referring to their forefathers who signed 'another covenant at the time of the persecutions in Scotland'. The Solemn League and Covenant of 1912 – to which Houston was comparing the Scottish model – was indeed the prime example of a process in which the anti-Home Rule struggle was identified with the language and symbolism of a Presbyterian, and Scottish, heritage.[13] The radical populism supplied by this heritage, what Arthur Aughey has recently called the notion of the 'Sovereign People' in Ulster Unionist ideology,[14] derived in large part from a history of grievance. Ian McBride has identified this in relation to the Siege

11 J. Buchan, *What the Home Rule Bill means* (1912).   12 Walker, 'The Presbyterian Anti-Home Rule Convention'.   13 Thomas Sinclair, the man mainly responsible for the drafting of the text of the covenant, was a Liberal Unionist Presbyterian who made much of his Scottish roots.   14 A. Aughey, 'The character of Ulster Unionism', in P. Shirlow and M. McGovern (eds), *Who are 'the people'?* (London, 1997).

of Derry commemorations;[15] arguably it was also instrumental in the making of 'the Ulsterman', and the shaping of an ethnic consciousness around notions of contracts and rights and entitlements to separate treatment.[16] Donald Akenson's study of the Ulster-Scots has illuminated such themes; Akenson perceives a process of 'Presbyterianization' of the wider Protestant community during the home rule era, culminating in a form of 'cultural hegemony'.[17] I would argue that this reached its peak in the 1911–1914 period when Presbyterian 'ethno-history' and Scottish aspects of Ulster's make-up were pressed tellingly into service for Ulster unionism.

III

Edna Longley has observed[18] that the cultural ideologies that won out in Ireland by 1921–2 in effect 'froze' in the posture they had by then assumed, and proceeded to dictate cultural and educational policy in both jurisdictions: in the new six-county Northern Ireland, a devolved unit within the United Kingdom; and in the twenty-six county Irish Free State on which was conferred Dominion status.

In Northern Ireland the ruling Unionist Party encouraged their Protestant communal constituency to continue to regard Ulster identity proudly, and – just as in the period of the home rule threat – 'Ulsterness' meant distinctiveness and difference from the rest of Ireland. However, Northern Ireland's status as a constitutional anomaly in the context of the UK[19] created difficulties: the impression was widespread in Britain that Northern Ireland was a 'place apart,' and unionists consequently felt that they had to work hard to demonstrate their British allegiance and loyalty. Hence the over – compensatory displays of patriotic pomp around events such as royal visits which Gillian McIntosh has ably discussed.[20] These displays were the popular cultural accompaniment to the political approach adopted by successive Unionist governments from the 1920s to the 1960s: that of remaining as far as possible step by step with Britain, and not therefore using devolution in any spirit of innovation or for the purposes of increasing autonomy. This glosses over an occasionally complex story,[21] but

15 McBride, *The Siege of Derry*. 16 On this theme see the seminal work by D. Miller, *Queen's Rebels: Ulster loyalism in historical perspective* (Dublin, 1978). 17 D.H. Akenson, *God's peoples* (New York, 1992), pp. 148–9; also Bew, *Ideology*, p. 48, regarding the views of James Bryce. 18 E. Longley 'An Irish Kulturkampf', in D. Kennedy (ed.), *Forging an identity* (Belfast, 2000). 19 Northern Ireland since 1921 has not been part of the British party system, and a convention quickly emerged after Northern Ireland's inception that the affairs of the Province would not be discussed at Westminster. 20 G. McIntosh, *The force of culture: unionist identities in twentieth century Ireland* (Cork, 1999). 21 For example, there was a serious debate within the Ulster Unionist Party in the post-World War Two years about the wisdom of Dominion status

essentially Unionists took no separatist risks with their powers until, that is, the premiership of Terence O'Neill from 1963.

O'Neill, in contrast to his predecessors, relished the potential of devolution; he visualized Northern Ireland leading the way to the rest of the UK in terms of policy and ideas, rather than meekly tagging on behind. It is perhaps no coincidence then that explicit efforts were made in the mid-1960s, with the support and the encouragement of the O'Neill government, to re-invigorate a local – Ulster – identity.[22] Again the Ulster–Scottish theme was strongly foregrounded. An Ulster-Scot Historical Society was set up at the Northern Ireland government's bidding, and in 1965 produced a booklet called *The Scotch-Irish and Ulster*. It makes familiar reading – a recycling of the kind of material found in the turn of the century 'Ulster Scot' blockbusters. Referring to what was termed as 'a wave of interest' in the USA regarding the Scotch-Irish, the anonymous author(s) of the booklet recalled that 'when American interest was at its peak at the beginning of this century, the Ulster-Scots or Scotch-Irish in Ulster were engaged in a prolonged and ultimately successful struggle to remain with their Scottish cousins within the United Kingdom when the rest of Ireland was breaking away to become in the end a Republic'.

The Ulster-Scot Historical Society claimed to be concerned with research into their forebears and ancestral homesteads. Of the latter, it was said in a 1965 pamphlet: 'No stately castles these but rather humble cottages not wholly unlike the log cabins which the Scotch-Irish built along the frontiers of America.' What is notable about this is the image of an essentially plain and unprivileged people – the picture Presbyterians had tended to paint of themselves in contrast to Church of Ireland wealth and finery. In this respect, it was somewhat ironic that the very Anglo-Irish and Church of Ireland figure of O'Neill – Eton-educated and aloof in manner – should seek to foster, or re-vitalize, a sense of identity for his devolved Province which once more fell back on the dour and indomitable stereotype of the Ulster-Scot.[23]

Shortly after the outbreak of 'the troubles' in 1969, Captain Bill Henderson, a senior Ulster Unionist from the O'Neill era and publisher of the *Belfast Newsletter*, gave evidence to the US Congress in which he equated the 'Ulster People' with the 'Scotch Irish' and referred to the Ulster Scottish origins of eleven US presidents.[24] At the same hearings, the Reverend Charles Reynolds, president of the Northern Ireland Service Council in New York, delivered a history lesson on the kingdom of Dalriada – an historical theme to

for Northern Ireland.   **22** See A. Gailey, 'The destructiveness of constructive unionism: theories and practice, 1890s–1960s', in D.G. Boyce and A. O'Day (eds), *Defenders of the Union* (London, 2001); M. Mulholland, *Northern Ireland at the crossroads* (Basingstoke, 2000) pp. 70–1. **23** See disparaging comments in James Kelly, *Bonfires on the hillside* (Belfast, 1995) p. 181.   **24** *Hearings before the sub-committee on Europe of the Committee on Foreign Affairs House of Representatives Ninety-second Congress Second Session* (Washington, 1972) p. 241.

be re-visited by Ulster unionists from the late 1970s onwards – and concluded: 'When we talk about a political union for the people of Northern
Ireland in the historical sense, it will be more natural to have it with Scotland
than with the Republic of Ireland if we go back to historical precedence.'[25]

As 'the Troubles' erupted, there may have been more appreciation of the
Ulster unionist case in Scotland than anywhere else, and fraternal links
through organizations like the Loyal Orders, were well-established and vig-
orous. In July 1970 it was noted by Prime Minister Edward Heath's
Conservative cabinet in London that trouble at Orange marches in Ulster in
the past had come from visiting contingents of Scots who were 'more aggres-
sive than local Orangemen'. Consideration was then given as to how the
number of Scots coming to Northern Ireland during 'the marching season'
might be reduced.[26] The murder of three Scottish soldiers by the IRA in
March 1971 resulted in the formation by Loyalist youths of 'Tartan Gangs',
and in Scotland there was no shortage of street demonstrations in support of
both sides, republican and loyalist graffiti, and topical additions to the respective Orange and Green repertoires of the supporters of the Rangers and Celtic
football teams in Glasgow.

Nevertheless, the predominant effect of the situation in Northern Ireland
on Scotland was to constrain sectarian passions from reaching a similar point
of outright conflict. There were crucial differences between both places in
respect of residential mixing, inter-marriage and a political context in Scotland
in which class issues were generally prioritised. Moreover, Scotland had in
general moved much further down the road to secularization. Echoes of the
Ulster troubles were certainly heard but the great majority of Scots recoiled
from the violence of extremists on both sides, and kept out of the political
argument. Among the Scottish political parties there was an unspoken consensus to leave Irish matters alone which was observed with only rare exceptions throughout the 1970s, 1980s and early 1990s.[27]

IV

The contemporary context of the peace process in Northern Ireland and con-
stitutional changes in the UK under the Blair Labour government has high-
lighted further manifestations of Ulster unionism's Scottish dimension.
Perhaps the most striking example has been the provisions in the Belfast
Agreement of Good Friday 1998 for the recognition and support of Ulster-
Scots speech, the equivalent of Scots or 'Lallans'. The inclusion of these pro-

25 Ibid.   26 PRO CAB 128/47, 21 July 1970.   27 See discussion in G. Walker, *Intimate
strangers: political and cultural interactions between Scotland and Ulster in modern times* (Edinburgh,
1995), chapter 6.

visions around Ulster-Scots in the Agreement has been widely viewed as a
political concession to Ulster unionists, designed to balance the support given
to the Irish language. There has been criticism of this as politically oppor-
tunist on the part of those who dispute the claim of Ulster-Scots (or 'Ullans')
to be a language in its own right, and who are sceptical about the number of
people who actually speak or use it.[28]

The debate around the language issue has perhaps obscured the wider significance of the rise in awareness of Ulster-Scottish cultural links, and the
extent to which the latter constitute a vital segment of the Province's cultural
mosaic. Ulster-Scots culture has the potential to be shared by both unionists
and nationalists in Northern Ireland, and the efforts of many of the Ulster-
Scots movement's activists to limit the politicization – and the 'sectarianiza-
tion' – of the issue have received too little consideration in the scholarly commentaries to date.[29] There has also been an extravagant emphasis on the theme
of 'British Israelism' in connection with Ulster Scots culture.

Nevertheless, the political lines have been drawn quite rigidly. Nationalist
jibes about Ulster Scots street signs and other phenomena have met the
unionist response that the Irish language and Gaelic culture have been used
politically for years with sectarian consequences. Wall murals celebrating the
Ulster-Scottish link have appeared in loyalist working-class areas with mes-
sages which seem to have the intention – although their creators may refute
it – of boosting the morale of that community. 'Dinnae houl yer whisht, houl
yer ain' proclaims one such mural: 'hold your own' indeed echoes traditional
unionist political slogans.[30] The involvement of leading unionist political figures in the movement such as Lord Laird of Artigarvan and Nelson
McCausland has reinforced the argument of those who perceive the current
revival of Ulster-Scots culture to be primarily about providing a 'cultural
booster' for Ulster unionist identity.[31] Certainly, as Edna Longley has demonstrated,[32] the 'Irish Culture War' has deep political roots, and cultural controversies make a profound political impact as a matter of course in a divided
society such as Northern Ireland.

In addition it might be argued that the Ulster-Scots issue has provided a
platform for some unionists (and indeed some favouring Ulster independence)
to promote an ethnic narrative which has been sketched out in the historical

28 See, for example, critical reflections of Malachi O'Doherty, 'Loyalists discover a language
and history', *The Scotsman*, 5 January 2001.   29 M. NicCraith, 'Politicized linguistic consciousness: the case of the Ulster Scots', *Nations and Nationalism*, 7:1 (2001), 21–37; C. McCall,
'Political transformation and the reinvention of the Ulster Scots identity and culture', *Identities:
Global Studies in Culture and Power*, 9 (2002), 197–218.   30 See J. Vannais, 'Out of the shad-
ows of the gunmen', *Fortnight*, 382 (January 2000), 21–3.   31 See McCall, op. cit.   32 E.
Longley, 'Multi-culturalism and Northern Ireland: making differences fruitful', in E. Longley
and D. Kiberd, *Multi-culturalism: the view from the two Irelands* (Cork, 2001).

work of Ian Adamson,[33] himself a unionist member of the Northern Ireland Assembly established by the Belfast Agreement. Adamson has attempted to provide an historical and cultural basis for Ulster identity which goes beyond the Plantation to the Cruthin, Cu Chulainn and the kingdom of Dalriada – a project which emphasises at once the antiquity of the Ulster – Scottish relationship and the ancient distinction between Ulster and the rest of Ireland. The works of Adamson might indeed take their place in the canon of ethnohistory which includes the Woodburn, Latimer, Harrison and Hanna books referred to above, if measured by their social, cultural and political effects.

However, assumptions of cultural affinities with Scotland, today as in the home rule era, are often made in a spirit of political exigency which hinders any significantly broad reciprocal gesture. Unionist insecurity has fashioned ossified perspectives which take little notice of the realities of contemporary Scotland. A talismanic and romanticized version of Scottishness has been a feature of unionist 'last resortism', part of the essential cultural baggage which would be taken into the final fight for survival if they were to be abandoned completely by the British government.

In this connection, and by way of a literary aside, it is notable how the problematic aspect – from an Ulster loyalist viewpoint – to the Ulster-Scottish relationship was highlighted recently by the Ulster playwright Gary Mitchell in his play *Marching On*.[34] The Ulster-Scottish theme is prominent throughout this play. A young loyalist extremist is clad in Rangers gear as he welcomes his Scottish visitor for the 12th of July celebrations. The Ulster-Scottish relationship is referred to as 'the link' throughout. The visitor is feted by his hosts, one of whom – a female admirer – thinks he is 'Just like Braveheart – only Protestant'. However, the relationship becomes strained when the Scottish visitor becomes increasingly bewildered and taken aback by the venom of his hosts' protests over a banned march. The young loyalist extremist's disillusionment with the Scotsman when the latter decides to leave during the protests echoes to a degree the sense of disappointment felt by Ulster unionists at the time of the Irish home rule controversies when it was felt that Scottish support was not all it could have been.

Notwithstanding this ethnic 'angst', the validity of Ulster-Scottish cultural expressions does serve as a reminder that Irish nationalists and republicans have generally failed to appreciate the range of identities with Ulster unionism/loyalism, and that terms such as 'Anglo-Irish' and binary oppositions of 'Irish and British' can be very misleading. There is a need, moreover, to unpack the concept of 'Britishness' and to recognize the wide diver-

33 I. Adamson, *The Cruthin* (Belfast, 1978); idem, *The identity of Ulster* (Belfast, 1981); idem, *The Ulster people* (Belfast, 1991). For a discussion of Adamson's work see B. Graham, 'The imagining of place: representation and identity in contemporary Ireland', in B. Graham (ed.), *In search of Ireland* (London, 1997). 34 This play was first staged in Belfast in 2000.

oity of meanings which it can assume. For too long commentators on the behaviour of Ulster unionists have seen contradictions where they should have seen ambiguities in the wider issue of British identity.

In Scotland today there is a strong tendency towards regarding British identity in a looser manner than before: devolution is identified with a wide degree of Scottish autonomy. Unionism in contemporary Scotland is for the most part 'lower case'. This is not gratifying to those Ulster unionists whose psychological and emotional needs crave a stronger pan-UK sense of belief in – or vision for – the Union's future.[35]

Nevertheless, it might be argued that the Blair government's constitutional reforms and the re-shaping of relationships with the British Isles bring with them opportunities for unionists. Edna Longley has recently written of the Ulster unionists' need to embrace a 'political life-wish'. She has called on them 'to face into the devolutionary reality that is creating a different kind of 'Britishness': one with overlapping affiliations rather than unitary imperatives. The East-West strand in the Belfast Agreement recognises that potential.'[36] The East-West strand referred to is in effect the British-Irish Council (or 'Council of the Isles') which has yet to develop into the pro-active body required to give political expression to the range of cultural, social and economic interactions to which Longley alludes.[37]

V

The Scottish dimension to Ulster unionism should alert us to the way that the Ulster Protestants' sense of British identity has been caricatured and misunderstood. It should help us to open up the category of 'British' and to appreciate that concept's variety. Ulster unionism faces the challenge of forging a new relationship with Scotland – and other parts of the UK – as well as reaching an accommodation with Irish nationalism. Ulster unionists have always faced in two directions: political structures in these islands are now beginning to reflect the layered identities and multi-cultural complexities which characterize the archipelago.

35 See P. Bew, 'Where is Burke's vision of the Union?', *Times Literary Supplement*, 16 March 2001. 36 Longley, 'An Irish Kulturkampf'. 37 For the British-Irish Council's potential significance see: V. Bogdanor, 'The British-Irish Council and devolution', *Government and Opposition*, 34 (1999), 287–98; G.Walker, 'The Council of the Isles and the Scotland-Northern Ireland relationship', *Scottish Affairs*, 27 (1999), 108–23; P. Lynch and S. Hopkins, 'The British-Irish Council: structure, programmes and prospects', *Irish Studies in International Affairs*, 12 (2001), 133–50.

'For we are the Brigton Derry Boys': social and political linkages between Derry and Glasgow in the nineteenth and early twentieth centuries

MÁIRTÍN Ó CATHÁIN

While a number of prominent historians have explored the links between Glasgow and Belfast none have, as yet, looked at the Derry-Glasgow connections in any depth, though many are well-acquainted with the strength and longevity of the connections between the two cities. Contemporary manifestations very obviously include the large Celtic support in Derry and the presence of visiting Scottish loyalist flute bands, manifestations every bit as legitimate as the hosting of Glaswegian writers, musicians and even tourist coach parties. It is not my intention, however, to try and locate every linkage from pre-Columban foundations up until 1865, suffice it to say that even by then the two cities were already closely tied. In fact, it is interesting to note that Glasgow's first official gathering of Derry exiles expressed what one speaker termed their 'peculiar right' to celebrate the link with Scotland on account of Colm Cille's mission to the heathen Caledonians in the sixth century.[1] Certainly, it is not unreasonable to assume that among the small band of Scots colonists who established themselves in Derry after 1600 there were at least a few natives of Glasgow.[2] Moreover, we can say that this number probably increased as the seventeenth century progressed, though it may well have been reduced by the predominantly Presbyterian outflow to North America in the decades after the siege. It was probably also from the eighteenth century that Glasgow University became an increasingly favoured location for the sons of many Derry Protestant families.[3] Derry Protestants also contributed a frequently unacknowledged supply to the annual seasonal exodus of migratory farm labourers in the harsh years after the Napoleonic wars. Indeed, as Graham Walker has established, by 1833–9, 22 per cent of seasonal migrants and 61 per cent of emigrants from Derry (city and county) to Scotland were

---

1 *Glasgow Observer*, 11 April 1896. The continued leading of the Apprentice Boys' Relief of Derry parade around the walls still gives pride of place to Glasgow's Blackskull Flute Band.
2 M. Perceval-Maxwell, *The Scottish migration to Ulster in the reign of James I* (London, 1973), pp. 69–70 & p. 303, n.23. Over 1614–15 alone, seven ships brought supplies, and probably migrants, from Glasgow to Derry.   3 Iain M. Bishop, 'The education of Ulster students at Glasgow University during the 18th century', unpublished MA thesis, Queen's University, Belfast (1987).

Protestants. The pattern was the reverse, however, at this point with regard
to Derry Catholics who contributed 88 per cent of seasonal migrants and only
39 per cent permanent emigrants.[4] Evidence for a significant influence of
Protestants from Derry may lie in the fact of a very early organizational form,
the appropriately named 'Old Revolution Club', which aimed from its inception in the 1740s, to perpetuate the memory of the Apprentice Boys and the
battle of the Boyne. This was a not altogether untoward ambition either in a
city that earlier in the eighteenth century had welcomed Governor Walker
with open arms and salutary honours.[5] The Orange Order, of course, made
its Glasgow debut in 1813 and would have almost definitely, like the mainly
benevolent body, the Glasgow Hibernian Society founded in 1792, contained
its quota of self-designated Derry or Londonderry natives.[6]

Increasingly, emigration from Derry was facilitated by faster and cheaper
vessels which could make the 139-mile trip to Glasgow in just under twenty
hours, though it was not until 1851 that Alexander Laird of Glasgow began
his famous service which he united with his main rival, the Burns Steamship
Company, in 1922 to form the Burns and Laird Line.[7] The potato famine
years of the late 1840s did not, as is often stated, fail to affect Derry and
while emigration to Scotland was not as dramatic as from other counties in
Ulster such as Donegal and Monaghan, it nevertheless did take place, and
Catholics began to form a greater share of the emigrants from this time.
Scotland's Irish-born population generally in the period from 1841 to 1851
almost doubled to over 200,000, while in the twenty-year-period from 1851 to
1871, Glasgow's Irish-born numbers went from around 60,000 to 70,000
people. These figures though, cannot give a true reflection of the Glasgow
Irish, because they enumerate only first generation immigrants and not the
second generation who were born in Scotland. This can be slightly rectified
by looking at Glasgow Catholic population figures and these totalled just over
100,000 (a sizeable number of whom were Highlanders), in a Glasgow population of about 400,000 by the 1860s, however this still leaves out the Scots-
born sons and daughters of Irish Protestants.[8] The figures, though, make clear

4 Graham Walker, 'The Protestant Irish in Scotland', in T.M. Devine (ed.), *Irish immigrants
and Scottish society, 1790–1990* (Edinburgh, 1991), p. 49.   5 Elaine McFarland, *Protestants first:
Orangeism in 19th century Scotland* (Edinburgh, 1991), p. 43; and Patrick Macrory, *The Siege
of Derry* (Oxford, 1980), p. 323.   6 McFarland, p. 51; and Bernard Aspinwall, 'A long journey: the Irish in Scotland', in Patrick O'Sullivan (ed.), *The Irish world wide: history, heritage,
identity, v: Religion and identity* (Leicester, 1996), p. 153.   7 Brian Mitchell, *The making of
Derry: an economic history* (Genealogy Centre, Derry, 1992), pp. 50–2. Even in the later twentieth century the Glasgow-Derry route could be a quite harrowing journey; see letter from an
American passenger in *Derry Journal*, 16 October 1950 about conditions aboard the steamers.   8
Donald M. MacRaild, *Irish immigrants in modern Britain, 1750–1922* (Basingstoke, 1999), pp.
18–19; and Aspinwall, pp. 154–5; and J.E. Handley, *The Irish in modern Scotland* (Cork, 1947),
p. 46.

that by the 1860s Glasgow had a large, visible and overwhelmingly Ulster Irish presence containing significant numbers of Derry men, women and children of differing denominations inhabiting overcrowded and insanitary streets around the town centre.

The 1860s were a period of rejuvenating militant Irish nationalism and the chief instrument of that revival was the Fenian movement or Irish Republican Brotherhood (IRB), founded in Dublin in 1858. The new body, heavily influenced by exiles in both its form and content, made its appearance in Glasgow within about a year of its formation and was aided in its early growth by a fraternal and open, but equally militant group known as the National Brotherhood of St Patrick. Few reliable and/or accurate remnants survive of these organizations that might indicate where their Glasgow adherents originally came from in Ireland, but from a list of Glasgow National Brotherhood of St Patrick stalwarts from 1864, the name John Magurk possibly indicates at least one Derry man.[9] Of perhaps more likelihood are the names of John O'Doherty and James Bradley, arrested in 1868 by Glasgow police investigating Fenian activities. Still, the entire process of linking name and locality is fraught with difficulty and can therefore only truly be posited with extreme caution.[10] We can be much more certain about the figure of Edward McCluskey, whom we know was both a Derryman and a very senior IRB commander in Glasgow, who was exposed by a police informer in 1866 and had to flee, first to Belfast and then to Dublin, where he was caught and imprisoned in December of that year. McCluskey later had the common option of continued incarceration or lifelong exile to the US, and after adopting the latter course he settled in Brooklyn where he appears to have lived out his remaining years.[11] McCluskey was very probably an IRB man before coming to Glasgow, but this was fairly unusual because the Fenians were poorly organized in the north-west of Ulster, and somewhat eclipsed by the Ribbon secret societies with their blend of anti-Orange, anti-landlord and pro-Irish Catholic nationalist sentiment. Having said that, the 1860s witnessed something of a coalescence between Fenians and Ribbonmen, and Derry was targeted by IRB men in Scotland as a point of entry on an insurrection breaking out. The prospect though, of a Scottish Fenian invasion induced little other than sarcasm from the pages of the *Derry Journal*. A column writer commented in 1866 that,

---

9 National Archives of Ireland (NAI), Fenian Briefs, letter dated 27 March 1864 from Thomas McPhillips, secretary, McManus Branch, National Brotherhood of St Patrick, Glasgow to the Governing Council, Dublin, Carton 6, Envelope 21.   10 Private information from Dr Patrick Quinlivan (1994).   11 NAI, Fenian Files, Habeas Corpus Suspension Act (HCSA), 1866, ICR, vol. 11, p. 244B, case of Edward McCluskey; and *United Irishman* (New York), 25 February 1888.

Neither in ancient or modern history was Derry valour ever subjected
to so severe a test as that which would be applied if seventy weavers
from Dundee, each armed with a shuttle and a read, and carrying his
web on his back like a knapsack, appeared before Ferryquay gate and
with infuriated looks stood shivering in the rain, demanding an uncon-
ditional surrender on behalf of the Irish Republic.[12]

The threat, however, was taken more seriously by the authorities when soon
after the *Derry Journal* piece they arrested two senior Fenians in Ballymoney,
County Antrim, and Derry, one of whom was a customs and excise officer
working on the Derry–Glasgow line. Interestingly, the other – who was felt to
be an IRB commander in north Derry and north Antrim – was a Protestant
named William McCrea.[13]

Fenians and Ribbonmen aside, however, it seems likely that many Derry
people in Glasgow had little time or money for such 'distractions'. In fact,
on occasion, even the close-knit bonds created while growing up in Derry
could dissolve in the alienating and harsh conditions immigrants faced in
Clydeside at this time. The Glasgow poor law records are an invaluable
marker of such rootlessness and abandonment and the case of just one Derry
woman who applied for poor relief gives an illustration of this. Mary Sweenie,
aged 58, was newly widowed (her husband had died in the street), and suffering from acute rheumatism when she approached the poor law guardians
in October 1862. An inspector's report from November ascertained her ill-
ness, that she had no dependants and lived with her sister in one room, three
stories up in the grim tenements of Glasgow's High Street, an area home to
a great many Irish immigrants. He described their accommodation as miser-
able and completely lacking in furniture or even a bed. A list of former res-
idences showed a litany of the kind of continual drifting from one squalid,
disease-ridden abode to another commonplace among the Glasgow Irish, and
Mary was duly admitted to the poorhouse where she eventually died on 27
April 1878.[14] The poor law records in Glasgow's City Archives reveal a host
of similarly sad stories where young and old Derry immigrants fell on
Dickensian hard times, had little option for help other than the grim façade
of places like Barnhill Poorhouse in Glasgow's east end, and the obligatory
pauper's grave in nearby Dalbeth Cemetery after the rigours and shame of
Victorian charitable institutionalization.

The collapse of Fenianism and the onset of the home rule agitation in the
1870s opened up a new vista for those immigrants willing, able and fortunate

12 *Londonderry Journal*, 6 January 1866.   13 NAI, Fenian Files, HCSA, ICR, vol. 11, pp.
252–5, case of Felix McCotter and William J. McCrea.   14 Glasgow City Archives (GCA),
Glasgow Poor Law Applications (GPLA), D-HEW, 10/4/26, p. 208, application of Mary
Sweenie.

to pursue activities outside work and household routines. Those that seized the opportunities were often far from being considered as even middle class and probably found coherence, familiarity and security, as well as conviviality (Fenians, Ribbonmen and Orangemen mostly met in pubs, home rulers held dinners and concerts), in gatherings of their fellow country- and countymen and women. Places of worship, particularly Catholic chapels were community focal points of a sort – Glasgow had a St Columbkille's in the suburb of Rutherglen founded in 1851, and a St Columba's in the north of the city by 1906 – but specifically Irish organizations were much sought after.[15] An example of this hunger for demonstrably Irish societies is apparent in the fact that when the Apprentice Boys of Derry were considering the possibility of chartering branches outside of the city, the first application came not from anywhere in Ulster, but from Glasgow, in 1872. Nearby Johnstone had even held a Relief of Derry commemoration in 1871, but it was not until much later that the Apprentice Boys of Derry actually conceded the formation of branches elsewhere, however the application underlines the fact that a Derry Protestant minority did exist in Glasgow, probably concentrated increasingly in the Partick and Whiteinch area as the century progressed.[16] Specifically Derry-influenced branches are harder to identify among the Glasgow home rulers, though the Home Government Branch – which was the biggest in Scotland with several hundred members – definitely contained Derry men. Its president, and Scotland's leading home ruler for years thereafter, was a prosperous Belfast Protestant named John Ferguson who was instrumental in persuading his friend, the Belfast provisions merchant Joseph Gillis Biggar to stand in the 1872 parliamentary by-election in Derry. Ferguson visited the city then and many times over the years as an advocate of home rule, though Biggar, as a Presbyterian, did not win the support of Derry's Catholic bishop and priests who counselled their flock to vote for the Liberal and Catholic candidate, and the Tory, Charles Lewis, took the seat leaving Biggar in third place.[17]

An intriguing development of the 1870s was the growing preponderance of skilled Irish Protestant workers in the shipyards of Glasgow, many from Belfast. They settled in areas such as Govan and Partick and their Orange lodges sprang up soon after their arrival. That more than the occasional Derry

---

15 *Catholic Directory for Scotland* (Glasgow, 1994), pp. 232 & 313. Many Derry-born Catholic priests also served in Glasgow over the years, with a majority trained for the Scottish mission in St Columb's College, Derry. Father Bernard Canning estimates that in the 150-year-period from 1829 to 1979, Derry contributed an impressive 76 priests, the sixth highest from all 32 counties in Ireland; see Bernard J. Canning, *Irish-born secular priests in Scotland, 1829–1979* (Inverness, 1979), p. 389, appendix I.   16 William S. Marshall, *The Billy Boys: a concise history of Orangeism in Scotland* (Edinburgh, 1996), p. 177; and McFarland, pp. 165 & 83.   17 Desmond Murphy, *Derry, Donegal and Modern Ulster, 1790–1921* (Derry, 1981), pp. 124–7; and *Londonderry Journal*, 17, 19 & 21 August 1872.

man drifted into other lodges is indicated by the names at least one or two, such as 'LOL 289 Derry Maiden Light', were given at their foundation. Whether some of the workers were later attracted to Derry from Clydeside when shipbuilding in the city re-animated in the 1880s and formed part of the distinctively 'Scottish' community based in Rosemount around streets such as Glasgow Terrace, Argyle Street, and Greenock Street (now Hawthorn Terrace), remains to be fully examined. If so, however, it may go some way to explaining why the 'Scotch' in Rosemount soon had their own Orange lodge and flute band.[18] This was hardly a definitively Scottish thing, and differs quite dramatically from the 'other' Scottish presence in nineteenth- and early twentieth-century Derry, which consisted of a wealthy merchant and manufacturing class, centred around such Glaswegians as the steamship owners, the McLellans, and Tillie and Henderson, the shirtmakers. These Scots, many of whom had built up considerable fortunes in Derry enjoyed their own patriotic conviviality in the form of annual St Andrew's Day banquets and celebrations in the city centre. In the decades after the First World War, the *Derry Journal* turned its occasional interest in the Irish in Scotland into a regular weekly feature and prominent visiting Scots in Derry could still create headlines, such as that which attended the visit to the city of anti-Catholic firebrand Alexander Ratcliffe in July 1933.[19]

Back in Glasgow a decade and more of largely ineffective Home Rule politics had led to a slow rejuvenation of the Fenian tradition, though the IRB in Scotland under its Glasgow-born leader, John Torley, was quite a placid and tactful organization, keen to calmly await rather than create another attempt at insurrection. This therefore allowed the Fenian torch to pass into Irish-American hands, and it was that redoubtable enemy of all things British, Jeremiah O'Donovan Rossa who capitalized on nationalist, historical and immigrant grievances. His organizers were in Glasgow in 1882 seeking to put together a team of dynamiters to carry out attacks in the city as part of a wider campaign in Britain in the early 1880s. Those attacks consisted of three bombings in Glasgow in 1883, which caused considerable damage and some injuries, though no fatalities. Of the ten Glasgow Irishmen subsequently convicted and jailed for these incidents, two were Derry men: James McCullough, a 33-year-old chemical works labourer, and Thomas Devaney, a 40-year-old quay labourer.[20] Both were jailed for life, despite the fact that their involvement appears to have been largely peripheral to the actual attacks. They were

18 McFarland, p. 105; and Walker, pp. 58–9; and B.J. Canning, H. Gallagher, J. Bradley, *Rosemount* (Derry, 1992), pp. 31 & 52–60.   19 Mitchell, pp. 52 & 104; and *Derry Journal*, 2 December 1885 for annual St Andrew's Day supper of the Londonderry Scottish Association, and 7 July 1933 for the Ratcliffe visit.   20 Máirtín Ó Catháin, 'Fenian dynamite': dissident Irish Republicans in late nineteenth century Scotland', in Oonagh Walsh (ed.), *Ireland abroad: politics and professions in the nineteenth century* (Four Courts, Dublin, 2003).

released in the later 1890s, but only McCullough re-involved himself politically, going on to become a prominent Sinn Féin member in the early 1900s.
Devaney became a sort of itinerant labourer, his wife having died and then
his son in a Glasgow poorhouse during his imprisonment, and after years of
wandering he collapsed and died on a remote roadside in the western highlands in 1909.[21]

Slightly more pedestrian pursuits, such as the Ancient Order of Hibernians
(AOH), and the Irish National Foresters (INF) indulged in, won many more
advocates than the dynamite war, the IRB or even the Home Rulers, and
Derry men were once again to the fore in these bodies. A large number were
attracted by the fraternal and benevolent character of such groups in a time
when many Irish immigrants still found it difficult to obtain certain kinds of
work because of religious and sectional antipathies, and when unemployment
and ill-health could quickly lead to severe impoverishment. Some, of course,
may simply have enjoyed marching and the 'wearing of the green' in public.
For much of the 1880s and 1890s the AOH in Scotland was riven with internal rivalries, and had wings favourable to Home Rule and to dynamiting. In
the former camp, Derry man Martin Devaney (no relation to the dynamiter),
was a close confidant of the Board of Erin AOH leader in Derry, John
Scullion, whom he accompanied on his frequent trips through Scotland.[22]
Not to be outdone though, the dynamite-leaning wing of the AOH, the
American Board, also contained Derry men, such as John Toner, and had as
their envoys to the city one James McNamee and even a priest, Father
William O'Shaughnessy, whose family were amongst the founders of Celtic
Football Club. Their leader in Derry was a man named John O'Kane, but
despite their best efforts the city remained a Board of Erin stronghold, though
incidents such as McNamee's arrest in an advanced state of drunken intoxi-
cation in a Derry street probably did little to help their cause.[23]

The INF, founded in 1877, were quite different from the AOH inasmuch
as they drew no creed line and welcomed into their ranks Irish people of all
denominations. Nevertheless, they utilized a wide array of avowedly nationalist icons and numbered some home rule MPs among their membership.
Among its senior figures in Scotland were a Derry-born undertaker named
Francis Gillespie (who was also an IRB man), and an engine-borer and occasional poet from Derry called Daniel Bradley. Bradley lived in the Anderston
district of Glasgow in a comfortable three-roomed house, worked for a steam-

21 Ó Catháin; and GCA, GPLA, D-HEW, 17/267, p. 73263, application of Thomas Devaney;
and *Glasgow Observer*, 27 March 1909. 22 Public Records Office (PRO), Colonial Office Papers,
CO 904/15; and NAI, Crime Branch Special (CBS) reports, 24207/S, report dated 18 February
1901 from Detective Sergeant Maguire, Royal Irish Constabulary, Glasgow to Attorney-General,
Dublin Castle, on AOH men John Scullion and Martin Devaney. 23 PRO, CO 904, Boxes
48 & 50, and CO 904/15; and *Glasgow Examiner*, 28 August 1897.

engine maker, and was active in the local Home Rule and League of the Cross
(temperance body) branches in addition to the Foresters. He died in Glasgow
in 1901, aged 48 and was brought home to Derry for burial in the city cemetery. Many of his poems though still lie in the pages of the newspaper of the
Irish in Scotland, the *Glasgow Observer*.[24]

With the Home Rulers in some disarray and division after the Parnell
split, other movements such as the Gaelic revival, labour politics and that for
county reunions gained ground, and all with people from Derry involved in
their progress. For example, at its outset in Scotland the Gaelic Athletic
Association had the firm support of senior Glasgow IRB men, John Brolly
and Joseph McFalls, both from Derry. Two other IRB men from Derry active
in literary society circles (Bernard Havilan and James Ward), were also heavily involved in the Anderston district with trade unions (the National Union
of Dock Labourers), with a body for ensuring Irish support for socialist
municipal election candidates (called the Anderston Workers' Association),
and in the Independent Labour Party.[25] Havilan and Ward were also instrumental in helping set up a Derry Reunion Committee in 1896 which aimed to
bring together all Derry exiles and their families every year for a grand con-
cert, meeting and dinner dance. While it can't be denied that the IRB had a
good foothold in the Reunion Committee (and much more so than in the
Donegal, Armagh, Monaghan or Tyrone Committees), and used this to some
effect in 1897 when its members initiated a 'Derry Defence Fund' to aid
nationalists in the city in their campaign against gerrymandering, most Derry
Reunion members were Home Rulers. The committee president, James
Feeney, who was born in Comber-Claudy in 1839 but lived and worked in
Derry for Tillie and Henderson before moving on to another shirt-maker in
Glasgow, is a case in point. In 1883 he began his own business in Glasgow,
had an active role in the St Vincent de Paul and was a total abstainer. He
married, had fourteen sons and served periods as a school board member and
parish councillor in Renfrewshire before his death in 1906.[26] This career is
comparable to that of another Reunion Committee member, James Barker,
born in 1857 who came to Glasgow and set up business in Anderston as a
draper. He was a founder of the Land League branch, and the local Home

24 *Glasgow Examiner*, 4 September 1897; and *Glasgow Observer*, 1 June 1901. I am indebted to
Mickey McGuinness, Harbour Museum, Derry, for drawing my attention to a small booklet
of Bradley's poems, for a typical example; see 'Ireland a nation again', *Glasgow Observer*, 13
May 1893. 25 NAI, CBS reports, 24032/S, report dated 18 January 1901 by Detective
Sergeant Harrington, Royal Irish Constabulary, Glasgow on IRB in the city; and *Glasgow
Examiner*, 12 February 1898. 26 *Glasgow Observer*, 11, 18 & 25 January, 1 & 8 February, and
4 & 11 April 1896 for Derry Reunion Committee, and *Glasgow Examiner*, 27 February, 17 April
& 21 August 1897 for the Derry Defence Fund, also *Glasgow Observer*, 21 July 1906 for James
Feeney obituary.

Rule branch in addition to being a member of the Glasgow Liberal Association and Young Men's Society. He died in 1915 when his son, a prominent Glasgow athlete, was with the British army in France.[27]

It is difficult to know merely from the Derry Reunion Committee's membership list whether or not it contained any Protestants though names such as Paton, Gilderson, Caldwell and Warren might indicate a presence. If not, then we may rest assured that another grouping, finally established in the Partick district of Glasgow and in the city centre in 1903 (the 'Murray' and 'No Surrender' clubs respectively) of the Apprentice Boys of Derry made up for any loss. The Glasgow club started with forty members and held a Relief of Derry march in August 1915 followed up by a Clyde cruise, known to generations of Glasgow people as a sail 'doon the watter'.[28] It is also recorded that Whiteinch Cross in Glasgow had been for many years – and before the Apprentice Boys clubs were founded – a favoured location for the annual ritualistic burning of Lundy. It is actually important to consider that as anyone wishing to join the Apprentice Boys had to come to Derry to be initiated, it is probable that Derry Protestant migrants maintained stronger links with their native city than Derry Catholics, few of whom ever appear to have returned. As an aside, there are currently some forty-two branch clubs of the Apprentice Boys of Derry stretching from Aberdeen to Irvine on the Ayrshire coast.[29]

There was also, it should be noted, a vibrant, completely non-political sectarian street gang culture in most working class districts of Glasgow which had been a fixture of the city's history throughout the nineteenth century. This mirrored, or perhaps parodied, the macro Irish immigrant politics of green and orange which held centre stage, and also indicates that territorial battles meant areas of Glasgow had a very definite perceived Irish Protestant or Irish Catholic character. Bridgeton, or 'Brigton' in local parlance, was one such area which despite having a sizeable Catholic parish, Home Rule bodies, a Gaelic League branch, a company of the Irish Volunteers (commanded by a brother of Count John McCormick), and even one of the first Celtic Brake Clubs, was always seen as Orange gang territory. Particularly in the years after the First World War when Glasgow's razor gangs were beginning to make a name for themselves, the area became home to the legendary 'Brigton Derry Boys', in memory of the youthful Derry apprentices, a gang later synonymous with the notorious 'Billy Boys' gang.[30] The name passed into folk legend however, and 'Brigton Derry', as well as forming part of one of Scotland's most famous sectarian anthems, is now almost something of a Glasgow catchphrase when discussing loyalism. Not to be outdone, and as an

27 *Glasgow Observer*, 1 January 1915. 28 *Glasgow Observer*, 11 April 1896; and Marshall, p. 177. 29 Marshall, pp. 177–8. 30 R.G. MacCallum, *Tongs Ya Bas* (Glasgow, 1994), pp. 3–8, pp. 34–5 & 121–2; for a Derry perspective on the gangs using the city's good name, see *Derry Journal*, 17 April 1936.

illustration of the two-way process and interchange between Derry and
Glasgow, the Waterside district of Derry has been and continues to be known
to those on the cityside as 'the Gorbals'.

As the twentieth century progressed, the Derry Reunion Committee's
gatherings took the more modest form of the Edwardian *conversazione*, rather
than the large concert-cum-banquet-cum-proto-political event of the 1890s.
This was in line with the fad for 'smokers', as they were known, whereby
exiles would gather for informal speeches, and talk among themselves over
tea and cigarettes – the idea was, it seems, to eliminate the drunken sing-a-
longs which the Glasgow Irish often excelled at, but which the clergy, Catholic
and Protestant alike, unanimously frowned upon. The Fermanagh exiles began
the trend and it was soon taken up by all but the Donegal Reunion
Committee, who continued with large rumbustuous gatherings regularly
addressed by members of John Redmond's Parliamentary Party.[31]

Of course, Sinn Féin in time made its appearance in Scotland and by 1907
formed a Coiste Ceantair na hAlban or Scottish executive council. Among its
first members were names redolent of Derry such as McLaughlin, Mellon, and
McGuirk, and its secretary was a shipyard worker from the Waterside in Derry
heavily involved in the AOH and IRB, Patrick McCauley.[32] McCauley was also
a pioneer of the Irish Volunteers in Scotland and later still an IRA officer in
Port Glasgow, as well as a founding member of the Independent Labour Party
in the town. Derry men had also made their mark in the IRB at this point in
the years leading up to the Easter Rising, and from about 1910 to 1914 the
overall command of the organization in Scotland rested with a south Derry
man named John Mulholland, while a leader in Motherwell on the eve of the
Rising was William Diamond, also from south Derry and possibly a relative of
the Glasgow Irish press baron, Charles Diamond.[33]

Glasgow witnessed the same scenes of consternation and jubilation caused
by the third Home Rule bill in 1912 as were witnessed in Derry, and as the
Volunteer movement (Ulster and Irish), gained ground and weapons, it is
clear that the sending of arms from the Irish in Scotland was a priority area.
The tradition continued and intensified on the IRA side throughout the
Anglo-Irish and Civil Wars, where arms and explosives shipped in small quan-
tities or carried by hand through Derry from Glasgow and on into rural
Donegal was commonplace.[34] A Derry IRA man who oversaw many of these

31 *Glasgow Observer*, 9 & 16 February 1901. 32 *Sinn Féin*, 30 November 1907. I am grateful to
Neil McCauley, Kilmacolm, Renfrewshire for all his help and interest. For more on McCauley's
return to Derry and activism in unemployed workers' struggles, see my forthcoming 'Struggle
or starve': Derry unemployed workers' movements, 1926–35', in *Saothar*, 28 (2004). 33 National
Library of Ireland, Patrick McCormick statement, MS. 15,337; and Owen Dudley Edwards, 'The
Catholic press in Scotland since the restoration of the hierarchy', in David McRoberts (ed.),
Modern Scottish Catholicism, 1878–1978 (Glasgow, 1979), pp. 169–73. 34 Handley, pp. 298–301;

operations and contacts between Derry, Glasgow and GHQ in Dublin was George Armstrong. In February 1921 along with another Derry IRA officer, Charles McGuinness, he succeeded in springing a Sligo brigade commander named Frank Carty from Derry Jail and getting him, eventually, to Glasgow where a re-arrest and failed escape attempt passed into Glasgow Irish folklore as the 'Smashing of the Van' incident.[35] The signing of the Treaty, however, effectively put an end to such dramatic events and though Derry exiles in Glasgow continued to be involved in Irish political and social activities on a smaller scale, ties to the city of their birth in years thereafter were maintained only *en masse* by organizations such as the Ancient Order of Hibernians and the Apprentice Boys in their frequent trips to the city.

The story of the migrants of Derry or Londonderry in Glasgow and vice versa is one with great divergences of experience. Some of those who went to Glasgow prospered and achieved a recognition in exile they may never have achieved at home, while some who came to Derry did extremely well and contributed much to the economic profile of the city. These however, may be seen as the minority. The story for most migrants was a tale of hardship and privation of every kind, often even for those who achieved the status of skilled workers. Many 'Scotch' in Derry had their success limited by economic decline in the city in the years after the First World War, as is partly illustrated by the experience of a Scottish Presbyterian stonemason who was the grandfather of John Hume.[36] Alternatively, the numbers of Derry migrants who appear in the dreary pages of the Glasgow Poor Law records are testament to the difficulties experienced by the mass of immigrants who poured into the city in the years after the potato famine. There is thus, no grand narrative that will neatly encapsulate the holistic experience of migrants from Glasgow and Derry in each other's cities. Many links remain to be uncovered – the full nature of the economic ties between Derry and Glasgow, the linguistic heritage, and even the sports linkages (Derry Celtic Football Club, founded around 1891 after its Glasgow namesake, and Jimmy and Billy 'Spider' Kelly, the Derry boxers and their experiences in the Glasgow boxing booths, where they gained their famous sobriquet). This article, however, has only been able to pick up a few threads of a much more expansive story, which remains to be told in full, but hopefully has contributed in some measure to our greater knowledge of the links between the peoples of the 'oak grove' and the 'dear green place'.

and Pádraig Ó Baoighill, *Óglach na Rosann* (Baile Atha Cliath, 1994), pp. 148–76.   **35** John McGuffin, Joseph Mulheron, *Charles 'Nomad' McGuinness* (Derry, 2002), pp. 43–68. I am indebted to my good friend, Stephen Coyle, for his help and voluminous knowledge about Irish republicanism in Scotland in the 1919–23 period.   **36** John Hume, *Personal views: politics, peace and reconciliation in Ireland* (Dublin, 1996).

II. EMIGRATION

Common ground in the Antipodes? Migration from Ulster and Scotland to New Zealand, 1800–1945

JOCK PHILIPS

Was the experience of those men, women and children who set off on the long journey to New Zealand from Scotland in the century and a half before 1945 similar or different to those who set sail from Ulster? Did Scots and Ulster folk perhaps achieve a common ground on the other side of the globe? This question may well be of more interest to inhabitants of New Zealand than to those in the homelands. Probably no more than about 7 per cent of those who left Ulster to go overseas in that period settled in New Zealand; probably about 10 per cent of Scots emigrants did so. By comparison with those who sailed to Canada, the United States, Australia or England the numbers of New Zealand emigrants are comparatively insignificant. From a New Zealand perspective, however, their contribution was important – almost a third of the total British migrant flow came from Scotland or Ulster – and perhaps a million people (of the present New Zealand population of four million) are descended from people who had lived their early lives in Scotland and Ulster. This fact is not one to which New Zealand historians, or New Zealanders generally, have given much attention. Traditionally as part of an ill-defined cultural nationalism, New Zealanders have preferred to locate the origin of their national traits in the experience of the new land. It was the encounter with the frontier and with the inhabitants of that frontier, the Maori, which are thought to have shaped the New Zealand worldview. To the extent that New Zealanders have explored their cultural inheritance they have lazily assumed that their inheritance was 'home county' English.

In the belief that culture was rather more determinative of New Zealand identity and suspecting that the 'Celtic fringe' was at least as important as England among New Zealand's founding populations, I initiated a project with two colleagues (Terry Hearn and Nicholas Bayley) to find out precisely who did come to New Zealand from Britain and Ireland and what traditions they brought with them. Using death registers, shipping lists and records of assisted migrants, we have been able to determine where people came from (down to a county level), when they arrived, and something about their occupational, religious and family backgrounds for the period 1800–1945. This paper draws on this research to explore whether the migration experience of

57

Table 1: Immigration to New Zealand, 1840

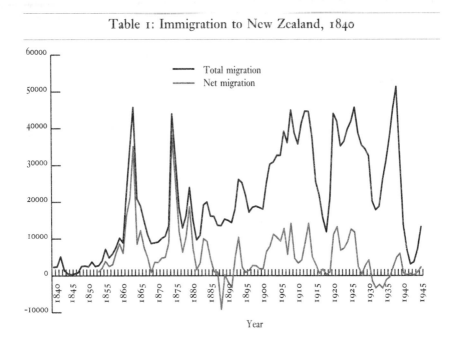

Year

the Scots and those from Ulster was similar or different, and then speculates
about what the statistical findings may suggest about the two peoples' cultural contribution.

We must begin with an overview of British migration to New Zealand
during those years. The crucial fact in interpreting table 1 is that New
Zealand had to work the hardest of all the settler societies to attract migrants
from the north. As the *Dublin University Magazine* said in 1845, New Zealand
was 'the most recent, remotest and least civilized of our colonies.'[1] The journey to New Zealand was halfway round the world – for much of the nineteenth century about 100 days in a cramped and leaky ship where the dan-
gers of storms or even fire at sea and disease on board were very real.
Naturally the cost of this voyage was high – about four times the cost to
North America. For the first half of the century, New Zealand had a reputation as a wild and dangerous place where the local inhabitants had unfor-
tunate cannibal tendencies. Normally people seeking a new life overseas would
prefer to go to more civilized places where they knew that acquaintances from
home had already paved a path.

1 Quoted in Donald Harman Akenson, *Half the world from home: perspectives on the Irish in
New Zealand, 1860–1950* (Wellington, 1990), p. 14.

Given these factors, people would only decide to set off on the long journey to New Zealand if they were given a special incentive. The lure of gold was one such carrot – and the large net migration of the 1860s is partly explained by the discovery of gold in Otago in 1861 and the West Coast in 1865. Some British migrants were brought out to their antipodes against their will: some of New Zealand's settlers before 1850 were ex-convicts who came across the Tasman; others were soldiers who were brought out to fight the Maori and then took their release in the 1840s and 1860s. Most common, however, the state lured migrants by deliberate campaigns to advertise the charms of New Zealand and then offer the desired migrants free passages. This practice began in the decade after 1840 with the New Zealand Company, a commercial enterprise, which offered free passages to migrants who would provide labour and a market for land. Provincial governments got into the act in the 1850s and 1860s; and then in the 1870s and early 1880s the New Zealand government brought over 100,000 people to New Zealand. These assisted passages were revived at the turn of the century, and then again in the 1920s. All told perhaps half of those who came to New Zealand during our period were assisted migrants.

Table 2: Percentages of United Kingdom migration to New Zealand

	Scots	Irish	Ulster
1800–39	20.4	15.6	
1840–52	20.6	13.5 [30.6]	4.3
1853–70	30.2	21.4	8.5
1871–80	20.9 [10.6]	22.4 [18.8]	9.4 [5.9]
1881–90	21.9	20.6	9.3
1891–1900	22.2	17.5 [12.5]	7.6
1901–10	21.6	10.0	5.1
1911–15	22.9	8.2	5.3
1919–45	28.7	8.6	5.3

Note: figures in square brackets are percentages of the United Kingdom population at the closest UK census. *Source*: Death registers

Those who received such assistance had of course to be desirable types – and here the differences between the Scots and the Ulster Irish begins. From the beginning of these assistance programmes, the Scots were a favoured group. They were regarded as a hard-working Protestant people, sober and reliable

and they were quickly targeted. The settlement of Otago from 1848 was largely
a Scots initiative. Recruiting agents, whether New Zealand Company, provincial or agents of the New Zealand government were sent north and throughout the periods of assisted migration Scots were consistently about a quarter
of those who were given free passages. The result is that, as table 2 shows, the
numbers of Scots migrating to New Zealand as a proportion of all migrants
from Britain and Ireland is remarkable stable. It remains over 20 per cent of
New Zealand's migrants, rising to even higher numbers in the twentieth century. Given the fact that during the nineteenth century the Scots comprised
about 10 per cent of the population of Britain and Ireland, we can see that
New Zealand became over twice as Scottish as the United Kingdom. Equally
striking is the fact that in terms of regional origin the Scots who migrated were
recruited from right around the country. There were some interesting regional
variations – a high proportion of people migrating from the northern islands
especially Shetland, slightly more from the Lowlands, but in general the
Scottish migration to New Zealand follows very closely the distribution of the
Scottish population as a whole (Table 3).

Table 3: Regional origins of Scots migrants to New Zealand (percentages)

	1842–52	1853–70	1871–90	1891–1915	1916–1945	UK Census 1871
Far North	6.1	5.9	10.6	3.8	5.1	3.1
Highlands	10.3	16	9.9	8.7	7.1	8.5
North-east	7.9	10.2	11.4	8.7	11.0	11.7
East Lowlands	36.2	32.7	26.9	34.3	32.7	31.5
West Lowlands	36.2	26.5	33.2	38.3	39.6	37.1
Borders	3.3	8.6	7.9	6.3	5.0	8.1

Source: Death registers

The Irish story is very different. New Zealanders at first made little distinction between citizens of Ulster and those further south, and in general the
Irish did not have a good reputation as desirable immigrants in New Zealand.
All were tarred with the same papish brush. There were strong negative
stereotypes of the Irish as drunken Catholics who were ill-educated and unre-
liable. So, initially no effort was made to draw them to New Zealand. Under
2 per cent of the New Zealand Company immigrants of the 1840s came from
Ireland. Until the 1850s the Irish were markedly under-represented among
New Zealand's British immigrants – less than half their representation in the

United Kingdom population of about 30 per cent. Those who did migrate in this early period tended to be those who came across the Tasman from Australia, and at least some of them must have been ex-convicts. They also gravitated strongly to the non-New Zealand Company settlement of Auckland; and indeed over a third of Auckland's immigrants from 1840 to 1852 were from Ireland. Some of these Auckland settlers were veterans of regiments who had come to fight in the Northern War (1845–6) and then stayed; and this may explain the large representation of people from Leinster (34.1 per cent) and from Dublin in particular (19.8 per cent) which was a favoured recruiting ground for the British army.

Table 4: Regional origins of Irish migrants to New Zealand (percentages)

	Leinster	*Munster*	*Ulster*	*Connaught*
1840–52	34.1	27.8	31.7	6.3
1853–70	19.9	31.7	39.8	8.5
1871–90	14.9	35.2	43.5	6.4
1891–1915	16.0	26.2	51.0	6.8
1911–15	20.0	20.0	56.0	4.0
1916–45	13.0	19.5	61.0	6.5
UK Census 1871	23.9	25.9	34.2	16.0

Source: Death registers

During the 1850s and 1860s the numbers of Irish began to increase. There were three reasons for this. Many came across from Australia to join the search for gold. Of Otago miners 31.5 per cent were from Ireland, a higher number than from Scotland (30.1 per cent). A high proportion of the Irish miners came originally from Munster (42 per cent of West Coast miners). Second the Irish were again well represented among the soldiers discharged after the New Zealand Wars – over half the British veterans who settled in New Zealand in these years were born in Ireland. Third the provinces, and especially Canterbury, began to draw a distinction between Protestant Ulster and the rest of Ireland and to look with greater favour on assisting immigrants from that area. Indeed among those who were assisted by Canterbury province from Ireland over 50 per cent came from Ulster. So during the 1850s and 60s, the numbers of Irish coming to New Zealand reached over 20 per cent of immigrants, and of these almost 40 per cent were from Ulster.

The gradual discovery of Ulster as a desirable source of sound Protestant migrants for New Zealand progressed further during the 1870s when in fact the percentage of United Kingdom migrants from Ireland reached 22.4 per cent, which was more than the Scots figure and higher than the Irish representation in the UK population as a whole (18.8 per cent in the census of 1871). Among those who came as assisted immigrants 27.5 per cent were from Ireland. Some of these were from Munster because the assistance scheme provided for the nomination of immigrants by settlers already in New Zealand; and there is clear evidence that those Munster folk who had come out in the 1860s made good use of this system to bring out their relatives. A good number, for example, settled in the area of south Canterbury known as Kerrytown.[2] But the really proactive recruitment came to focus heavily upon Ulster. In 1873, 41 of the 54 New Zealand agents in Ireland were to be found in Ulster,[3] and special efforts were made to recruit Ulster women as domestic servants and potential wives given the imbalance of the sexes in New Zealand.[4] So during the 1870s Ulster people comprised over two-fifths of the Irish immigrants to New Zealand; and compared with their representation in the UK population (5.9 per cent) as a whole, 9.4 per cent of New Zealand's immigrants came from Ulster. The counties especially prominent were those around Belfast, Antrim and Down. For the remaining years of the century both Irish and in particular Ulster people were well represented among the immigrant flow, although the absolute numbers were not high. When assisted migration resumed at the turn of the century, there was a change. The total Irish representation dropped and remained low for the rest of our period. But among those Irish who did come, a good majority, about 60 per cent, were from Ulster throughout the twentieth century.

At first sight then, it looks as if the pattern of Irish and Scots migration to New Zealand is rather different – with the Scots consistently well represented over the century and a half and the Irish low at either ends of the period and reaching a highpoint between 1850 and 1890. But when we isolate the Ulster representation the perspective alters. True, Ulster representation is low until the middle of the nineteenth century; but then as New Zealanders begin to think of Ulster Protestants as desirable types their recruiting efforts are rewarded and the numbers start to flow. Ulster immigrants come to be regarded in a similar light to those from Scotland – as solid Protestant citizens to be distinguished from those unruly people further south.

That it was their Protestantism which was a key factor may be inferred from evidence of the religious affiliation of the Irish immigrants (table 5). Clearly one must use these figures with caution since the denomination is derived from the

2 Sean G. Brosnahan, *The Kerrytown Brosnahans* (Timaru, 1992). 3 Alasdair Galbraith, 'The invisible Irish? Rediscovering the Irish Protestant tradition in colonial New Zealand' in Lyndon Fraser (ed.), *A distant shore: Irish migration and New Zealand settlement* (Dunedin, 2000), p. 46. 4 Charlotte Macdonald, *A woman of good character: single women as immigrant settlers in nineteenth-century New Zealand* (Wellington, 1990).

affiliation of the presiding cleric who completed the death certificate. But the figures are nevertheless valuable. They suggest that from the earliest there was a tendency for Catholics to be under-represented among Irish migrants to New Zealand; and among the Ulster community they were very significantly under-represented by comparison with their place in the community at home. Further there was a tendency among the Ulster migrants for Presbyterians to become more prominent over time, so that in the twentieth century they comprised over two fifths of those from Ulster. To this extent too, the similarity of the Ulster community with the Scots became greater. By the twentieth century both Scots and Ulster people were being welcomed to New Zealand on the assumption that their Protestantism implied a hard-working reliability.

Table 5: Religious denominations of Irish immigrants to New Zealand (percentages)

	Catholic	*Church of Ireland*	*Presbyterian*	*Other Protestant*
Irish 1840–52	56.8	27	9	
Irish 1853–70	53.8	26.2	15.6	4.3
Irish 1871–80	55.8	22.6	15.6	6.0
Irish 1881–1915	54.8	15.3	22.5	
Ireland 1851	*80*	*10.7*	*8.1*	
Ulster 1853–70	20	39.4	33.5	7.1
Ulster 1871–80	23.7	31.4	33.7	11.2
Ulster 1881–1915	21.8	21.1	42.9	14.2
Ulster 1916–45	15.7	27.4	41.2	15.7
Ulster 1861	*50.5*	*20.4*	*26.3*	

Source: Death registers

Turning to the occupational background of the two groups, contrasts once again appear. The figures in table 6 are derived from the occupations of the subjects' fathers as recorded on the death registers. This is therefore evidence at one remove from the occupations of the immigrants themselves, and it may have an element of unreliability since the certificate was completed by people across the other side of the globe from where the father actually lived and worked. Nevertheless the figures are again of some value. They suggest that migrants to New Zealand were of a strongly agricultural background, and this in part reflects the activities of the recruiting agents who were asked to attract rural rather than urban industrial types. But this tendency is even more marked among the Irish than the Scots. A significant difference between the two is the much higher number of people with a craft and industrial background among the Scots. Of course these figures include all the Irish migrants, and those outside Ulster were likely to be even more from a peasant background than those further north. But even in the twentieth century, when Ulster migrants became dominant and Ulster itself was the most highly industrialized part of Ireland, the contrast with the occupational background of the Scots remains.

Table 6: Occupations of fathers of immigrants to New Zealand
(percentages)

	Agriculture	Builders	Crafts	Industrial	White collar
Scots 1840–52	43.1	9.4	14.9	7.2	10.5
Irish 1840–52	38.3	6.9	12.7	4.9	14.7
Scots 1853–70	42.9	8.6	20.3	2.7	9.9
Irish 1853–70	58.3	4.9	9.1	1.2	10.8
Scots 1871–90	29.9	7.8	22.7	8.4	6.8
Irish 1871–90	59.5	3.2	10.2	1.0	6.2

Source: Death registers

Having looked at the immigrants at home, what happened once they got on the boat and sailed to New Zealand? Probably many Scots and Ulster people were on the same boats, because few ships sailed direct from Ireland and many from Ulster would have begun their journey by going to Glasgow to catch the ship. But once in New Zealand they were likely to settle in rather different places, as table 7 makes obvious. Although the Scots were welcomed throughout New Zealand, and in 1871 comprised at least 15 per cent of the United Kingdom-born population in all provinces except for Taranaki, there were only two provinces, Otago and Southland, which had an above average number of Scots. These two, the most southern provinces, had an overwhelming dominance of Scots – in 1871 over half of Otago's foreign-born came from Scotland and over 60 per cent of Southland's. There were some other communities with large numbers of Scots – in 1842, for example, over 500 people came from Paisley to Auckland and between 1853 and 1860 over 800 Highlanders came to Waipu in Northland after a long sojourn in Nova Scotia.[5] But these were relatively isolated examples, and nowhere could match

5 Maureen Molloy, *Those who speak to the heart: the Nova Scotian Scots at Waipu, 1854–1920*

the overwhelming Otago and Southland Scottishness. It was not for nothing that Dunedin was the Edinburgh of the south. Even forty years later, in 1911, the census showed that these two provinces remained more than twice as Scots-prone as the New Zealand average.

Table 7: Provincial residence of people born in the United Kingdom, 1871
(percentages)

	English	*Scots*	*Irish*
Auckland	54.9	17	27.2
Taranaki	69.6	9.5	20.5
Hawke's Bay	55.2	20.9	23.2
Wellington	63.5	20	15.4
Nelson	56.4	15.9	25.9
Marlborough	62.1	20.4	16.4
Canterbury	62.7	16.9	19.4
Westland	40.1	19.9	37.9
Otago	31	51.5	16.9
Southland	24.4	61.4	13.9
New Zealand	49.7	27.3	22

Source: 1871 New Zealand census

As table 7 suggests, the Irish pattern was very different. The two places where the Irish were not to be found in any numbers were Otago and Southland. The most Irish community in New Zealand in 1871 was the West Coast of the South Island and this remained true even in 1911 when the province was proportionately about twice as Irish as the country as whole.[6] The West Coast Irish were, as we have noted, people who had come across the Tasman, often from the Victorian goldfields to the new goldfields beneath the Southern Alps, and many were from Munster rather than from Ulster. In the years 1853–70, 42.1 per cent of Westland's Irish were born in Munster, only 29.3 per cent hailed from Ulster. The high numbers of Irish in Nelson also reflected these factors since it was in the part of that province in the gold district around Greymouth that the Irish were to be found.

A second community with strong Irish representation was Auckland. As we have noted Irish settlement in this area began early and in 1852 Auckland town was almost one third of Irish birth. Even in 1871 the UK-born popu-

(Palmerston North, 1991).   6 See also Lyndon Fraser, 'Irish migration to the West Coast', *New Zealand Journal of History*, 34:2 (October 2000), 197–225.

lation of Auckland province was over 27 per cent Irish. But in contrast with the West Coast story these Irish settlers were very likely to be Ulster Protestants. As table 8 shows almost half of Auckland's Irish settlers between 1853 and 1870 were from Ulster. Some of these Ulster Protestants were people who had been settled south of Auckland, around Pukekohe, as part of the Waikato immigration scheme. This was in a sense a plantation, not dissimilar in style or even intent from the seventeenth-century plantation in Ulster itself. As in Ireland, the Pukekohe scheme had a political purpose – it was intended to protect Auckland from Kingite Maori further south. Some 3000 people were settled and of these about half were Ulster Protestants.[7] The Ulster connection did not stop there. In the following decade an Ulster gentleman from Ballygawley, County Tyrone, George Vesey Stewart obtained land in the vicinity of the Bay of Plenty township of Katikati in return for settling Ulster Protestants. He recruited tenant farmers, using his Orange Lodge connections and two ship-loads sailed from Belfast in 1875 and 1878.

Table 8: Irish in NZ provinces, 1853–70 (percentages)

	Ulster	Munster
Canterbury	59.6	18.5
Auckland	48	26
West Coast	29.3	42.1
New Zealand	39.8	31.7

Source: Death registers

Another place which attracted considerable numbers of Ulster Protestants was Canterbury. As table 7 shows, the proportion of Irish-born in Canterbury in 1871 was not even up to the national average. But the numbers in real terms were quite large, and what is of special significance is that almost 60 per cent of Canterbury's Irish in the 1850s and 60s were from Ulster. This followed the quite deliberate targeting of that area by the province's recruiting agents. Through the process of chain migration people continued to leave Ulster and travel to Canterbury; and by 1911 Canterbury had the highest proportion of Irish-born after the West Coast. The vast majority of these were Ulster Protestants. It was not for nothing that within 10 kilometres of Christchurch city was a small township called 'Belfast'.[8]

7 Alasdair Galbraith, 'A forgotten plantation: the Irish in Pukekohe, 1865–1900', unpublished paper, 2001.   8 See also Lyndon Fraser, *To Tara via Hollyhead: Irish Catholic immigrants in nineteenth century Christchurch* (Auckland, 1997).

What has this survey of the statistical evidence thrown up? It has suggested that the contrasts of Ulster and Scots settlement in New Zealand are greater than the similarities. Although both groups eventually came to be regarded as welcome immigrants because of their Protestant identity, Ulster folk took much longer to gain this status than the Scots and the timing of their migration flows was more erratic than the Scots. There were clear differences in the occupational background of the two migrant groups with the Scots more likely to come from a craft or industrial background; and the two communities tended to settle in different parts of New Zealand – the Scots overwhelmingly in Otago and Southland, the Ulster Protestants more likely to be found in Auckland and Canterbury.

It is worth following the communities a little deeper into New Zealand society and exploring, in a somewhat speculative manner, their respective contributions. Is this still a story of contrast? In part because the Scots were so numerically strong in Otago and Southland, they had a base from which to establish and nourish Scottish culture in the antipodes. The Presbyterian Church provided a strong centre of Scottish tradition. Caledonian and Scottish societies were established to provide a place where Scots could meet and encourage the Scots association. Statues of Robbie Burns appeared in some half dozen places in the south. Because Dunedin was the wealthiest community in the country for much of the nineteenth century, its influence spread. Scottish traditions of education, to give one example, were very influential in New Zealand. The first university was in Dunedin and both the structure of the degree and many of the early teachers in universities came from Scotland. The first girls' secondary school was in Dunedin, again following Scots precedents. Scots played an important role in such movements as temperance. Scottish games such as golf, bowls and curling were quickly established, and at least the first two spread quickly out of the south throughout the country.

At the end of the century there was a colonial invention of the highland tradition, echoing British patterns. In Waipu, just as the first generation of Gaelic speakers died out, a tradition of Highland games became established. In 1896 the Southland town of Invercargill saw the establishment of the Caledonian Pipe Band of Southland, the first such organized group in the world outside the homeland. From 1907 there was a national pipe band contest, and competitions of highland dancing and piping spread throughout New Zealand.[9]

This is not to say that Otago and Southland remained islands of Scottish culture. It is interesting how quickly 'English' traditions such as the playing of cricket flourished in the south too. But clearly Scottish culture and patterns of behaviour made a visible difference to New Zealand and there were self-conscious institutions dedicated to the promotion of Scots traditions.

9 G.L. Pearce, *The Scots of New Zealand* (Auckland, 1976); Jim Hewitson, *Far off in sunlit places: stories of the Scots in Australia and New Zealand* (Victoria, 1998).

The Irish Catholic community also found ways of keeping alive its traditions in the new world. West Coast pubs, oral traditions of story-telling, radical labour activism – arguably such phenomena grew out of an Irish Catholic
heritage, even if this is hard to prove. The most explicit vehicles for perpetu-
ating the Irish culture were the Catholic Church and school. Catholicism in
New Zealand was dominated by members of an Irish background, and the
church itself came under Bishop Paul Cullen's Irish empire from 1870.[10] Priests,
nuns and bishops were usually trained and often born in Ireland. The church
spawned a separate school system and by 1890 there was a Catholic primary
school in every parish. The long fight to gain state funding for parochial and
convent schools, which began in 1877 and was not successful until 1975, helped
define the community.[11] Other institutions followed from church and school
and helped to give the Irish Catholic community its own separate identity.
These included the Hibernian Benefit Society, Marist sporting teams and
Catholic scouts. New Zealanders of an Irish Catholic background even today
remain forcefully aware of their distinctive ethnic and cultural heritage.[12]

What of the Ulster Protestant community – do they, like the Scots and
Irish Catholics, still have a distinct visible presence within New Zealand life?
The Ulster migrants did create their own special institution, the Orange
Lodge, which first appeared in Auckland in 1858 and then spread throughout the country. By 1876 there were eighteen lodges.[13] There was some open
conflict between Orangemen and Catholics on the West Coast in 1868 and
in Canterbury in 1879.[14] At this stage the battle of the Boyne was commem-
orated, and in 1874 more than 700 people are said to have attended the 12th
of July celebrations in Auckland. When Stewart's followers settled in Katikati
they quickly established an Orange Lodge and built a 'Protestant Hall'. But
membership of the Orange order dropped off from the turn of the century;
and as Don Akenson notes, even in Katikati where the numbers of Ulster
Protestants was great, Orangeism soon lost its energy.[15]

Unlike the Scots and the Irish Catholics, Ulster Protestants did not have
particular religious denomination which could serve as a centre for their identity. A good proportion of Ulster Protestants were members of the Church
of Ireland and on arrival in New Zealand they were quickly subsumed within
the Anglican Church. In Auckland, for example, Irish-born comprised about

---

10 Fraser, *To Tara*, pp. 64–72; Akenson, *Half the world*, p. 124.   11 Richard Davis, *Irish issues
in New Zealand politics* (Dunedin, 1974) pp. 71–101.   12 See, for example, Jane Tolerton,
Convent girls (Auckland, 1994), pp. 15–16.   13 J.A. Carnahan, *A brief history of the Orange
Institution in the North Island of New Zealand from 1842 to the present time* (Auckland, 1886);
Rory Sweetman, '"The importance of being Irish": Hibernianism in New Zealand', in Fraser,
Distant Shore, p. 139; Davis, *Irish issues*, pp. 51–2.   14 David McGill, *The lion and the
wolfhound: the Irish rebellion on the New Zealand goldfields* (Wellington, 1990); Sean G.
Brosnahan, 'The "Battle of the Borough" and the "Saige O Timaru"', *New Zealand Journal of
History*, 28:1 (1994), 41–59.   15 Akenson, *Half the world*, pp. 150–2

one tenth of the city's Anglicans in the late nineteenth century,[16] which was hardly larger enough to make a big difference. Similarly Ulster-born Presbyterians were easily swallowed up by the Scots who dominated that church. Irish-born comprised no more than one fifth of Auckland's Presbyterians. As Galbraith and Akenson have suggested, Ulster members may have contributed a distinctive low-church flavour to both churches (especially in the North Island), but in neither case did the church become a real mechanism for articulating a distinctive Ulster Protestant perspective.

As Irish Catholicism became a more divisive issue within New Zealand – especially with a series of controversies which broke out as a consequence of the Easter uprising in 1916 and the Great War[17] – so Irish Protestants were encouraged to hide their Irish roots and identify strongly with the British Empire. Indeed rather than articulating a distinctive Irish Protestant inheritance, Ulster migrants may have been among the leading proponents of the importance of the 'British' inheritance to New Zealand. During much of the nineteenth century New Zealand settlers had continued to make distinctions between parts of Britain and to recognize that people from Cornwall or Yorkshire or the Highlands or Dublin brought their own accents and traditions to the new land. But as second and third generations began to appear, and as conflict, first in South Africa and then in the Great War, called for a collective loyalty to the Empire, so there emerged a stronger sense of the 'British' inheritance of New Zealand. New Zealanders began to think of themselves as proud upholders of this 'British' inheritance, one that was Protestant and loyal to Empire, and they presented a view of New Zealand as expressing the finest distillation of this inheritance – a 'Better Britain' no less. It may be that Ulster Protestants, unable to find an identity in distinctive Ulster traditions were peculiarly important in articulating this 'British' inheritance. Certainly one of the more ardent promoters of the vision was the Protestant Political Association which emerged to fight alleged Catholic disloyalty during the Great War and probably had a strong infusion of former Orangemen. More important, some of New Zealand's more significant political leaders during this period had a background in Northern Ireland. John Ballance, for example, born in Glenavy, County Antrim, was a leading thinker and the first prime minister of the Liberal Party which took office in 1890. William Ferguson Massey, born in Limavady, County Londonderry, and member of an Orange Lodge, was prime minister throughout the First World War and the public spokesperson for New Zealand's role in defending the British Empire. Such sons of Ulster appear to have played a leading role in articulating New Zealand's sense of their British inheritance.[18]

16 Galbraith, in Fraser, *A distant shore*, p. 50.   17 P.S. O'Connor, 'Sectarian conflict in New Zealand, 1911–1920', *Political Science*, 19:1 (1967), 3–16; Rory Sweetman, *Bishop in the dock: the sedition trial of James Liston* (Auckland, 1997).   18 Galbraith, in Fraser, *A distant shore*, pp.

A particularly good example of how Ulster migrants lost a sense of their distinctive regional roots and promoted British traditions (by which they come to understand essentially 'English' traditions) may be found in the Mulgan family. The family came to Katikati with Vesey Stewart's party of Ulster settlers in 1875. The Reverend W.E. Mulgan was a Church of Ireland clergyman and he was a leader of the Katikati settlers. His grandson was Alan Mulgan, born in Katikati, and his mother was also the daughter of an Ulster cleric who had brought his family out from County Antrim. So Alan Mulgan was brought up in a strong Ulster lineage; but when he decided to go 'home' in the 1920s it was England, not Northern Ireland, which he went to visit because: 'To a boy who had been born in New Zealand, and had never been out of it, Ulster was a shadowy place. England and English things were always before my eyes ... I had some affection for the country of my parents, but infinitely more for England.'[19] Westminster Abbey, Lords cricket ground, Kew gardens – these, not the Giant's Causeway, were what made Alan Mulgan's heart pound. In the next decade Alan Mulgan's son also went abroad. John Mulgan went off to Merton College, Oxford. He worked for the Clarendon Press and joined the British army which sent him to garrison duty in Northern Ireland which he found tedious and frustrating. The novel he wrote in 1938, *Man Alone*, has come to be regarded as one of the finest explorations of New Zealand identity, and his autobiographical account, *Report on Experience*, contains wistful nostalgia for the land and people of his birth. For John Mulgan, of pure Ulster Protestant stock, home was not Ireland, but England and New Zealand.

So once in New Zealand the Ulster Protestant community, unlike the Scots or the Irish Catholics, lost a sense of their distinctive regional roots and came to identify with a highly English definition of their 'British' identity. So was there any common ground at all with the Scottish migrants? Perhaps a point of agreement may be found in the way New Zealanders came to understand their Britishness. The Scots, as we have noted, did keep alive particular Scottish traditions, but they also accepted a definition of New Zealand as 'British' and indeed as a 'Better Britain'. What made New Zealand better than the old country was partly the absence of huge cities with belching smoke-stacks and disease. More important it was better because the country was thought to be more democratic, less elitist and free from the pretensions of upper-class toffs. Both Scots and Ulster Protestants, in part through their common Presbyterian traditions, shared a resistance to English aristocratic pretensions; and they may have joined in a determination that New Zealand identity, though 'British', should be more democratic and classless than England. Perhaps, here, in a shared definition of a 'Better Britain', common ground in the Antipodes between Scots and Ulster Protestants was found.

48–9. **19** Alan Mulgan, *Home: a colonial's adventure* (London, 1929), p. 7.

'Black '97': reconsidering Scottish migration to Ireland in the seventeenth century and the Scotch-Irish in America

PATRICK FITZGERALD

The impetus behind this paper is largely drawn from the confluence of two impressions which I have formed over the course of the last five years. The first, relates to the changing historical perspective upon eighteenth century Ireland's economy and society and the contemporary trans-Atlantic migration streams which emanated there, most prolifically in Ulster. The prodigious research and publication of economic historians such as Cullen, Dickson and Crawford has fashioned a view of eighteenth-century Ireland, at the beginning of the twenty-first century which is markedly different from that which prevailed in the middle of the twentieth century. In short, there is a significantly greater awareness today of the evolving economic dynamism and regional diversity which characterized Ireland's eighteenth-century experience.[1] The implications of this changing perspective for those studying contemporary emigration could not be long ignored. A major issue for historians of migration has always been the question of why people move and thus the developing historiography of the conditioning economy and society inevitably impinged upon the agenda of historians interested in emigration and settlement. The ripples of a shifting emphasis amongst Irish historians of the eighteenth century were to be detected in the writings of those interested in the immigration to colonial America of those dubbed the Scotch-Irish, principally Presbyterians of Scottish birth or ancestry, predominantly settled in the province of Ulster. The best summation of this influence at work was offered by Maldym Jones in his 1991 article entitled 'The Scotch-Irish in British America'.

To be sure, the character of Scotch-Irish immigration had changed over the six decades preceding the Revolution. Those arriving in the early 1770s were conspicuously poorer, less Scottish, more secular, and more liberal than the pioneers of 1717–1718, and they came from an

---

1 D. Dickson, *New foundations: Ireland, 1660–1800* (Dublin, 2000), pp. 109–43 provides a useful summation of the contemporary historical perspective on the economy and society of eighteenth-century Ireland.

Ulster transformed by a rapidly growing population and by economic
and social change.[2]

In many ways Jones's differentiation between immigrants of different eras
was a welcome antidote to a Scotch-Irish historiographical tradition which
was often transfixed with differentiation from that preoccupying 'other' – the
Irish Catholic immigrant. It also served as a useful corrective to the developed tendency to portray the essentially static continuity of Scotch-Irish folk-
ways, not only over decades but often centuries. For our purposes here, however, the key point was that one needed to consider carefully the chronology
of a migrant's exit from the Old World and entry to the New World in order
to set their migratory experience in it's proper context. In accepting the value
of this approach it becomes obvious that the same principle applies to an
understanding of Scottish migration to Ireland during the seventeenth century. Even if one accepts the view that Scotland was not changing as rapidly
in the seventeenth century as Ireland, and particularly Ulster, was in the eighteenth century, one could not simply equate the outlook and character of the
Scots settler of 1615 with that of a settler in 1695. The importance of this
point was arguably accentuated by the persistence of two commonly held mis-
conceptions, held with particular tenacity on the far side of the Atlantic.
Firstly, that Scottish migration to Ulster was most voluminous in the decades
between the establishment of the government-sponsored Ulster Plantation
scheme of James VI & I and the outbreak of the native Irish Rising of 1641.
Secondly, that the vast majority of those leaving Ulster for America in the
decade after 1717 were the third and fourth generation descendants of those
pre-1641 Scots planters.

    Thus an awareness of the need to fully appreciate the 'sequencing' of
migrations between Scotland, Ireland and America in the seventeenth and
eighteenth centuries coalesced with a second significant impression. In examining the evidence relating to the migration of Scots to Ulster during the
course of the seventeenth century it becomes clear that in both relative and
absolute terms the decade in which the greatest volume of movement occurred
was in fact the 1690s. Not only was one struck by the extent to which this
movement was obscured from much of what had been written on this subject but also by the manner in which the motivation behind the migration
was often presented. In short, the 1690s, particularly the years between 1695
and 1698, witnessed the worst famine in Scotland's history. The 'ill years' or
'lean years', as this crisis was collectively recalled in folk memory, saw an
estimated decline in Scotland's population of between 5 and 20 per cent

2 M. Jones, 'The Scotch-Irish in British America' in B. Bailyn & P.D. Morgan (eds), *Strangers within the realm: cultural margins in the first British empire* (Churchill, N.C., 1991), p. 312.

(within the range of relative demographic decline experienced during the Great Irish Famine of the 1840s).[3] This factor did not seem to feature as consistently or prominently in published accounts of the significant upsurge in migration to Ulster which occurred at the same time. What, one wondered, might explain this apparent quietude?

Before addressing that particular issue I would like to make some preliminary observations about the peopling of Ireland with British settlers during the course of the seventeenth century and then focus in on events in Scotland during the 1690s. Perhaps the first point to stress about migration flows across the Irish Sea in the seventeenth century is that they were cyclical in nature and that there was significant return migration from Ireland. All migrations can be analysed at the simplest level in terms of push and pull factors. Most migrants, not surprisingly, tended to come to Ireland when conditions there were most favourable and when conditions in their place of origin were least favourable. The second decade of the seventeenth century witnessed, for example, a particularly voluminous migration of British settlers into Ulster.[4] These years were generally marked by bountiful harvests and favourable leasing terms in Ulster. Whilst the 1610s were not marked by serious dearth in England, there was depression in the cloth trade after 1614 and more significantly an increasingly unfavourable balance between population and resources, which stoked the fires of pauperization.[5] Equally the impetus to return to Britain reflected potential and relative prospects there but perhaps most forcibly the influence of powerful push factors in Ireland. For instance, the most dramatic and sizeable return flow occurred in response to the outbreak of the native Irish Rising in October 1641 but the notoriety of this episode should not obscure earlier instances of return migration. When Ireland experienced a run of failed or poor harvests in the late 1620s and early 1630s there is clear evidence of settlers returning to England from Munster and from Ulster to Scotland. In the latter case, poor harvests at the end of the 1630s combined with Wentworth's Black Oath encouraged many more Scots to return across the North Channel.[6] The peopling process was shaped by war,

3 I.D. Whyte, *Scotland before the Industrial Revolution: an economic and social history, c.1050–c. 1750* (London, 1995), p. 124; R.E. Tyson, 'Famine in Aberdeenshire, 1695–99: anatomy of a crisis' in D. Stevenson (ed.), *From lairds to louns* (Aberdeen, 1986), p. 50.   4 M. Perceval-Maxwell, *The Scottish migration to Ulster in the reign of James I* (Belfast, 1973), pp. 160–83, 217–28; P. Robinson, *The Ulster Plantation: British settlement in an Irish landscape, 1600–1670* (Dublin, 1984), pp. 212–24; N. Canny, *Making Ireland British, 1580–1650* (Oxford, 2001), p. 211.   5 J.A. Sharpe, *Early Modern England: a social history, 1550–1760* (London, 1987), pp. 51–2; K. Wrightson, *English society, 1580–1680* (London, 1982), pp. 140–2.   6 On return migration see K. Lindley, 'The impact of the 1641 Rebellion upon England and Wales, 1638–41' in *Irish Historical Studies*, 70 (1972), 143–76; P. Fitzgerald, '"Like crickets to the crevice of a brew-house": poor Irish migrants in England, 1560–1640' in P. O'Sullivan (ed.), *The Irish worldwide: history, heritage, identity*, i, *Patterns of migration* (Leicester, 1992), pp. 13–36, N. Canny,

politics, government intervention, the role of landholders and many other factors but the pattern of migration clearly bore a strong correlation with fluctuations in the agricultural economies of Britain and Ireland. It is difficult to overstate the centrality of the harvest yield to the lower orders in the early modern period. It could literally be a life and death issue.

The second point worth emphasis in relation to British settlement in seventeenth-century Ireland is the varied geographical origins in Britain of those who crossed the Irish Sea. An older model of Ulster plantation shaped by lowland Scots and Munster plantation shaped by those from south-west England now obscures as much as it enlightens. Whilst these regions might be thought of as core feeders, it is clear that those who migrated to Stuart Ireland, north and south, were drawn from every corner of England, Wales and Scotland. British settlement was not restricted to areas of official plantation and by 1641 an active market in land helped to ensure that no Irish county remained untouched by these 'newcomers'.[7] It should be born in mind, for example, that the ten-fold increase in Dublin's population during the course of the century was fuelled to a considerable extent by migration from Britain. Canny, who has done most work on settlement across the island of Ireland in the seventeenth century, suggests that in the period between 1603 and 1641 approximately 100,000 people migrated from Britain to Ireland of whom a minimum 70,000 were English and Welsh and a maximum of 30,000 Scots. Whilst the Scots were predominantly settling in Ulster, it is important not to overlook the significant English and Welsh component within Planter society in Ulster. There continued to be a strong flow of English settlers into Ulster after 1650.[8]

This immigration which appears to have been at its heaviest in the 1650s and in the years around 1680 was primarily into Belfast Lough, down the Lagan valley, along the south shore of Lough Neagh, along the Clogher valley and ultimately into County Fermanagh.[9] These were the areas where Anglicanism, Quakerism and Methodism were most strongly established by the nineteenth century, but it should not be forgotten that there were also Presbyterian immigrants in the second half of the seventeenth century who hailed from the North of England. Even in the Ulster of 1700 one could not simply equate Presbyterianism with Scottish origins. In drawing attention to the diversity of Ulster society in the seventeenth century it is also worth

op. cit. (Oxford, 2001), pp. 394–5.   7 N. Canny, op. cit., pp. 362–402; M. O'Dowd, *Power, politics and land: Early Modern Sligo, 1568–1688* (Belfast, 1991).   8 N. Canny, 'English migration into and across the Atlantic during the seventeenth and eighteenth centuries' in N. Canny (ed.), *Europeans on the move: studies on European migration, 1500–1800* (Oxford, 1994), pp. 62–3; W. Macafee & V. Morgan, 'Population in Ulster, 1660–1760' in P. Roebuck (ed.), *Plantation to partition: essays in Ulster history in honour of J.L. McCracken* (Belfast, 1981), pp. 46–63.   9 Macafee & Morgan, op. cit. (1981), pp. 54–5.

pointing out that those who took up land in Ulster under the Plantation scheme were not exclusively from the Scottish lowlands. As Hill has demonstrated, a number of those who most successfully adapted to the challenging environment of early seventeenth-century Ulster had been drawn from the Scottish Highlands and Islands.[10] Finally, it is perhaps wise to caution against any assumption that virtually impermeable ethnic boundaries existed during the seventeenth century. It is clear that intermarriage between settler and native, though by no means unknown, was very much the exception in this period but we know less about the extent of segregation between Scots and English settlers, particularly after mid-century. It does seem clear, however, that cultural influences mixed relatively freely. In short, the development of a society that bore traits unique to Ulster began early and that a century after the beginning of British settlement it was not easy to identify people who were in any meaningful sense genetically or culturally 'pure'.[11]

Returning to Scotland, let me try to sketch out the basic chronology of the developing crisis of the 1690s. The first reports of difficulty emanate in 1693 and 1694 when there were reports of deficient harvests. These bad conditions were restricted, however, to the North of Scotland and appear not to have caused exceptional levels of distress. The year 1695, at least in hindsight, was not a propitious one for Scotland. The launch of the Company which would undertake Scotland's ambitious expedition to Darien in Central America was initially greeted with much national fervour. However, the very significant sums of money invested in the project would eventually sink without return over the course of the proceeding five years. Darien, in short, drained the Scottish economy of capital at a time when it was most vulnerable. The cause of that vulnerability related in large measure to the severe shortage of basic foodstuffs which followed the widespread harvest failure of 1695. The Scottish privy council responded to this crisis through the relaxation of restrictions on the importation of foodstuffs, primarily grain. In such circumstances contemporaries, having done their best to make good the shortfall through import, tried to ensure that as much seed corn as possible could be retained for ploughing with a view to the following season's harvest. Then one simply kept one's fingers crossed and prayed hard for clement weather. The biggest danger to pre-industrial economies was the repetition of harvest failure and this was precisely what unfolded in Scotland. The harvest of 1696 failed to the same

---

10 J.M. Hill, 'The origins of the Scottish Plantations in Ulster to 1625: a re-interpretation' in *Journal of British Studies*, 32 (1993), 24–43. It should also be noted that whilst the vast majority of those Scots coming to Ulster in the 1690s were lowland Presbyterians there was a movement into north Antrim and the Glens of Highland Catholics.   11 The issues of intermarriage and wider cultural mixing in seventeenth-century Ulster are in need of further research. See the discussion re. intermarriage in J.G. Leyburn, *The Scotch-Irish: a social history* (Chapel Hill, N.C., 1962), pp. 133–9, 143, 153.

extent as that of the previous year and thus in the autumn of 1696 the worst effects of the crisis began to bite in the Scottish countryside. The harvest of 1697 was generally good, improving the food supply and affording some relief to the hard pressed population. Relief, however, was short lived, as a severe winter and late spring followed and lead to significant livestock mortality and a further harvest failure in 1698. A second peak in the crisis subsequently set in with widespread distress and increased mortality lasting through another particularly cold and wet winter. It was not until the plentiful harvest of 1699 was gathered until a substantive recovery began. The absence of further deficient harvests over the following decade provided space for what appears to have been a fairly strong and rapid recovery.[12]

This represents a basic framework of events during the later 1690s but obviously only takes us so far. It might be deemed somewhat surprising that there has not been more published work dealing with the events of these years. The last decade in Ireland has seen books or articles published on the harvest crises of the early seventeenth century by Gillespie, the crises of the later 1720s and the early 1780s by Kelly and the Famine of 1740–1 by Dickson.[13] Whilst there has been a great deal of exploration of Scottish economy and society in the early modern period during the last decade also, there still is no single publication dealing with the national impact of Scotland's worst famine. Although the range of primary sources are inferior it is not perhaps, entirely inappropriate to compare the deluge of publication which marked the 150th anniversary of the Great Irish Famine with the relative quietude in Scotland during the 300th anniversary of the 'ill years' of Williamite Scotland.[14] One can nonetheless attempt to address some of the key questions about the 1690s crisis.

A primary issue with all subsistence crises and famines is to attempt to measure their demographic impact and quantify the relative significance of excess mortality and migration in shaping population decline or displacement. The most recent estimate of Scotland's population before the onset of famine is presented by Robert Tyson and based on the hearth tax returns of the 1690s. Tyson suggests a total population at this date of 1.23 million.[15] Ian Whyte has

12 This summary draws largely upon I. Whyte, *Agriculture and society in seventeenth century scotland* (Edinburgh, 1979), pp. 246–51; M. Flinn, *Scottish population history from the seventeenth century to the 1930s* (Cambridge, 1977), pp. 164–86.   13 R. Gillespie, 'Harvest crises in early seventeenth-century Ireland' in *Irish Economic and Social History*, 11 (1984), 5–18; J. Kelly, 'Harvests and hardship: famine and scarcity in the late 1720s' in *Studia Hibernica*, 26 (1991–2), 65–103; J. Kelly, 'Scarcity and poor relief: the subsistence crisis of 1782–84' in *Irish Historical Studies*, 28 (1992–3), 38–62; D. Dickson, *Arctic Ireland: the extraordinary story of the Great Frost and Forgotten Famine of 1740–41* (Belfast, 1997).   14 Since the beginning of the sesquicentenary commemoration of the Great Irish Famine in 1995 there have been at least two dozen monographs or collections of essays published relating to the subject.   15 R.E. Tyson, 'Contrasting regimes: population growth in Ireland and Scotland during the eighteenth century' in S.J.

concluded that 'it is likely that Scotland's population was cut by around 13 per cent' during the course of the years 1695–1700.[16] In real terms, thus, Scotland lost somewhere in the region of 160,000 people. Whyte suggests that 'about half of this was due directly to increased mortality, the remainder to a drop in the birth rate and to emigration'.[17] Estimating the projected loss through a decline in the birth rate, that is averted births, is very difficult. If one were to apply the estimated reduction rate deployed by Joel Mokyr with respect to the Irish Famine of the 1840s it could be considered that about a fifth of the missing 160,000 could thus be accounted for, in other words about 32,000 missing births between 1695 and 1700.[18] We are thus left with some 48,000 Scots who disappeared in this period through migration.

The next obvious, but no less difficult, question is where did these migrants go? Perhaps the most obvious destination was England with which Scotland, of course, shared a land border. There has been little work done on the movement of Scots into England in the seventeenth century as a whole. Northern towns like Newcastle upon Tyne had a fairly substantial dockside Scots community of keel men by this stage and there was undoubtedly reinforcement during the late 1690s.[19] Overall, however, pending further research we might estimate that England received only a few thousand Scots migrants during these crisis years. Seventeenth-century Scotland had developed significant trading and migration routes with continental Europe. Indeed, in the first half of the century movement to Scandinavia and Poland alone was more than double the migration to Plantation Ireland. Movement to Europe was less significant after mid-century but there is evidence to suggest a fairly significant and vibrant Scots mercantile and military community in the Netherlands by 1700.[20] Overall one might tentatively propose that migration to Europe in the later 1690s was probably similar in volume to that across the border to England.

The other alternative destination to Ireland for Scots during the 1690s was America, or more accurately the Americas. It has been estimated that approximately 7,000 Scots crossed the Atlantic during the second half of the seventeenth century, with some two-thirds of these migrants ending up in the Caribbean.[21] There is some evidence for an acceleration in such migration during the 1690s. Some of this was driven by the demand to settle Darien but

Connelly, R.A. Houston and R.J. Morris (eds), *Conflict, identity and economic development: Ireland and Scotland, 1600–1939* (Preston, 1995), pp. 64–77.   16 Whyte (1995), p. 124. On outward migration from Scotland in this period see T.C. Smout, N.C. Landsman and T.M. Devine, 'Scottish emigration in the seventeenth and eighteenth centuries' in N. Canny (ed.), *Europeans on the move: studies on European migration, 1500–1800* (Oxford, 1994), pp. 76–113.   17 Whyte, op. cit. (1995), p. 124.   18 J. Mokyr, *Why Ireland starved: a quantative and analytical history of the Irish economy, 1800–1850* (London, 1983).   19 Whyte, op. cit. (1995), pp. 120–1.   20 Ibid., p. 120; S. Murdoch, *Britain, Denmark, Norway and the house of Stuart, 1603–60* (Eliston, 2000).   21 Whyte, op. cit. (1995), p. 120.

also instances of ships like the *Liloo of London* which left Montrose in February
1696 with 112 men, women and boys on board destined for Pennsylvania.[22]
Perhaps 2,000 Scots went west across the Atlantic in this decade. Thus taking
these migration streams into account it would appear that approximately 7,000
of the estimated 48,000 Scots who left their homeland during the 1690s were
destined for England, Europe and the Americas. So by a process of elimina-
tion we arrive at an estimate for migration from Scotland to Ireland in the
1690s of 41,000. Any attempt to correlate this estimated immigration against
Irish population figures is made problematic by the notoriously treacherous
demographic evidence for early modern Ireland.[23] The most detailed work on
population in Ulster in this period was carried out in the 1970s. An article on
population in Ulster, 1660–1760 by Bill Macafee and Valerie Morgan, published in 1981, does not offer any concrete estimate for Scots immigration in
the 1690s but what it does demonstrate is the very strong growth in the number
of British households in Ulster between the 1660s and the 1740s.[24] At its most
dynamic, this expansion could manifest itself in a rise from 308 British households in the barony of Loughinsholin, County Londonderry, to 2,572 British
households by the 1740s – an extraordinary increase of 735 per cent (without
immigration the natural growth rate might have been anticipated to have
increased Settler population during this period by around 60 per cent). An
interesting pattern to emerge from this work, however, was the differentiation
between the expansion of British settler population in this period in eastern
and western Ulster. Baronies in western Londonderry and Donegal generally
expanded between 1660 and 1740 by 200–300 per cent, whilst those in county
Antrim expanded by only 60–80 per cent. As the authors conclude,

> The evidence suggests that the influxes of the latter years (of the sev-
> enteenth century) were concentrated in the west. At the same time it
> must not be forgotten that there was undoubtedly secondary internal
> migration from the more densely settled Scottish areas of counties
> Antrim and Down'.[25]

The problems, then of assessing with any degree of accuracy the scale of the
Scots flow to Ireland in the later 1690s on the basis of what is known today

22 I. Adams & M. Somerville, *Cargoes of despair and hope: Scottish emigration to North America,
1603–1800* (Edinburgh, 1993), p. 21.   23 For a fuller explanation of these problems see L. M.
Cullen, 'Population trends in seventeenth century Ireland' in *Economic and Social Review*, 6
(1974–5), 149–65; L.A. Clarkson, 'Irish population revisited, 1687–1821' in J.M. Goldstrom &
L.A. Clarkson (eds), *Irish population, economy and society: essays in honour of the late K.H. Connell*
(Oxford, 1981), pp. 13–36; D. Dickson, C. Ó Gráda, S. Daultrey, 'Hearth tax, household size
and Irish popultion change, 1672–1821' *Proceedings of the Royal Irish Academy*, 82C, no. 6
(1982), 125–55.   24 W. Macafee & V. Morgan: see n. 8 above. 'Population in Ulster 1660–1760'
in P. Roebuck (ed.), *Plantation to partition: essays in Ulster history in honour of J.L. McCracken*
(Belfast, 1981).   25 Ibid., pp. 58–9.

about Irish demography at this juncture, are considerable. Can we hope to find firmer evidence in the comment of contemporary observers? There were contemporaries who offered purely general commentary upon the migration flow. For example, a report of 1698 which described the multitudes of Scots who went over to Ireland every day.[26] Others speculated over a longer time-frame. Bishop Synge, for example, suggested that between the revolution (1689) and 1715, some 50,000 Scottish families had come to Ireland.[27] We have, however, three more specific estimates. The most conservative of these, offered by the author of a *Discourse concerning Ireland*, published in 1698, put forward the figure of 14,000 Scots immigrants as having entered Ireland during the course of the previous year.[28] Another contemporary commentator believed that between 1690 and 1698 approximately 50,000 Scots had crossed to Ulster. This total was broken down to the years between 1690 and 1696 when 30,000 were estimated to have made the move and the years between 1696 and 1698 when another 20,000 followed.[29] The largest estimation of this *fin de siècle* migration was presented by a pamphlet of 1698, whose author argued that no less than 80,000 Scots families had come to Ireland since the revolution.[30]

Setting these estimates alongside the demographic evidence from Scotland and the estimated migration flow of some 41,000 Scots to Ulster in the later 1690s, it is clear that the observations of contemporaries were not wildly at variance with the calculations of historical demographers. The estimation that 50,000 Scots crossed to Ulster in the years between 1690 and 1698 sits fairly comfortably with the Scottish population figures. The observations of 50,000 Scots families arriving in Ireland in the quarter century after the Revolution and, in particular, the claim that 80,000 Scots families came in the eight years after 1690 alone, in this context appear exaggerated and require some explanation.

Scottish settlement in post-Restoration Ireland was very closely correlated with Presbyterianism, not least in the minds of Irish Anglicans. Between 1689 and 1707 the number of Presbyterian ministers and congregations appears to have expanded by about 50 per cent.[31] Spectacular growth which did not really subside until the second decade of the eighteenth century. As Seán Connolly observes, 'by the 1690s Presbyterians outnumbered Anglicans in Ulster' and 'Anglicans had before them the dreadful example of Scotland, where Presbyterianism had only a few years before supplanted episcopacy as the established religion'.[32] Thus in the 1690s the apparent unity which had brought together dissenter and churchman in defence of the Protestant interest (most graphically at the Siege of Derry) soon gave way to an atmosphere of sectarian

26 *Some thoughts on the bill* (London, 1698), p. 7.   27 BL Add. MS 6117, f. 50.   28 *Discourse concerning Ireland* (London, 1698), p. 34.   29 BL Add. MS 2907, f. 218.   30 *HMC Ormonde*, new series, iv (1906), p. 126.   31 S. Connolly, *Religion, law and power: the making of Protestant Ireland, 1660–1760* (Oxford, 1992), p. 167.   32 Ibid.

competition and near paranoia. This sense of perceived threat presented to the established church at the time is perhaps most palpably communicated by Tobias Pullein, the bishop of Dromore. In 1697 Pullein published a pamphlet responding to Joseph Boyse's pamphlet of a few years before entitled 'The case of the dissenting Protestants of Ireland.[33] Boyse, a non-conformist minister in Dublin, was a vocal proponent of religious toleration. Pullein's response is interesting because it does not simply engage with Boyse, as was so often the case, on the basis of theology but rather sets his argument within a contemporary social context. It is worth quoting a passage from Pullein's pamphlet in full:

> For though the Vindicator (Boyse) tells us, that this present toleration can tempt none to leave Scotland, yet I'm sure it has not hindered many thousand families from coming thence, and settling in this Nation within these five years, and tis observable, that the dissenting ministers among em, are all zealous for the Covenant, and tis not to be doubted but that the whole body of the people (except some few Highlanders) are of the same persuasion with those teachers: And all of em being lately come from a Kingdom where episcopacy is abolished, and Presbytery established, and having solemnly sworn to exterpate Prelacy; and their aversion to our eclesiastical polity being so deeply rooted in their natures, and their obligation to destroy it so strongly inforced upon their consciences, there is great reason to fear, that when their power and numbers are increased, they will employ their utmost strength, and most vigorous endeavours to overturn (now their hand is in) this truly Apostelical Government of the established church: And therefore for the preservation of the public peace and safety of the nation, tis advisable that we should deal with their preachers at their first coming over as tis usually done with those that come from a country infected with the plague: they should all be obliged to perform their quarantine, and undergo some religious tests and probations before they be publicly allowed to preach in their Conventicles.[34]

The language employed by Pullein is of interest because it suggests the notion of Scots settlers and particularly immigrant ministers spreading Presbyterianism in a way which was analogous to contagious disease. This, I would suggest, betrays the classic psychological state of an individual host reacting defensively against what they perceive to be a sudden flood or influx of outsiders who were deemed to be different and threatening. Similar language, for example, was often used in England and North America in relation to Irish immigration in

33 T. Pullein, *A defence of the answer to a paper entitled The Case of the dissenting Protestants of Ireland* (Dublin, 1697); J. Boyse, *The case of the dissenting Protestants of Ireland* (Dublin, 1695).
34 Pullein, op. cit. pp. 8–9. Reproduced in facsimile in D.W. Hayton (ed.), *Ireland and the Glorious Revolution, 1692–1715* (PRONI, 1976), doc. 226.

the later 1840s. Famine immigrants not only represented a real threat as carriers of typhus and other diseases but could, according to the popular press at least, spread the perceived evils of popery and idleness in a similar fashion.[35]

What is clear is the fact that the significant Scots migration to Ireland in the 1690s formed an important backdrop against which relationships between Protestants in Ireland were forged in the wake of the Williamite war. An indication of the stresses and fissures within the Protestant interest in Ireland is the debate surrounding the application of ethnic labels during these years. Connolly points to those few contemporaries who now talked of the Irish and the British, rather than the Irish and the English. Perhaps, most revealing of all was the response of the lord chancellor, Porter, to those attached to Capel who in 1695 sought to promote the all-encompassing term 'British' to Irish Protestants of both English and Scottish lineage. He not only rejected this new unifying terminology but held out the prospect in the future of having to arm Irish Catholics in order to put down a rebellion by the Ulster Scots.[36] One should be wary of underestimating the depth of suspicion and antagonism between English and Scottish interests in Ireland before the English and Scottish Union of 1707.

Having established the volume and impact of movement from Scotland to Ireland during the 1690s the next critical issue to address is that of motivation and the socio-economic profile of the migrants. Perhaps the best starting point is an acknowledgment that, as with most strong migration flows, powerful push and pull factors were active. We have already referred in detail to the push exercised by famine in the four years after 1695, but it is clear that there was already by 1695 a significant Scots migration underway and that this movement was more strongly conditioned by pull factors. The availability of cheap land in the wake of the Williamite war was undoubtedly the central explanation for this movement. From October 1691 when the signing of the Treaty of Limerick, brought the war in Ireland to a close, probably earlier in Ulster, there began an upsurge in the number of Scots settling the land.[37] Whilst the conflict of the preceding three years was generally less physically disruptive or destructive than the wars of the 1640s it nonetheless forced significant numbers of tenants to desert their holdings.[38] Thus as warfare subsided and peace returned, a priority for estate owners in Ulster and elsewhere in Ireland was to attract tenants to re-people their lands and ensure that rent rolls continued to realize capital. It was in these circumstances, what we might refer to today as a 'buyer's market', that tenants could hope to secure the most favourable leasing terms and lowest rent from landowner or land agent. Many of those

---

35 N. Kissane, *The Irish Famine: a documentary history* (Dublin, 1995), pp. 158–9; F. Neal, *Black '47: Britain and the Famine Irish* (Basingstoke, 1998), p. 162.   36 Connolly (1992), p. 118.   37 BL Add. MS 2902 f.218, W.H. Crawford, 'Landlord-tenant relations in Ulster 1609–1820' in *Irish Economic and Social History*, 2 (1975), 10.   38 J. Childs, 'The Williamite War, 1689–1691' in T. Bartlett & K. Jeffery (eds), *A military history of Ireland* (Cambridge, 1996), pp. 188–210.

who came to Ireland in the early 1690s in order to take advantage of the attractive market either to rent or purchase land have been identified by David Dickson, as 'yeoman migrants with some resources'.[39] Indeed, Louis Cullen has suggested that this migration stream was a positively active force in stimulating the Irish economy in the post-war period as a result of the capital which these Scots brought with them.[40] This pull factor did not neatly switch off in 1695 and there undoubtedly were migrants continuing to take up attractive leasing arrangements in the later 1690s. To quote one example, we know that a Scots family agreed a 21-year lease with the agent of the Essex estate in County Monaghan in the autumn of 1697 when the same family decided to move on to the American colonies when the lease fell in 1718, the lease was renegotiated at triple the rental value of 1697.[41] It should also be acknowledged that many Scots traders and merchants also appear to have established themselves in Ireland at this time. We know that the Scots were very prominent amongst those who victualled the Williamite forces during their campaign in Ireland and many did well as a consequence of the victorious campaign. The Scots mercantile community in Ulster ports such as Belfast and Londonderry received reinforcement during and after the Revolution but southern ports such as Sligo and Limerick also saw the establishment of some Scots traders.[42]

Having established the presence of Scots migrants 'with means' during the 1690s, the obvious question, to some extent begged by a reading of the historiography, is were those who came in large numbers after the onset of famine in 1695 generally drawn from a lower social level and materially poorer. The strongest evidence from contemporary sources that this was indeed the case is located in a memorandum simply entitled 'The Scots in Ireland, 1697'. In this document it is estimated that the second wave of Scots migration to Ireland, that predominantly driven by famine conditions comprised '20,000 poor'.[43] The wider evidence relating to subsistence migration conditioned by food crises in early modern Europe would support, not surprisingly, the correlation between an increase in the volume of poor migrants and the occurrence and intensity of periods of dearth.[44]

Rab Houston, in studying geographical mobility in Scotland between 1652 and 1811, notes that in periods of crisis there were likely to be 'bouts of extraordinary movement' characterized by the migration of 'more families and a

---

39 D. Dickson, *New foundations: Ireland*, p. 48. 40 L.M. Cullen, *An economic history of Ireland since 1660* (London, 1972), p. 29. 41 PRONI, MIC 170/2, Edmund Kane, Clones, to Hon. Dacres Barrett, Essex, Sept. 20 & Dec. 18 1718. 42 J. Bardon, *A history of Ulster* (Belfast, 1992), p. 171. I am grateful to Roger Dixon, Librarian, Ulster Folk and Transport Museum, for enlightenment on this point. 43 'The Scots in Ireland, 1697', University of London MS 30, ff. 11–12. 44 M. Livi Bacci, *The population of Europe* (Oxford, 2000), pp. 52, 141; H. Kamen, *European society, 1500–1700* (London, 1971), pp. 35–40; J.D. Post, *Food shortage, climatic variability, and epidemic disease in preindustrial Europe: the mortality peak of the early 1740s* (New York, 1985).

wider range of ages ... especially among the lower classes'.[45] Adding weight to Houston's assertion was the comment offered by local governors in the borders town of Hawick, who in 1697 noted that 'extreme dearth' had created a flood of 'mendicating persons and familys'.[46] The migrant poor throughout the British Isles in the sixteenth and seventeenth centuries were notable for the extensive geographical range of their mobility. Periods of harvest crises in Ireland, Scotland or Wales in this period consistently lead to a significant influx of poor migrants and beggars from the 'Celtic fringe' into London. The Irish poor even turned up in significant numbers on the continent of Europe at such times.[47] It would therefore not be surprising to find Ulster included within the perceived migration field of the rural poor, particularly perhaps in southern and western Scotland. The draw of Ireland in the later 1690s was undoubtedly enhanced by the fact that the country miraculously escaped the inclement weather and famine conditions that struck Scotland with such devastating force. Push and pull factors were thus exercising maximum force as the agricultural economy in Ireland geared up to meet the export demand for foodstuffs across the North Channel.[48]

Another area in which one might look for evidence of increasing pauper migration from Scotland would be in the field of provision for the poor in Ireland. The absence of any compulsory national poor law in Ireland until 1838 left much to the discretion of individual parish vestries. One notable pattern of concerted action to address the problem did emerge in east Ulster during the decade after 1699. At least six parishes in east Ulster set in motion the operation of a badging scheme to identify the local and deserving poor as being worthy of relief. This method of distinguishing the worthy from the unworthy poor had been a central component of poor relief practice in Scotland during the seventeenth century. It seems very likely that Scottish influence was at play in, at least, shaping the response to the challenge imposed by the poor.[49] The fact that concerted action was taken at the level of local government suggests an increased pressure exerted by growing numbers of paupers.

The County Antrim grand jury may have been looking back over the preceding decade, when in 1707, it advocated badging as a response to the 'great increase of vagrant persons and idle beggars'.[50] Lists of those transported to

45 R.A. Houston, 'Geographical mobility in Scotland, 1652–1811: the evidence of testimonials' in *Journal of Historical Geography*, 11 (1985), 391. 46 Cited in Houston, op. cit. (1985), p. 391. 47 A.L. Beier, *Masterless men: the vagrancy problem in England, 1560–1640* (London, 1985), pp. 32–47; L.M. Cullen, 'The Irish diaspora of the seventeenth and eighteenth centuries' in Canny (ed.), *Europeans on the move*, p. 132. 48 L.E. Cochran, *Scottish trade with Ireland in the eighteenth century* (Edinburgh, 1985), p. 100. 49 D. Dickson, 'In search of the old Irish poor law' in R. Mitchison & P. Roebuck (eds), *Economy and society in Scotland and Ireland, 1500–1939* (Edinburgh, 1988), p. 151; P. 'Fitzgerald, poverty and vagrancy in Early Modern Ireland' (QUB, PhD, 1994), pp. 271–80. 50 W.N.C. Barr and W.C. Kerr (eds), *The oldest register of the parish of Derriaghy, County Antrim, 1696–1772* (Derriaghy, 1981), pp. 91–2.

colonial America in the 1730s from Ulster strongly suggest, on the basis of surname, that those indicted as vagabonds included men and women of Irish, English and Scottish lineage.[51]

As stated at the outset of this paper much of what has been written about the Scots in Ulster and migration from Ulster to colonial America has tended to underplay the significance of the Scots migration to Ulster in the 1690s and the role of famine as a conditioning force behind that movement. John Harrison, author of a slim volume entitled *The Scot in Ulster*, published in Edinburgh in 1888, drew upon Lecky in presenting the migration of the 1690s as a movement propelled by a sense of opportunism in land and trade.[52] Latimer, writing about the history of Irish Presbyterians, fourteen years later, briefly notes 'many thousands of Presbyterians came to Ireland between the years 1690 and 1698 to occupy farms laid waste by the ravages of war.'[53] Those in North America, writing on the history of the Scotch-Irish, such as Hanna and Ford tended to follow suit by stressing the motivational pull of land rather than the push of famine.[54] In the context of the largely Irish catholic and famine induced influx of the 1840s it is not difficult to see why those writing sympathetically about the largely protestant influx of the colonial era might not stress the role of famine in the migration of Scots to Ulster or of Ulster emigrants to America. It is only in the last two decades that the strength of the correlation between the cycle of subsistence crises in Ireland and the ebb and flow of trans-Atlantic emigration before 1750 has been fully recognised.[55]

In conclusion, may I say that this paper is intended as an initial exploratory foray designed to float ideas rather than the conclusion to extensive or detailed archival work. At least it highlights a number of interesting avenues for further research. Work in the archives in Ireland and Scotland could help to reveal more about the character of this migration whilst American archives might yield up material which sheds light on the perceptions of those who came to the New World in the generation after 1690. It would, furthermore, be interesting to explore more fully the writings of those before and after the Great Famine who referred to the Scots influx of the 1690s, in order to determine shifts in explanatory emphasis.

51 P. Fitzgerald, 'A sentence to sail: the transportation of Irish convicts and vagrants to colonial America in the eighteenth century' in P. Fitzgerald and S. Ickringill (eds), *Atlantic crossroads: historical connections between Scotland, Ireland and North America* (Newtownards, 2001), pp. 114–31. 52 J. Harrison, *The Scot in Ulster: sketch of the history of the Scottish population of Ulster* (Edinburgh, 1888), p. 81. 53 W.T. Latimer, *A history of the Irish Presbyterians* (Belfast, 1902), p. 250, 258. To be fair to Latimer he does later briefly acknowledge the role of famine in fuelling the Scots migration. (p. 267). 54 C.A. Hanna, *The Scotch-Irish or the Scot in North Britain, North Ireland, and North America* (New York, 1902), i, p. 614; H.J. Ford, *The Scotch-Irish in America* (New York, 1941), p. 186. 55 G. Kirkham, 'The origins of mass migration from Ireland' in R. Kearney (ed.), *Migrations: the Irish at home and abroad* (Dublin, 1990), p. 86.

The Scots and Ulster in the seventeenth century: a Scandinavian perspective

STEVE MURDOCH

A Scandinavian angle to Scottish relations with Ulster, or Ireland in general, may not be immediately apparent to historians of relations between the two countries. Rosalind Mitchison once said that 'Neither Scotland nor Ireland can be studied for the seventeenth century without attention to their relationships to England and to the effects on both countries of decisions made in England.'[1] While that is so, recent research, particularly that spear-headed by the Northern European Historical Research Network has demonstrated that neither can the three kingdoms be studied without also considering the wider European dimension.[2] Alexia Grosjean has demonstrated, for instance, that had there been no sub-state Scottish-Swedish alliance in the 1630s, there would have been no Scottish Army of the Covenant in 1639 with which to fight the Bishops' Wars.[3] Without this severe challenge to Stuart authority, it is not certain that there would have been an uprising in Ireland in 1641 or, indeed, an English Civil War. Speculation on that point will undoubtedly continue for some time, yet more certainly Scottish migration to Ulster ultimately led to the presence of soldiers from Ireland in Scandinavia. Levies from Ireland were frequently orchestrated by Scottish officers using kith and kin networks among the plantation population to fill their regiments with settlers and native Irish alike.[4] These emigrations from Ireland in turn facilitated several episodes of 'Swedish' involvement in the political struggles within the British Isles, Ireland included, but only when there was a significant Scottish input into them.

Seventeenth-century Ulster is often seen as the major destination for Scots, particularly Lowland Presbyterian Scots. Mitchison has robustly challenged

---

1 R. Mitchison, 'Ireland and Scotland: The seventeenth-century legacies compared' in T.M. Devine and D. Dickson (eds), *Ireland and Scotland, 1600–1850* (Edinburgh, 1983), p. 2. 2 See for example the recent NEHRN publication, A.I. Macinnes, T. Riis and F.G. Pedersen (eds), *Ships, guns and Bibles in the North Sea and the Baltic states, c.1350–1700* (East Linton, 2000). 3 A. Grosjean, 'General Alexander Leslie, the Scottish Covenanters and the *Riksråd* debates, 1638–1640' in Macinnes et al., *Ships, guns and Bibles*, pp. 115–38. 4 For more on these episodes see S. Murdoch and A. Grosjean, 'Irish soldiers in Scandinavia, 1618–1648' in M. Ó Siochrú (ed.), *Ireland and the Thirty Years War* (forthcoming). For specifically Ulster-Scottish involvement, see P. Robinson, 'Ulster Scots ettles wi tha Thrittie Years' Weir' in *Cairn*, 2 (1998), 15–22.

estimates by Thomas Wentworth, first earl of Strafford, of 50,000–150,000 Scots arriving in Ireland in the 1630s and other figures of 80,000 more between 1650 and 1672. She suggests a much lower figure of between 10,000 and 20,000 by 1652 with another larger wave in the 1690s, perhaps as many as 40,000 according to Paddy Fitzgerald.[5] Given the numbers involved and the impact they had on their new land – for better or for worse – the belief in 'destination Ulster' for the itinerant Scot is hardly surprising. However, Ulster was only one of a number of locations that attracted the Scots during this period, even if it is the place Irish historians associate most with Scottish settlement. Indeed, the Ulster angle has perhaps been overstated in that regard. Not only does it miss out Scottish migrations to other parts of Ireland, but also the more significant movement of Scots to Scandinavia and Northern Europe.

Norway in particular sustained numerous Scottish communities around Stavanger, Bergen and Trondheim drawn there by trading opportunities. So important was the timber trade in these parts that in Norway it is still called *Skottehandlen* – the 'Scottish trade' – while the sixteenth and seventeenth centuries are known as 'the Scottish period' of Norwegian history.[6] Added to the numbers of Scottish entrepreneurs in Scandinavia were up to 50,000 Scottish soldiers who participated in the anti-Habsburg armies, especially those of Sweden and Denmark-Norway, during the Thirty Years War (1618–48).[7] Many of these men took their families and servants with them, considerably increasing the numbers of Scots in the region – albeit that many of them went directly to Germany rather than Scandinavia proper.[8]

The Scots also emigrated and spread into the southern Baltic towns at a phenomenal rate. The Scottish community in Poland-Lithuania in the seventeenth century has been shown to have been both large and influential.[9]

5 Mitchison, 'Ireland and Scotland', p. 7. See Fitzgerald's chapter in this book for further details. 6 See A. Espelland, *Skottene i Hordaland og Rogaland fra aar 1500–1800* (Norheimsund, 1921), p. 31; A.M. Wiesener, 'Axel Movat og hans slegt' in *Bergins Historiske Forening Skrifter*, 36 (Bergen, 1930), 98; F. Tennfjord, *Stamhuset Rosendal* (Oslo, 1949), pp. 7–8; E. Vaage, *Kvinnherad* (Bergen, 1972), pp. 206–213; A. Næss, 'Skottehandelen på Sunnhordland' in *Sunnhordland Tidskrift*, 7 (1920); A. Lillehammer, 'The Scottish-Norwegian timber trade in the Stavanger area in the sixteenth and seventeenth centuries' in T.C. Smout (ed.), *Scotland and Europe, 1200–1850* (Edinburgh, 1986), pp. 97–111. 7 For numbers of Scots in various armies see S. Murdoch, 'Introduction', in idem (ed.), *Scotland and the Thirty Years War, 1618–1648* (Leiden, 2001), pp. 9–14. 8 A. Grosjean, 'Scots and the Swedish state: diplomacy, military service and ennoblement, 1611–1660' (unpublished PhD thesis, University of Aberdeen, 1998), pp. 140–7; M. Glozier, 'Scots in the French and Dutch armies during the Thirty Years War' in Murdoch, *Scotland and the Thirty Years War*, pp. 131–7. 9 A.F. Steuart (ed.), *Papers relating to the Scots in Poland, 1576–1793* (Edinburgh, 1915); A. Biegańska, 'Scottish merchants and traders in seventeenth and eighteenth century Warsaw', *Scottish Slavonic Review*, no. 5 (Autumn 1985); A. Biegańska, 'A note on the Scots in Poland, 1550–1800' in T.C. Smout (ed.), *Scotland and Europe, 1200–1850* (Edinburgh, 1986), pp. 157–165; A. Biegańska, 'In search of tolerance: Scottish Catholics and Presbyterians in Poland', *Scottish Slavonic Review*, 17 (autumn

Indeed, if reports of 30,000 Scots in 1620 are correct, there can be little doubt that Poland-Lithuania and the Baltic cities under her influence hosted among the largest settled Scottish diaspora communities outwith Scotland.[10] Some Scots, like the community in the Lithuanian town of Kedainiai, appear to have been attracted by the lure of establishing a Calvinist utopia under the protection of Duke Radziwill in the 1630s. They left at a time when many believed Charles I might be successful in pushing through his Anglican reforms in Scotland.[11]

In terms of Scots seeking religious freedom, mercantile or military opportunities abroad, Scandinavia and the Baltic offered an alternative, and more lucrative destination than Ulster. However, the two pronged nature of the Scottish exodus east and west invariably led to members of Scots in one part of the diaspora calling on their family and friends to join them where opportunities presented themselves in the other. This could either lead to Scots from Ireland being drawn to the Baltic or *vice versa*.

A QUESTION OF IDENTITY

Many contemporaries living on the continent erroneously perceived the Scots and the Irish as a single ethnic group. This has clouded the interpretation by many scholars as to who is Scottish and who is Irish and what their role was in the history of the two nations. In one example, confusion still abounds about Irish military service in the Swedish army largely caused by the Stettin woodcut of 1631. In it, four men are shown and described as 'Irrlander' which is translated as Irish when it actually means, in this case 'Gael'. The confusion arises from the seventeenth-century Scottish practice of referring to Highlanders as *Erse* or Irish. However, the identity of the Stettin 'Irrlander' has been firmly established as being Highlanders from Donald Mackay, first Lord Reay's Scottish regiment since they formed the Stettin garrison at exactly that period, though this does not prevent Irish scholars from continually using the image to depict Irishmen.[12] In fact, the regiment was composed initially of Scots from the Highlands and Lowlands, but after several years of fighting included a few Germans, English and Irish by the mid

1991); R. Frost, 'Scottish soldiers, Poland-Lithuania and the Thirty Years War' in S. Murdoch (ed.), *Scotland and the Thirty Years War* (Leiden, 2001), p. 192. 10 There are at least two contemporary sources for this piece of information. See *Calendar of state papers domestic* (hereafter *CSPD*) *1619–1623* ed. M.A.E. Green (London, 1858), p. 237, Chamberlain to Carleton, March 24, 1621; William Lithgow, *The totall discourse of the rare adventures and painefull peregrinations of long nineteene yeares travayles from Scotland to the most famous kingdomes in Europe, Asia and Affrica* (Glasgow, 1906), p. 368. 11 L. Eriksonas, 'The lost colony of Scots: unravelling overseas connections in a Lithuanian town' in Macinnes et al. (eds), *Ships, guns and Bibles*, pp. 173–83. 12 I. Grimble, *The chief of Mackay* (London, 1965), p. 103.

1630s.[13] Interestingly, some Swedes are still caught up in the confusion and in one recent publication there is a drawing of 'Irländska Höglandmusketerare' or Irish-Highland musketeers based on the woodcut.[14] Either the authors are genuinely confused or are simply hedging their bets as to the origin of the soldiers they depict in their book. Leaving the Gaels aside for a moment, there is an additional problem of how to describe people of non-Gaelic origins who arrived in Scandinavia from Ireland.

The Stuart ambassador to Sweden between 1611 and 1632 was the Scotsman, Sir James Spens of Wormiston. In a scathing attack on a member of the Butler family in 1626, Spens described the man as 'Anglus-Hibernus', or Anglo-Irish.[15] Spens therefore distinguished between individuals of English as opposed to Gaelic origin from Ireland. Yet when it comes to those of Scottish origins, the difference is not so clear cut. As noted above, many Scottish Gaels defined themselves as linguistically Irish but politically Scottish until well into the eighteenth century.[16] The Macdonalds in particular had made inroads into Ireland since the fifteenth century.[17] Here there were complications as it was possible to have two branches of the same family with one being classified as subjects of the crown of Scotland and the other being considered subjects of the crown of England in Ireland. Thus throughout the 1580s and 1590s, the Macdonalds of Dunnyveg were Scottish subjects, bound by oaths to the Scottish council and king, while the Macdonalds of Glenluce variously swore allegiance to the English and Scottish crowns.[18] This complication in identification did not go unnoticed and indeed, in 1620, James Macdonald of Dunnyveg was described by the Spanish ambassador in London as both 'Escoces y Irlandes' – Scottish *and* Irish.[19] In addition to the Macdonalds, there were also several other branches of Scottish Gaeldom operating in the north of Ireland, each with varying degrees of loyalty to James VI & I.

Lowland Scots also started to appear in Ireland during this period, mostly settling in Ulster. Circumstances sometimes saw these people leave Ireland for Scandinavia where historians and genealogists today regard them as Irish, although that is probably not how they viewed themselves. Two branches of the Scottish Hamilton family in Sweden exemplify this. Archibald Hamilton (*c.*1580–*c.*1659), archbishop of Cashel and Emly, was the son of Claud Hamilton of Cochno in Dumbartonshire, Scotland, and his wife Margaret

13 For a breakdown of the regiment's component nationalities see J. Fallon 'Scottish mercenaries in the service of Denmark and Sweden' (unpublished PhD thesis, Glasgow, 1974).   14 G. Göransson, *Gustav Adolf och hans folk* (Stockholm, 1994), p. 275.   15 Swedish State Archive (hereafter SRA), Anglica V, Spens to Oxenstierna, 26 November 1626.   16 See for instance *A vocabulary of the Irish dialect spoken by the Highlanders of Scotland* (1702).   17 D. J. Macdonald, *Clan Donald* (Loanhead, 1978), p. 233.   18 Ibid., pp. 249–50 and p. 269.   19 A. Ballesteras Beretta (ed.), *Documentos para la historia de España: correspondencia oficial de Don Diego Sarmiento de Aaina, Conde de Gondomar*, 4 vols (Madrid 1936–1945), i, p. 287, Gondomar to Philip III, 29 March 1620. I would like to thank David Worthington for this reference.

Betoun.[20] In 1598 Hamilton matriculated at Glasgow University where he obtained his MA degree. He spent several years working at the college, initially as a master in 1602–3, a regent from 1605 to 1612, and finally a Doctor of Divinity in 1617. He had already become the minister for the parish of Paisley in 1610, and a member of the General Assembly that year. By 1621 he had approached King James VI requesting a bishopric, which the king subsequently promised him in Ireland. Alexander Seton, first earl of Dunfermline, then intervened on Hamilton's behalf suggesting that the bishopric of Cashel would be suitable. However, two years later he was appointed bishop of Killala. Hamilton also held the bishopric of Achonry on King Charles I's recommendation. It was not until 1630 that Hamilton became the archbishop of Cashel and Emly on the death of the previous archbishop, Malcolm Hamilton. During the Irish revolt of 1641, Archibald Hamilton and his family were forced to flee Cashel, being initially sheltered by some friendly Catholic neighbours. Eventually they left Ireland, losing goods and property worth £9000 in the process. Hamilton obtained a recommendation for Charles I from the Scottish cleric John Durie, but as the king himself was engaged in three civil wars he probably found little comfort at the Stuart court.[21] Hamilton thereafter petitioned the prince of Orange, who ensured he was employed as a professor of Theology in the Dutch Republic in 1644.[22] From his base there, he eventually moved to Sweden where he died at about the age of 80 in 1659. The labelling of this bishop as an Irishman is clearly erroneous since, despite a strong Irish connection, he is unlikely to have viewed himself as such, and clearly the natives concurred and drove him out. Yet even once Hamilton arrived in Sweden, and hopes of him ever returning to Ireland were long gone, he always signed himself 'Casseliens', perhaps as an act of defiance, but certainly adding to the confusion.[23] Thus, when the Swedish ambassador Christer Bonde referred to Hamilton, his bafflement at the bishop's identity extended to calling him both Irish and English in the same letter without mention of his Scottish birth, parentage or upbringing.[24] What is clear though is that Hamilton managed to escape to the Continent with the help of Scottish patrons like John Durie and though he retained his Irish title, there is no evidence whatsoever that he considered himself anything other than a Scot.

Archibald Hamilton succeeded in the episcopalian archbishopric of Cashel from Malcolm Hamilton who held the position between 1623 and 1629.[25]

20 Lt. Colonel George Hamilton, *A history of the house of Hamilton* (Edinburgh, 1933), p. 251
21 Hartlib papers, CD Rom, folio 3/1/16A–16B, John Durie to Samuel Hartlib, 3 December 1643. 22 J.A. Worp, '*De Briefwisseling van Constantijn Huygens'*, iii, *1640–44* (The Hague, 1914), p. 368. 23 See for example SRA, Ericsbergsarkivet, Autografsamlingen, Storbritannien, vol. 269. Archibald Hamilton to Gabriel de la Gardie, c.1650. 24 M. Roberts (ed.), *Swedish diplomats at Cromwell's court, 1655–1656* (London, 1988), pp. 163–4. Christer Bonde to Charles X, 28 September 1655. 25 Hamilton, *A history of the house of Hamilton*, p. 1013.

Like Archibald, Malcolm was a Scot, the son of Archibald Hamilton of Dalserf in Lanarkshire. Probably due to the commonality of surnames and position, Archbishops Malcolm and Archibald are often confused in Swedish and Irish sources, Lodge's *Peerage* suggesting that Malcolm's sons Hugh and Ludowick (Louis) were the sons of Archibald.[26] In fact, Malcolm had at least four sons, Hugh, Ludowick, Alexander and John. Three of these men, Hugh, Ludowick and Alexander served in the Swedish army, drawn to that country's service during the Thirty Years War along with tens of thousands of protestant Scots eager to serve both the Stuart and/or 'Protestant' cause.[27]

In the Swedish peerage, the Hamiltons are listed as being Irish as they used, among others, the name Hamilton of Balygally.[28] The issue of whether they viewed themselves as Scottish, Irish or British in Ireland remains unresolved and in some doubt. True, Hugh Hamilton claimed to have been born in Ireland while securing his Irish baronage in 1661.[29] If that is so then he must have left Ireland barely as a teenager as his father only moved to Ireland about 1611 while Hugh left for Sweden as a soldier in 1624 or 1628. Whatever the truth of his age or place of birth, his Scottish heritage was of great importance to him and his brothers. In Sweden, they served initially in Scottish regiments and were viewed by their contemporaries as fellow Scots of which we have written proof. In both Robert Monro's diary for 1632 and in Sir Thomas Urquhart of Cromarty's classic work, *The Jewell*, Hugh Hamilton and other Scots from Ulster like Sir Frederick Hamilton are referred to as Scottish officers.[30] Indeed, the Scots appear to have recognised anyone born of Scottish parents as a Scot, regardless of where they were born. This led to comments from the likes of James Turner about one 'Johnstone a Scot, but born in Ireland'.[31] Other foreign-born Scots reaffirmed their Scottish nationality by registering themselves as native Scots under the Great Seal of Scotland, a route taken in 1634 by the Dutch-born Scots, Thomas Cunningham and James Weir. Cunningham in particular went on to serve his country by running more arms to the Scots during the Bishops' Wars of 1639–40 than any other individual.[32] Urquhart of Cromarty wrote about a

26 J. Lodge, *The peerage of Ireland; or a genealogical history of the present nobility of that kingdom*, 7 vols (Dublin, 1789 edition), ed. M. Archdall, ii. 27 Many Catholic Scots were influential in raising troops for the 'Protestant' armies fighting for the cause, as they saw it, of Elizabeth of Bohemia. See Murdoch, *Scotland and the Thirty Years War*, introduction, pp. 15–18. 28 G. Elgenstierna, *Den Introducerade Svenska Adelns Ättartavlor, med tillägg och rättelser* (hereafter *SAÄ*), 9 vols (Stockholm, 1925–36), iii, pp. 453 and ix, pp. 244–5. 29 *Calendar of state papers Ireland* (hereafter CSPI), *1660–1662*, ed. R.P. Mahaffy (London, 1905), p. 186: Hamilton to Nicholas, 18 January 1661. 30 R. Monro, *His expedition with the worthy Scots regiment called Mac-keyes*, 2 vols (London, 1937) i, List 2, 'The list of the Scottish officers in Chiefe anno 1632'; R.D.S. Jack & R.J. Lyall (eds), *Sir Thomas Urquhart of Cromarty: the jewell* (Edinburgh, 1983), p. 93. 31 Sir James Turner, *Memoirs of his own life and times* (Edinburgh, 1829), p. 111. 32 J.M. Thomson (ed.), *Register of the Great Seal of Scotland, AD 1634–1651*,

Norwegian-born Scot, Admiral Axel Mowatt as his countryman and of whom he said 'Mowat living in Birren [Bergen] in whose judgement and fidelity such trust is reposed, that he is as it were Vice-King of Norway'.[33] Robert Monro also mentioned another foreign-born Scot, Daniel Sinclair, in a contemporary document. Monro noted that the island of Laaland 'is plentiful of wood for building of ships, where his majesty every yeare hath some builded by his owne master builder, a worthy gentleman begotten of Scots ancestors, called Mr Sinclaire, who speaks the Scottish tongue, and is very courteous to all his countrymen which come thither'.[34] The fact that Sinclair was born in Scandinavia did not prevent him from being considered a fellow Scot, at least not by Monro. From such evidence as this, of which numerous other examples survive, it can be concluded that the Hamiltons born in Ireland did not consider themselves as Ulster-Scots or Scotch-Irish. They were, like foreign-born Scots elsewhere, simply Scots.

MARITAL LINKS AT THE CORE OF THE SCOTTISH COMMUNITY

The links between the 'Irish' and the Swedish-Scots, particularly the Macleans in Gothenburg, were frequently strengthened by marriages. Catherine Cochrane, the daughter of Sir John Cochrane and Grace Butler (cousin of James Butler, twelfth earl and first duke of Ormond) married one of John Maclean's sons, Colonel Jacob Maclean.[35] This marriage undoubtedly facilitated, or at least in some part explains the organizing of military supplies from Sweden to Ormond in 1650. Charles II wrote to Ormond noting that corn ships were being used to conceal 1,000 suits of armour, 900 pistols and powder and match. These had been organized by Patrick Ruthven, earl of Forth and Brentford, and several Swedish merchants.[36] In fact we know the merchant to have been John Maclean and the organizer of the corn ships to have been Cochrane. When Charles II effectively sacrificed James Graham, fifth earl and first marquis of Montrose to the Scottish parliament in 1650, the impact of these actions on the foreign Scottish community was profound. Extreme Royalists working for Montrose felt betrayed at the sacrifice of their friends and waste of their own endeavours. Hence, the much maligned

ix (Edinburgh, 1984), p. 95, nos. 232 and 233; E.J. Courthope (ed.), *The Journal of Thomas Cuningham of Campvere, 1640–1654* (Edinburgh, 1928), p. xiii. **33** Jack & Lyall, *The jewell*, pp. 94–5. **34** Monro, *His expedition*, i, p. 42. **35** *SAA*, v, p. 143. **36** Historical Manuscripts Commission (hereafter HMC), *Pepys manuscript* (London, 1911), p. 253: Charles II to Duke of Ormond, 25 April/4 May 1649 and p. 292: five letters of Patrick Ruthven, 17 March to 7 April 1649; HMC, *Report on the manuscripts of the marquis of Ormond*, ii (London, 1899), p. 93. Robert Long to Ormond, 21 May 1649; S. Murdoch, *Britain, Denmark-Norway and the house of Stuart, 1603–1660* (East Linton, 2000), p. 154.

Royalists, Sir John Cochrane, Sir John Henderson, General James King and General Patrick Ruthven (and John Maclean) ceased to actively support Charles II and, indeed, some changed sides.[37] Cochrane bolted with the corn ships in order, no doubt, to try to recoup the investment of Maclean and his business partners. In 1650 after Cochrane left the Royalist camp with their funds, one English Parliamentarian said of him, 'I believe he hath wit enough to keep the whole money to himself, for if neither the Scots nor the English suffer him to return, that money will be little enough to maintain his Irish lady and her Hangbyes.'[38] The suggestion here is that there may have been more Irish women in the company of Grace Butler. More importantly, once more the presence of a group of Irish in Scandinavia came as a result of inter-marriage with Scots. Yet further, that marriage led to support for events in Ireland (the supply of arms) which, without the family bond, would probably not have been realized.

As a member of the Scottish nation in Sweden, it should come as no surprise that at least two of Hugh Hamilton's three wives came from the Scottish community there, Margaret Forrat (a widow of Sir James Spens) and Susan Balfour.[39] It is very probable that his third wife, Joachamin, was also a Scot. Hugh Hamilton was a major player in the Scottish community. He lent money to fellow Scots on behalf of the Swedish crown, and certainly maintained his usage of the Scots language abroad.[40] On one occasion in the Swedish *Riksråd* (royal council), the scribe stopped recording a debate between Hamilton and fellow Scottish councillor Robert Buchan noting that 'Hammelton tahlte Hånom till på Schottsche' – Hamilton spoke to him in Scots (and please note that even a humble seventeenth century Swedish scribe knew it was Scots not 'bad English').[41] Hugh and his brother Ludowick were ennobled in Sweden under the name of Hamilton of 'Deserf', a corruption of the Scottish place-name 'Dalserf', reflecting their family's Scottish origins. When Hugh Hamilton did press for his Irish peerage, he only did so because the Scots, John, first earl of Middleton and John Maitland, second earl and later first duke of Lauderdale, intervened on his behalf with Charles II.[42]

37 Murdoch, *Britain, Denmark-Norway and the house of Stuart*, pp. 156–9. 38 *Sixth report of the Royal Commission on Historical Manuscripts, Part I, Report and Appendix* (London, 1877), p. 431: Bradshaw to Frost, 3 September 1650; ibid., p. 427: Bradshaw to Acton, 19 June 1650. 39 HMC, *Supplementary report on the manuscripts of his grace the duke of Hamilton*, ed. J.H. McMaster & M. Wood (London, 1932), p. 40. 40 *Svensksa Riksrådets Protokoll* [hereafter *SRP*], xv, 1651–53 (Stockholm, 1920), p. 408, 23 May 1653. The subject of the loan to Gordon was brought up again in 1690. See SRA, Biographica 5, E01463, 5/8. Hugh Hamilton's relation of Lord Glenawley's estate, Dublin, 3 November 1690. 41 *SRP*, xv, p. 425, 20 July 1653. For more on the use of the Scots language in Europe at this time see Dauvit Horsbroch 'Nostra Vulgari Lingua: Scots as a European language, 1500–1700' in *Scottish Language* 18 (1999), 1–16. 42 *CSPI, 1660–1662*, p. 186: Hamilton to Nicholas, 18 January 1661. 43 *SAÄ*, iii, pp. 452–3 and vii, p. 429.

Their intervention being a success, Hugh Hamilton retired to his estates in Balygally, County Tyrone, in 1662 as Baron Hamilton of Glenawley. After his wife Margaret Forrat died in 1653, Glenawley married the Scot Susan Balfour and their daughters married into the Irish peerage.[43]

It was not just the Hamilton men who had travelled to Sweden in the 1650s. Hugh Hamilton's sister, Lillian, also travelled to Sweden and married the Gothenburg-based Scottish merchant, John Maclean first Baron Duart, in 1655.[44] Another marriage linking the Hamiltons and the Macleans came through the marriage of Malcolm Hamilton to Christina Maclean, a daughter of John Maclean. Despite his Irish birth, Malcolm Hamilton had arrived in Sweden from Scotland and took up service as an officer in 1654.[45] He was the son of John Hamilton and Janet Somerville of Comnethon, as well as being a nephew of the above-mentioned Malcolm, Ludowick and Lillian.[46] This degree to which his marriage bound the two families together reveals itself when one considers Lillian Hamilton. Not only was she Malcolm Hamilton's blood aunt, but also his wife Christina's stepmother. Malcolm had a younger brother, Hugh (known as Hugo in Sweden), who had been born in May 1655 in Mone Castle, Ireland. After some cavalry service in the Stuart Lifeguard, Hugo was called to Sweden by his elder brother around 1680 and served in Malcolm Hamilton's regiment. The marriage between Christina Maclean and Malcolm Hamilton made Malcolm a brother-in-law of Colonel Gustavus Maclean, a veteran of Stuart, Dutch and French service. Hugo requested a transfer to Maclean's regiment as his brother's saw little action in their garrison at Gothenburg. Maclean was keen to help Hamilton and frequently interceded to ensure that he received promotion.[47]

Given the above information, it is safe to conclude that culturally, militarily and linguistically, this branch of the Hamiltons was very much linked to the Scottish diaspora both in Ireland and Scandinavia. Once in Sweden they continued to cement this link through marriage alliances and various other cultural ties. This did not mean, however, that these families now felt rooted to Sweden and many members of both the Hamilton and Maclean families returned to the British Isles, many to Ireland.

44 J.N.M. Maclean, *The Macleans of Sweden* (Edinburgh, 1971), p. 26. On 2 March 1641 a group of unnamed Irishmen raised their family standard in Gothenburg. They had come to Sweden to learn the art of war (although they were forbidden from fighting) and some of them stayed for as long as seven years. They are reckoned to have had some links with Kilkenny and were partially funded in Sweden by John Maclean. Who they were exactly is still to be established, but that they were in Sweden at all was certainly due to their Scottish patron. See S. Skarback, *Göteborg på 1600-talet* (Gothenburg, 1992), pp. 83–6.   45 His arrival from Scotland not Ireland is noted in F. Rudelius, *Kalmar Regementes Personhistoria 1623–1927*, 2 vols (Norrköping, 1952), i, p. 101.   46 *SAÄ*, iii, p. 453; P. Sørensson, *Generalfälttygmästaren Hugo Hamilton en karolinsk krigare och landshöfding* (Stockholm, 1915); *Svenska Man och Kvinnor*, iii (Stockholm, 1946), p. 269.   47 Sørensson, *Generalfälttygmästaren Hugo Hamilton*, p. 269.

RETURNING TO IRELAND

Ireland had long been a retirement destination for Scottish soldiers after their Scandinavian service. Anna Catherina Montgomery's claim of a familial relationship to Gustav I Vasa of Sweden is certainly indicative of such a return migration.[48] Another Scot, Sir Frederick Hamilton of Manor Hamilton, served under the Swedish General Åke Tott between 1631 and 1633.[49] He levied troops for his regiment in both Scotland and Ireland via his lieutenant-colonel, Arthur Forbes.[50] On returning from Swedish service, Frederick became a 'guildbrother' in Edinburgh before moving to Ulster to claim his inheritance from his wife's father Sir John Vaughan, former governor of Derry. The 1641 rebellion broke out and his family suffered great misery, Hamilton being deprived of his income of £3,000, his tenants and estates and he was forced to appeal to his friends in Scotland for help.[51] Hamilton went on to form 'Hamilton's Horse', which served in the army of the Solemn League and Covenant. This was mostly in Scotland, but in 1645 and 1646 they were among the Covenanters in Ireland where he died in 1647.[52] Frederick was the father of the Barons Hamilton of Stackallan and, more importantly, Gustavus Hamilton, Viscount Boyne.[53]

Even Major General Robert Monro, victor over Phelim O'Neill and vanquished by Owen Roe O'Neill during the 1640s, retired and lived out his life in Ireland after a long career in Scandinavia.[54] This tradition of retiring to Ireland continued among numerous other 'Swedish' Scottish families, indeed too many to list here. However, just among the families already mentioned in this paper there were returnees to Ireland. Jacob Maclean and Catherine Cochrane apparently chose to follow the itinerant Stuart court around Europe in the 1650s rather than remain in Sweden.[55] After the Restoration in 1660, Jacob became a gentleman of the bedchamber to Charles II and found a role

48 Public Record Office of Northern Ireland [hereafter PRONI], Calendar of T.1089, no. 6, Genealogical Extract to shew relationship between King Gustavus I and Anna Matherine Montgomery née Dunbar; ibid., no. 32, Pedigree (in Swedish) attested in 1896 in Stockholm to show this relationship. I have written twice to the PRO in Northern Ireland in order to obtain copies of these documents, but have never heard back. I would like to thank Professor Jane Ohlmeyer for bringing them to my attention. 49 R. Monro, *His expedition with the worthy Scots Regiment called Makays*, 2 vols (London, 1637), ii, p. 102 and 02 verso; *De Svenska Ätterna Hamilton en släktkrönika*, by Hamiltonska Släktföreningen 1 (Göteborg, 1936), pp. 102, 116–17; 'The humble remonstrance of Sir Frederick Hammilton, knight and colonell, to the right honourable the committee of both kingdoms' (London, 1643), pp. 2–3. 50 *The register of the privy council of Scotland* (RPCS), second series, iv (1630–1632), ed. P. Hume Brown (Edinburgh, 1902), pp. 319–20, 348–51, 626–7. 51 'The humble remonstrance of Sir Frederick Hammilton, pp. 2–3. 52 E. Furgol, *A regimental history of the Covenanting armies* (Edinburgh, 1990), pp. 146–8. 53 Sir James Balfour Paul, *The Scots peerage*, 8 vols (Edinburgh, 1904–11), i, pp. 43–4. 54 See Monro's entry in S. Lee (ed.), *Dictionary of national biography*, xiii (London, 1909). 55 SRA, Brev till Brahe 8, 1658.

in a regiment in Ireland.[56] He died in 1663 in dubious circumstances. Some reports say that his wife murdered him, others that in he threw himself on his own sword during a fit, but either way he died in Ireland.[57]

During their brief time in Ireland, Jacob and Catherine Maclean would have had the company of their relatives, the Butlers (through Catherine's mother) and the Hamiltons through the other marriage alliances already discussed. As noted above, Hugh Hamilton, Baron Glenawley, retired to his estates in County Tyrone in 1662. His brother Ludowick intended to join him but died during the return trip from Sweden. Ludowick's Swedish wife, Anna-Catherina Grubbe-Stjernfelt, completed the journey to Ireland where she was styled Lady Hamilton of Tullykeltyre, County Fermanagh, and where she continued her own Scottish link by marrying Captain James Somerville of Tallacht.[58] While Lady Hamilton enjoyed her new married life in Ireland, her sons from her first marriage, Gustavus and Malcolm Hamilton, were both gaining military experience in the Swedish army. Like their father before them, these men thought nothing of flitting between the various locations of the Scottish diaspora and both retired to Enniskillen in the mid-1680s. Gustavus Hamilton, styled 'of Castleton' in Ireland, had been married in Sweden to Lettice Gore and with her had a son called William. After her death he took a Scottish wife, marrying Margaret Cooper, who bore him several children including Ludowick, born in Enniskillen in 1686.[59] Gustavus's brother Malcolm also married a Scot, Jane Sanderson, and they had a son, also called Malcolm.[60] Their relative, Swedish-born Baron James Hamilton (1664–1726), a son of Malcolm Hamilton and Christina Maclean, also retired to Ireland after military service where he died unmarried.[61]

THE WILLIAMITE WARS

It is clear from these return migrations that the 'Swedish-Scots' maintained an interest in Ireland. This was also true of the government in Sweden, particularly during the change of regime in the British Isles between 1688 and

---

56 Maclean, *The Macleans of Sweden*, p. 27; *SAÄ*, v, p. 143.   57 For the two descriptions see *SAÄ*, v, p. 139; Uppsala University Library, manuscript collection, Palmskiöldska Samlingen, vol. 225, p. 21.   58 Given that two of the Hamiltons (John and Lady Hamilton) married Somervilles in Ireland, it is very possible that the following may be of use to scholars following up these families. See PRONI, Calendar of T.1089, no. 53: Hamilton, Somerville and Dunbar families, Chancery Bill & Testamentary Extracts.   59 G. Hamilton, *A history of the house of Hamilton* (Edinburgh, 1933), pp. 1014–15; *SAÄ*, ix, p. 244. Young Ludowick Hamilton kept the close nature of Hamilton marriages going when he married Mary Cooper, probably his cousin.   60 *SAÄ*, ix, p. 244.   61 Swedish Military Archive [SKRA], Muster roll, 1683/8,17,19; 1685/13; 1697/7; 1691/6; 1696/8,9; Hamilton, *A history of the house of Hamilton*, pp. 1104–5 and 1083.

1690. Agents in Ireland such as J.N. da Costa informed the Swedish resident in London about various matters including the landing of Schomberg in Ireland, the progress of the allies there and expressing the hope that 'God would bless the weapons of the armies of Scotland'.[62] The Scandinavian monarchies of Denmark-Norway and Sweden both raised significant armies in support of William of Orange. The Danes originally intended to support William with 6,000 foot and 1,000 horse and thousands of Danish troops saw service in Ireland. The arrival of these men in Scotland and Ireland is well documented.[63] Among their ranks could be found first and second generation Scots from Scotland, Ulster, Denmark-Norway and Sweden. Tracing the numbers of common soldiers involved is not so easy, especially given the variety of Scandinavian alternatives used for Scottish names. But among the 'Danish' officers we find individuals such as Ensign Gideon Ferguson, Lieutenant John Livingstone and Captain John Seaton.[64] Joining these Scots in Danish regiments fighting James VII & II were Irishmen, like Felix O'Neill and Francis Butler, although Butler apparently regarded himself as a Scot.[65] The service of Swedish troops who supported William of Orange is not as well known as the Danish levy, yet it amounted to yet amounted to at least 6,000 men.[66]

As early as September 1689 news circulated in Edinburgh that the Swedish king, Karl XI, had travelled to Gothenburg to oversee the embarking of as many as 8,000 men for transporting to Ireland.[67] Although destined for Ireland, most of the Swedish troops supported the Dutch in the continental theatre. At least some made it to Ireland however, and even as late as May 1691 a mixed army of Swedes, Germans and Dutch were rumoured to be mustering in The Netherlands for transport to the British Isles.[68] Nonetheless, all of those

62 SRA, Anglica 190 (D)., J.N. da Costa to Christoffer Leijoncrona, 10 December 1689. The latter reference was probably to the Scots-Dutch brigade who served in William's army and other Scottish regiments raised for service in Ireland. 63 See for example *CSPD, 1689–1690*, ed. W.J. Hardy (London, 1895), p. 255. Newsletter, 14 September 1689; ibid., p. 458, 11 February 1690, noting arrival of Danish horse in Edinburgh; ibid., p. 571, 21 March 1690, noting fear of Danes among Jacobite soldiers. 64 T. Riis, *Should auld acquaintance be forgot*, 2 vols (Odense, 1988), ii, pp. 88, 91, 94. 65 Both men are mentioned in J. Jordan, 'Wild Geese in the North' in *An Cosantoir*, 14:2 (1954), 79–80. Although he does not say so, Jordan is quoting from J.C.W. Hirsch and K. Hirsch (eds), 'Fortegnelse over Dansk og Norske officerer med flere fra 1648 til 1814 (12 volume manuscript in Denmark's Rigsarkiv, compiled 1888–1907), ii, part III. The Norwegian scholar, O. Ovenstad on the other hand, notes that Hirsch says Butler was Irish, but says that the man himself actually claimed to come from a 'high' [noble] family in Scotland. See O. Ovenstad, *Militærbiografier: Den Norske Hærs Officerer*, 2 vols (Oslo, 1948), i, p. 194. 66 H.H. van der Burgh, *Gezantschappen door Zweden en Nederland, 1592–1795* (The Hague, 1886), p. 53: 'Conventie betreffende het door Zweden te leveren contingent troepen van 6000 man infanterie', Stockholm 12 September 1688; ratified Stockholm, 17 September 1688. 67 *CSPD, 1689–1690*, p. 255. Newsletter, 14 September 1689. 68 *CSPD, 1690–1691*, ed. W.J. Hardy (London, 1898), p. 319. Newsletter, 22 May 1691.

with an Irish interest traced to date that did make it to Ireland from Sweden were of Scottish birth or heritage. And not all of those were officers. Johan Adolf Leijonjanker (aka John Young) was one of the 32 children of the Scottish merchant in Stockholm, Daniel Young, who had been ennobled with the name Leijonjanker in 1666.[69] Johan Adolf served as a simple musketeer in the Swedish Guard of the Brandenburg regiment in Ireland for a year and a half. During that time he campaigned in Drogheda, Cork, Kinsale and Limerick before moving on to fight for the Dutch in Flanders.[70]

Among the Scottish officers of the Swedish levy sent to the Netherlands was Captain Samuel Zeedtz who eventually commanded the regiments when they left Dutch service to return to Sweden in 1698.[71] Lieutenant-Colonel James Jeffereys also transferred from the Swedish service of King Karl XI to that of William III and certainly took part in the 1690 campaign, arriving in Ireland with three servants and seven horses sometime after May.[72] He became governor of Cork by 1698 and held the rank of brigadier-general by 1702.[73] Trying to establish his national identity is, once more, a complicated business. His name marks out his Scottish origins and yet references to him as an Irishman exist in secondary sources.[74] Both before and after his Swedish service in the 1680s, Jeffereys had some association with Ireland. Even once finally settled there, he returned to Sweden on several occasions and kept up a significant correspondence with the Swedish authorities.[75] One of his Swedish-born sons, Gustavus, remained in Swedish service where he was killed in action against the Danes in 1700. His second son, James Bavington Jeffereys, returned to Ireland to study at Dublin University, 1697–1701, where he received the degree of BA. The youngest son, Charles, received his commission into Queen Anne's army in 1710.[76] Yet the most frequent references to the family are as Englishmen, due no doubt to the fact that James Bavington Jeffereys worked as an agent of the British (Hanoverian) crown in Sweden, Russia and the Baltic.[77] His missions were erroneously interpreted

69 Johan Kileberg (ed.), *Svenska Ambetsverk, Del. VI:I Kammarkollegium, 1634–1718* (Norrköping, 1957), p. 67; *SAÄ*, iv, p. 523.   70 Rudelius, *Kalmar Regementes Personhistoria*, i, p. 184. Leijonjanker eventually reached the rank of Captain in 1708.   71 *SAÄ*, ix, p. 148.   72 *CSPD, 1690–1691*, p. 23: pass for Lt. Colonel Jeffereys and his companions, 30 May 1690.   73 J. F. Chance (ed.), *British diplomatic instructions 1689–1789, i, Sweden, 1689–1727* (London, 1922), p. 39; R. Hatton (ed.), 'Captain James Jeffereys letters to the Secretary of State, Whitehall from the Swedish army, 1707–1709' in *Historiska Handlingar*, 35:1 (Stockholm, 1954), 8.   74 P. Englund, *The battle of Poltava: the birth of the Russian empire* (London, 1992), p. 82 and Biographical Appendix, p. 269. In the text, Englund calls James Bavington Jeffereys an Englishman while the biographical appendix refers to him as the son of an Irish officer in Swedish service.   75 See for example SRA, Ericsbergsarkivet, autografsamling, letters dated: 8 Feb. 1699 and 11 Apr. 1699 till Eric Dahlberg. 20 Apr. 1699, kopia till överste lt. Joakim Christian von Beijer och assessor Sam. Adlerberg; SRA, Stafsundsarkivet, Reinhold Johan von Fersens Arkiv. 2 letters *c.*1700.   76 Hatton, 'Captain James Jeffereys', pp. 8–10.   77 SRA Anglica, vol. 523, 'Memorial Jefferyes

by Swedish contemporaries as only representing the English court and thus
he has been historically proclaimed an Englishman despite his Swedish birth,
Irish upbringing and Scottish heritage.[78]

In addition to the 'Swedish-Scots' who returned from abroad to fight in
William's army, other Irish-based Swedish veterans also became caught up
in the conflict. For instance, the retirement of the Swedish-born Hamiltons
in Ireland was short lived after King James VII & II forfeited both Lady
Hamilton and Gustavus in 1689. In response, Gustavus raised six regiments
for William of Orange, two of which were drawn from Enniskillen and pop-
ulated by other 'Swedish-Scots'.[79] For Gustavus's services, his widow
Margaret was granted £600 per year as a pension in 1703.[80] Gustavus's
brother Malcolm served as major (and acting lieutenant-colonel) in his
brother's regiment while Gustavus himself also acted as governor of the
Enniskillen until his death.[81] In Sweden, Hugo Hamilton had been disappointed not to be part of the Swedish auxiliary troops sent by Karl XI to
William of Orange for his British and Irish campaigns. He therefore sought
and received leave to privately 'go abroad and study the art of war'.[82] He took
the opportunity to return to Ireland where he joined his cousin Gustavus at
Enniskillen.[83] It was perhaps he who, along with one Allen Cathcart, served
as agents for the Enniskillen men at their own expense in Scotland raising
arms and ammunition for the regiment.[84] If so it reaffirms the strong links

1711–1715'; E. Carlsson (ed.), 'Kapten Jefferys bref till Engelska regering fran Bender och
Adrianopel 1711–1714, från Stralsund 1714–15' in *Historiska Handlingar*, 16:2 (Stockholm, 1897),
50–101; Hatton, 'Captain James Jeffereys', passim.   78 For an example see *Karolinska Krigares
Dagböcker IV* (Lund, 1908), p. 252. 'Kansli-dagbok från Turkiet till största delen förd av J.H.
von Kocken 1709–1714', 2 Feb. 1714.   79 This man has previously been confused with
Gustavus Hamilton, Viscount Boyne (1639–1723) who commanded the garrison of Colraine
and later became governor of Athlone for William III. See J.S. Crone, *A concise dictionary of
Irish biography* (Dublin, 1937), p. 87. For more on Boyne see his entry in the *DNB*, though
the sources used suggest at least some of the actions cited might have belonged to the Swedish-
born Gustavus; J.G. Simms, *The Williamite confiscation in Ireland, 1690–1703* (London, 1956),
p. 90; E. Black (ed.), *Kings in conflict: Ireland in the 1690s* (Belfast, 1990), p. 220. I would like
to thank Dr Paddy Fitzgerald for bringing Viscount Boyne to my attention.   80 *SAÄ*, ix, p.
244.   81 *CSPD, 1690–1691*, p. 445: 'List of officers in Ireland holding rank of Lt. Col. By
virtue of brevets from the General', 13 July 1691; Hamilton, *A history of the house of Hamilton*,
pp. 1014–15; *SAÄ*, ix, p. 244.   82 SRA, Reduktionskommission till Kung. Maj., vol. 14, 27
April 1689; Sørensson, *Hugo Hamilton*, p. 4; *Svenska Män och Kvinnor*, iii, p. 269.   83 Hugo
Hamilton also used the 1690 visit to Ireland to try to settle some family business regarding his
uncle, Lord Glenawley's estate: see SRA, Biographica 5, E01463, 5/8. Hugh Hamilton's relation of Lord Glenawley's Estate, Dublin, 3 November 1690. However, he had to return to
Sweden for in his absence his Swedish regiment had mutinied near Gothenburg. See
Gothenburg Landsarkiv, Förteckning över landshövdingens i Göteborg och Bohus län skrivelser till Kungl. Maj;t 1657–1840: letter to Karl XI, 13 February 1690.   84 *CSPD, 1689–1690*,
p. 465: duke of Schomberg to William III, 17 February 1690.

the 'Swedish-Scots' maintained with both Ireland *and* Scotland. He certainly took the opportunity thereafter to ship at least ten consignments of goods between June 1691 and May 1697 from Sweden to Britain, although quite what those cargoes were is not yet clear.[85]

The Protestants of Enniskillen and Derry have been mentioned as the saviours of Ireland for the British crown.[86] That several of the commanders should be a product of the Scottish-Scandinavian diaspora, especially Gustavus Hamilton named after the Swedish 'Lion of the North' is perhaps quite apt *if* viewed through a seventeenth century Scottish Protestant lens.

SCOTTISH-IRISH JACOBITE LINKS IN THE NORTH

The link between the Scottish and Irish communities in Scandinavia continued long after the Williamite Wars, and found new expression during the increased Jacobite activities surrounding the 1715 rising. Remarkably, some of the protagonists of the Williamite Wars were still involved including Hugo Hamilton, commandant and vice-governor of Gothenburg at the time of the revolt. George I of Great Britain and Ireland had bought the secularized bishoprics of Bremen and Verden from Denmark in 1715 and thus extended his electorate of Hanover. The Danes had seized these locations from Sweden in 1712 while the Swedish king was a 'guest' of the Turks. Karl XII returned to Sweden in 1714 and wanted his bishoprics back. Due to the fact that the George I now owned them, Karl XII had been approached by Jacobite sympathisers to support James VIII & III, the 'Old Pretender', against George who, as elector of Hanover, had proved to be quite hostile towards Sweden anyway.[87]

In 1715, the Pretender's councillor and illegitimate half-brother, James Fitzjames, duke of Berwick, held negotiations with the Swedish ambassador in Paris, Erik Sparre. They proposed that Hugo Hamilton should lead a pro-Jacobite Swedish invasion force against Scotland from Gothenburg. A French ambassador informed his government that Karl XII liked the plan, and that Hamilton should be sent to Scotland with 4,000 men as soon as possible. Many contemporaries even believed that Karl XII invaded Norway as a preparatory move towards this invasion.[88] Three individuals in Stockholm,

85 C. Dalhede, *Handelsfamiljer på Stormaktstidens Europamarknad*, 3 vols (Partille, 2001), iii, CD Rom; Hugo Hamilton, no. 1512.   86 I. Adamson, 'The Ulster-Scottish connection', in I.S. Wood (ed.), *Scotland and Ulster* (Edinburgh, 1994), p. 16.   87 For more on this subject see S. Murdoch, 'Soldiers, sailors, Jacobite spy: Russo-Jacobite relations 1688–1750' in *Slavonica*, 3/1 (1996/7), 7–27; M.K. Schuchard, 'Leibniz, Benzelius and the Kabbalistic roots of Swedish Illuminism' in A.P. Coudert, R.H. Popkin & G.M. Weiner (eds), *Leibniz, mysticism and religion* (Boston, 1998), pp. 98–100.   88 Chance, *British diplomatic instructions, 1689–1789*, pp. xxii and xxv.

messers Campbell, Jarrot and Dobson, were observed by the Swedes to be paying for and sending many shiploads of victuals to Scotland and Ireland in August 1715. There was no mention as to which side they were supplying, but Vice-Admiral Lewenhaupt in Gothenburg was ordered *not* to hinder the vessels suggesting that they did indeed belong to Jacobites.[89] However, the full Swedish attack never occurred as the rising in Scotland ended before the Swedes had mobilized – if indeed they were ever going to.

The end of the uprising saw hundreds of Jacobite exiles head to the continent. The Swedish minister in France agreed to employ some of these men in Sweden at the same rank and station as they enjoyed under James VIII & III.[90] In February 1716 a French ship carrying Jacobite officers arrived in Gothenburg, among them Kenneth Sutherland, third Lord Duffus.[91] His arrival in particular greatly annoyed the Hanoverian authorities and they specifically asked that he would not receive employment or shelter in Sweden.[92] Elsewhere, John Erskine, sixth or eleventh earl of Mar,[93] wrote to the tsar of Russia's physician and councillor, Dr Robert Erskine, recommending that 'if your master thought fit to employ some of them [Jacobites], I am sure he could not be better served'.[94] With opportunities opening up for the exiles in both Sweden and Russia, despite British attempts to block them, the Jacobites saw the advantage in ending the hostilities between the two northern powers.[95] The scene being set for some serious negotiations, Scottish and Irish Jacobites were identified in the two northern empires who

89 Gothenburg Landsarkiv, Förteckning över landshövdingens i Göteborg och Bohus län skrivelser till Kungl. Maj;t, 1657–1840. Letter dated 20 August 1715. The three men were erroneously described as Englishmen.   90 Chance, *British diplomatic instructions, 1689–1789*, pp. 86–7: Townsend to Sir John Norris, 3 July 1716. Lord Duffus became an admiral in Russia after the close of the Great Northern War. See R.C. Anderson, 'British and American officers in the Russian navy' in *Mariners Mirror*, 33 (1947), 21–2; Murdoch, 'Soldiers, sailors, Jacobite spy', p. 9.   91 Gothenburg Landsarkiv, Förteckning över landshövdingens i Göteborg och Bohus län skrivelser till Kungl. Maj;t, 1657–1840. Letter to Karl XII, 28 February 1716.   92 SRA, Kanslikollegiets skrivelser till Kungl. Maj:t 1656–1718, Robert Jackson's memorials on Scottish Jacobite refugees in Gothenburg, 10 March 1716 and 21 March 1716. Kanslikollegiets notes on Jackson's memorial, 11 April 1716; Chance, *British diplomatic instructions, 1689–1789*, p. 83: instructions to Sir John Norris, 10 May 1716. Before her death, Queen Anne had specifically asked Karl XII not to allow Jacobites, especially the 'Pretender', shelter in Swedish dominions. See SRA, Anglica 523 Didymotica. Via James Jeffereys, 2 January 1713/14.   93 *Dictionary of national biography*, xvii (London, 1889), pp. 426–31.   94 HMC, *Calendar of the Stuart papers belonging to his majesty the king, preserved at Windsor Castle*, 7 vols (London, 1902–1923), ii, 323: Mar to Erskine, 3 August 1716.   95 HMC, *Reports on the manuscripts of the earl of Egglington* (London, 1885), p. 169: 13 November 1716; Revd R. Paul, *Letters and documents relating to Robert Erskine, physician to Peter the great czar of Russia*, Miscellany of the Scottish History Society, II (Edinburgh, 1904), p. 420, Contained in a letter from Mr Gustavus Gyllenberg to Count Gyllenberg based on information received from the earl of Mar via Dr Erskine, 17 November 1716.

might prove helpful to the cause. When a Jacobite emissary was to visit Sweden in 1716 to broach this subject, he was advised to get in touch with Hugo Hamilton and only to complete his journey if Hamilton supported it.[96] In Russia, Field-Marshal James Bruce was appointed as one of the main Russian plenipotentiaries to the treaty negotiations while Hugo Hamilton was chosen to represent Sweden.[97]

Reports filtered back to Britain that Karl XII was contemplating 'pouring a body of forces into Scotland or the north of England from Gothenburg' in order to draw George I's forces away from the Baltic.[98] Mar proposed a confederacy between Russia, Sweden, Prussia and the Jacobites. An estimated 10,000 troops were earmarked as the Swedish contribution to an invasion of England backed, if possible, by another 3–4000 under Hamilton landing in Scotland.[99] James Butler, second duke of Ormond, sponsored by Scottish Jacobites, particularly Dr Erskine, negotiated with the Tsar directly and throughout 1718 rumours spread of final agreement between Sweden and Russia.[1] In the end however, the Jacobite intriguing came to naught. Karl XII was killed during his Norwegian campaign and Russia's new treaty included Prussia but not Sweden. Without an agreement over the Russo-Swedish War, Tsar Peter also declined to support the confederacy and instead vigorously renewed hostilities against Sweden. With only limited Spanish support the Jacobites pressed on with their plans, resulting in the abortive attempt of 1719.

It could all too easily be assumed that the Scottish and Irish communities in Northern Europe in the post-1690 period were composed exclusively of Jacobites, particularly given the sort of intrigues noted above. That is something of an over simplification and indeed many Scots and Irishmen across the northern empires appear to have expressed little interest. The Irishman and former Royal Navy officer, Gaspard Guillaume Morgane (aka Jaspar Ó Morugh) saw fit to leave the northern arena in order to establish a Swedish colony in St Marie in Madagascar for which he was ennobled.[2] His countryman Denis O'Brian simply sought privileges from the Swedes to open a salt processing plant.[3] Even John Jordan could not contrive a Jacobite role for

96 Sørensson, *Hugo Hamilton*, p. 54; *Svenska Män och Kvinnor*, iii, p. 269.   97 D. Fedosov, 'The first Russian Bruces' in *The Scottish soldier abroad* (Edinburgh & Stockholm, 1992), p. 63; Murdoch, 'Soldiers, sailors, Jacobite spy', p. 10.   98 Chance, *British diplomatic instructions, 1689–1789*, pp. 92–3: Extract of a letter from the Secretary of State in England, 15 September 1716 O.S.   99 HMC, *Stuart papers*, iii, pp. 115–17: Mar to Sir Harry Sterling, 21 October 1716; ibid., pp. 132–3, Charles Erskine to Mar, 24 October 1716; Chance, *British diplomatic instructions*, pp. xxiv–xxv; HMC, *Stuart papers*, v, pp. 560–2: Mar to Baron Sparre, 25 July 1717.   1 HMC, *Stuart papers*, vi, p. 183: Ormond to James VIII, 24 March 1718; HMC, *Stuart Papers*, vii, p. 81: F. Panton to the duke of Mar, 23 July 1718.   2 B. Schleger och C.A. Klingspor, *Den med sköldebref förlänade men ej å Riddarhuset introducerade Svenska Adelns Ättartavlor* (Stockholm, 1875), p. 404.   3 SRA, Kommerskollegii underdåniga skrivelser 1651–1840:

Ireland's most famous officer in Russia during the Great Northern War, General Peter Lacy, despite the fact that he had served James VII & II in 1691.[4]

Over and above the disinterested were those who positively supported the anti-Jacobite faction. The Scot, George Mackenzie, for instance, served as the resident British minister to Russia in 1714–17.[5] James Bavington Jeffereys is another example of a Hanoverian operating in Scandinavia and the Baltic.[6] He served as a volunteer in the army of Karl XII in Russia between 1707 and 1709 placing him in the same orbit as Hugo Hamilton. However, while in Swedish service, Jeffereys served as a British agent reporting back to Dr John Robinson (1650–1723), the long-term British resident in Stockholm.[7] After capture by the Russians at Poltava in 1709 he travelled to England to await further instructions.[8] Jeffereys returned to the court of Karl XII where he remained between 1711 and 1716. He thereafter moved from his Swedish base to serve as British minister in St Petersburg thus placing him in direct opposition to the Jacobites at the Russian Court such as Admiral Thomas Gordon, Dr Robert Erskine and Sir Henry Sterling.[9] Like his father before him, Jeffereys' Swedish service ended with his promotion to the governorship of Cork and adjacent forts in 1719.[10] His departure did not herald the end of Scottish or Irish Hanoverian agents in the north.

Two purported Irish Jacobites, Mr O'Brien and Mr O'Connor arrived in Russia looking for Russian support of 8–10,000 men. Through collaboration with the Scottish Jacobite network in St Petersburg, they got direct access to the tsar.[11] When O'Brien left he instructed Admiral Gordon and Sir Henry Sterling to continue the negotiations on his behalf. Sterling clearly trusted the men although in July 1625, it became clear that O'Connor was a Hanoverian agent. He informed the British authorities in Russia about Jacobite intentions with a promise to deliver up further information and letters to George I.[12]

5 letters of Denis O'Brian, 1723–25.   4 J. Jordan, 'Wild Geese in the North (Russia)', in *An Cosantóir*, 14:4 (April 1954), 192–5.   5 S. Dixon et al. (eds), *Britain and Russia in the age of Peter the Great* (London, 1998), nos. 142, 147, 149–150, 153 and 165; Chance, *British diplomatic instructions, 1689–1789*, p. 66. For his Jacobite sympathies and masonic connection with the tsar, see Murdoch, 'Soldiers, sailors, Jacobite spy', p. 8.   6 SRA Anglica, vol. 523, 'Memorial Jefferyes 1711–1715'; E. Carlsson (ed.), 'Kapten Jefferys bref till Engelska regeringen från Bender och Adrianopel 1711–1714, från Stralsund 1714–15' in *Historiska Handlingar*, 16:2 (Stockholm, 1897), 50–101; Hatton, 'Captain James Jeffereys', passim.   7 SRA, Svenske Sändebuds till Utlandske Hof och Deras Sändebud till Sverige, unpublished manuscript, 1841, p. 85; *DNB*; Chance, *British diplomatic instructions*, pp. xii–xiv, xvi and 14–38; Dixon et al., *Britain and Russia in the age of Peter the Great*, nos. 48 and 75.   8 Chance, *British diplomatic instructions*, p. 39.   9 Ibid., p. 40; HMC, *Stuart papers*, v, p. 550: Mr Weddle to Sir R. Everard, 8 August 1717; Murdoch, 'Soldiers, sailors, Jacobite spy', pp. 10–12.   10 Hatton, 'Captain James Jeffereys', pp. 26–7.   11 M.W. Bruce, 'Jacobite relations with Peter the Great' in *Slavonic and East European Review*, 14 (1936), p. 349.   12 Dixon et al., *Britain and Russia in the age of Peter the Great*, no. 272: Thomas Consett to Lord Townsend, 17 July 1725.

Even Hugo Hamilton's Jacobite sympathies are questionable. It is not unreasonable to assume that a Williamite soldier like Hugo could go over to the Jacobite cause after the Hanoverian Succession. After all, the second duke of Ormond, a leading Williamite, had done just that. The assumption that Hamilton acted out of Jacobite sympathies, however, does not allow for the fact that he had other loyalties. True, the reason for the choice of Hamilton as commander of the proposed British invasion was due to his 'Scottish background'.[13] It is also true that as Commandant of Gothenburg he did nothing to arrest or hinder Lord Duffus or the other Jacobites who arrived in Sweden.[14] However, Duffus had every right to feel safe in Gothenburg despite Hamilton, as in 1711 he had married the Swedish noblewoman Charlotta Christina Siöblad, daughter of Erik Siöblad, governor of Gothenburg and Båhus.[15] Supposing Hamilton even wanted to arrest the Jacobites, Duffus's Swedish father-in-law outranked him. The familial link between Duffus and Siöblad was even expressly mentioned in Swedish correspondence at the time.[16] Then there are questions regarding Hamilton's other loyalties. Yes he was of 'Scottish background' and Irish birth, but he was also a Swedish nobleman. Perhaps he was selected as the contact point for the Jacobites *not* because he had Jacobite sympathies, but because he was the best equipped in terms of language and knowledge of the geography of the British Isles to lead an invasion force simply as a loyal soldier of Karl XII. Whatever the truth the fact remains that the Scottish and Irish community in Scandinavia and the North once more schemed to effect political change in the their home islands.

CONCLUSION

Throughout the Early Modern period, the Scots proved to have a high degree of mobility travelling as far as the Scandinavia, Russia, the Americas, Java, China and Cambodia.[17] Frequently they would travel and settle in a particular destination without feeling confined by the land they were born in. Despite that, they did maintain a strong sense of community and identity. Those feelings of kith and kin encompassed the whole of the Scottish community regardless of where an individual found themselves at any given time. The

13 Sørensson, *Hugo Hamilton*, p. 54; *Svenska Män och Kvinnor*, iii, p. 269.   14 An examination of the Duffus papers in the Swedish Riksarkiv could perhaps yield further information. However, they were removed from their box in December 1981 for restoration, and have not been seen since. Some papers belonging to his son Eric Duffus are still there. See SRA, Ericsbergsarkivet, Autografsamlingen, Storbritannien; Duffus–Murray, vol. 269.   15 *SAÄ*, vii, p. 284.   16 Gothenburg Landsarkiv, Förteckning över landshövdingens i Göteborg och Bohus län skrivelser till Kungl. Maj:t 1657–1840: letter to Karl XII, 28 February 1716.   17 S. Murdoch, 'The good, the bad and the anonymous: a preliminary survey of the Scots in the Dutch East Indies, 1612–1707' in *Northern Scotland*, 22 (2002), 1–13.

geographical proximity of Scotland to Ulster and the density of the settlement there meant that to many Scots, large parts of Ulster were like an extension of Scotland itself. Yet a move from Scotland to Ulster did not equate
to the final stage of the migratory process and within a generation many Scots
from Ulster engaged in a secondary migration to Scandinavia. Many of these
people became imbued with ideas of Protestant ascendancy throughout Thirty
Years War period and beyond. This movement and those ideas guaranteed
that, with very few exceptions, where there were Irish folk in Scandinavia,
they were there due to a familial link with members of the Scottish
Presbyterian ex-patriate community.

From the evidence discussed in this chapter it is clear that migration from
Scotland was not necessarily an end in itself. The family case studies noted
here prove the interest of the foreign born Scots in maintaining contact with
their, or their parents place of birth. That interest extended to trying to influence political change in Scotland and Ireland, albeit with varying degrees of
success. The two attempts to support the Stuarts between 1649 and 1651,
and 1715 and 1720, had little impact. However, when it came to support of
the Williamite cause in 1690 there was greater success. But the numerous
conflicts in Ireland should not be seen as the only times when Scandinavian-
Scots showed an interest in Ireland. As shown above, many individuals
returned to Ireland in times of peace as well, albeit they were often caught
up in warfare thereafter. In combination with the more dramatic military
episodes, it should have become clear that there was a Scandinavian aspect
to Scottish-Irish relations in the Early Modern Period through the input of
the extended Scottish-Ulster diaspora.

The New England and federalist origins of 'Scotch-Irish' ethnicity

KERBY A. MILLER

Since the early 1700s Ulster Presbyterians' ethnic identity – its nomenclature, definition and social and political implications – have been sharply contested issues in America as well as in Ireland.[1] Between 1650 and 1776 merely 10 per cent of Ulster emigrants settled in New England, yet their leaders and descendants contributed disproportionately to these controversies. Of the early combatants, few were as important as the Reverend James McGregor and his followers who in 1719 settled what became the township of Londonderry, New Hampshire.

James McGregor was born in 1677 near Magilligan Point in the parish of Tamlaghtard in northwest County Londonderry. According to tradition, McGregor received part of his education in Europe, but he graduated from the University of Glasgow and had returned to Ulster by 1701, when he was ordained as Presbyterian minister of Aghadowey parish, on the banks of the lower Bann river, in northeast County Derry. In 1704 the synod of Ulster 'severely admonished' McGregor for intemperance, but marriage in 1706 may have settled him, and in 1710 the synod commissioned him to preach in Ulster Irish (then virtually interchangeable with Scots Gaelic) to additional congregations in Derry, Antrim and Tyrone.

McGregor was still pastor of Aghadowey in 1717 when he and several other clergymen in the Bann valley determined to transport themselves and their flocks to New England, as encouraged by Samuel Shute, royal governor of Massachusetts. Thus, in early 1718, at the nearby port of Coleraine, McGregor delivered a farewell sermon, charging that he and his people were fleeing Ireland 'to avoid oppression and cruel bondage, to shun persecution and designed ruin, to withdraw from the communion of idolators and to have an opportunity of worshipping God according to the dictates of conscience and the rules of His inspired Word'.

---

1 To conserve space, footnotes have been minimalized. This essay is an abridged version of chapter 49 in Kerby A. Miller, Arnold Schrier, Bruce D. Boling, and David Noel Doyle, *Irish immigrants in the land of Canaan: letters and memoirs from colonial and revolutionary America, 1675–1815* (New York, 2003), henceforth cited as Miller et al., *Land of Canaan*. Full citations can be found in chapter 49 and the Sources section of that volume.

It is notable that McGregor complained of harassment not from Ulster's despoiled Catholics, but from magistrates and clergy of the Church of Ireland 'by law established,' and his sermon set the tone for subsequent interpretations of Ulster Presbyterian emigration as a communal exodus from 'Egyptian bondage'. Anglican critics dismissed McGregor's and other ministers' claims of religious and political persecution as mere pretenses, arguing that their real reasons for emigration were economic. Historians generally agree, citing the sharp rent increases and severe distress that afflicted Ulster in the 1717–20 period. Indeed, by 1718 McGregor's own salary from his congregation was three years in arrears. Yet his sermon was not entirely disingenuous. Although by 1717–18 the times of severe persecution under Queen Anne (1702–14) had ended, Presbyterians remained bitterly aggrieved by the Irish results of a Glorious Revolution that had returned to power an Anglican establishment that questioned their loyalty to the crown, belittled their sacrifices at the siege of Derry (1690), and in 1704 imposed a Sacramental Test Act that excluded Presbyterians from all civil and military offices. Some Anglicans contended that Ulster's Presbyterians were 'a more knavish, wicked, thievish race than even the natural Irish of the other three provinces'. Thus, it was not illogical for McGregor to interpret his flock's departure in political and religious terms, and his sermon was designed in part as a warning to officials in Dublin and London that northern Ireland might lose its Presbyterian garrison to emigration if the Test Act was not repealed. In fact, the Act was suspended in 1719, a year after McGregor's company arrived at Boston, but Presbyterians remained aggrieved by tithes and other disabilities.

McGregor may also have calculated his words to appeal to the sympathies of New England's Congregationalists, to their own memories of past persecutions at Anglican hands. If so, he must have been disappointed, for the approximately 800–1,000 Ulster immigrants who landed at Boston in summer 1718 met a hostile reception from New Englanders who feared that ships from Ireland brought only famine, disease, paupers, and 'papists.' However, in late October McGregor successfully petitioned governor Shute for a grant of land on the frontier of Maine, Massachusetts' northeastern province, and although McGregor himself first settled near Boston, his brother-in-law James McKeen and about 300 immigrants went north and spent an uncomfortable winter at Casco Bay. In spring 1719 McKeen's family and about twenty others abandoned Maine and sailed south to the Merrimac and up the river to Haverhill, Massachusetts, where they disembarked and traveled overland twenty miles northwest to an unsettled tract called Nutfield for its abundance of chestnut, butternut, and walnut trees. On 12 April McGregor joined them, preached a memorable sermon describing their new home as 'a great rock in a weary land' (Isaiah 32:2), and agreed to be pastor and effective leader of the first major Ulster Presbyterian settlement in the New World.

Unfortunately, Nutfield was an area disputed by the governments of Massachusetts and New Hampshire, and although Shute was royal governor of both provinces, rival groups of proprietors and speculators, backed by their respective legislatures in Boston and Portsmouth, jealously contested ownership of the upper Merrimac valley. Furthermore, Shute and Massachusetts legislators were angry that the Ulstermen had left Maine, and so in June 1719, when MacGregor and McKeen petitioned Boston for a land grant on the Merrimac, they were refused on the grounds that Nutfield belonged to Haverhill's proprietors. Consequently, in October Nutfield's settlers sent a similar petition to New Hampshire's legislature. New Hampshire's lieutenant governor, John Wentworth, although Shute's nominal subordinate, was much more sympathetic to the Nutfield colonists, perhaps because of his own family's Irish connections, but certainly because western settlements would increase New Hampshire's trade and population, create a barrier against Indian incursions, and strengthen his colony's claims to the upper Merrimac valley.

While their petition to Portsmouth was pending, McGregor and McKeen fortified their claim to Nutfield by purchasing from Colonel John Wheelright of Wells, Maine, the old deed to the area that Wheelright's grandfather had purportedly bought from the Indians in 1629. Despite this move, however, during the winter of 1719–20 Nutfield's settlers were harrassed, legally and violently, by rival claimants from Haverhill and Boston, who alleged that the Ulstermen were not only illegal squatters but also 'poor Irish,' 'not wholesome inhabitants,' and, most damning of all, Roman Catholics. To refute those charges, and to assert his people's claims to their settlement, that winter McGregor wrote a petition, titled 'The Humble Apology of the People of Nutfield,' to Governor Shute in Boston. 'We were Surprised to hear our Selves termed *Irish People*,' McGregor protested, 'when we So frequently ventured our all for the British Crown and Liberties against the Irish papists & gave all tests of our Loyalty w[hich] the Government of Ireland Required …' Moreover, McGregor argued, his people's legal right to Nutfield was superior to that of Haverford's proprietors, for the former was based on Colonel Wheelright's 'Indian … Deed being of Ninety Years Standing,' whereas the Haverford claim was merely 'twenty Years Old.'[2]

McGregor's petition may have had its intended effect, for in April 1720 Governor Shute authorized Nutfield's inhabitants to choose their own officials. Furthermore, in June 1722 New Hampshire's government gave the settlers full incorporation, with a grant of land ten miles square, for a 'town'[3]

2 The only extant 'original' copy of McGregor's petition, in the Jeremy Belknap papers at the Massachusetts Historical Society, Boston, is dated 27 February 1720. However, a semi-legible marginal note suggests McGregor may have written it in late 1719.   3 Londonderry was denominated a 'town' according to colonial New England usage, but it was analogous to what in

whose inhabitants, a year later, officially renamed Londonderry. Meanwhile, the settlement had grown rapidly – to 360 inhabitants by April 1721 – as Ulster immigrants converged on the upper Merrimac valley, attracted by the free lands, Presbyterian worship, and refuge from Puritan prejudice that Nutfield/Londonderry offered. However, Londonderry's conflicts with Haverhill and Boston were just beginning, as the settlement now became the focal point of an intense political struggle between Massachusetts and New Hampshire. The result was a boundary war, spearheaded by the Haverhill proprietors, that assumed a variety of forms: endless petitions, arrests and trials for trespassing, seizures of property for non-payment of taxes, destruction of crops and farm buildings, mob violence, and physical assaults. On 5 March 1729, the Reverend McGregor died in the midst of the strife, but in a town meeting held on 15 December 1729, Londonderry's inhabitants voted to send James McKeen, town moderator, and John McMurphy to Portsmouth, to petition the New Hampshire government concerning 'our Grivances with respect to Law Shuits that arises from our neighbouring town (viz.) Heverhill.' The petition itself, probably written by McMurphy as town clerk, was in turn forwarded by Lieutenant Governor Wentworth to London, as part of his own strategy to persuade the crown to recognise New Hampshire's title to the disputed area. Unlike the settlers' first petition, which had focused primarily on legal issues, McMurphy dwelt more heavily than had McGregor on the Londonderry settlers' identity, reputation, and loyalty. 'We could bear the many scandalous & unjust reflections which [our critics from Boston and Haverhill] cast upon us by saying we are romans and not good Subjects to his present Majesty,' McMurphy wrote, 'being well assured your Hon[our] well knows to the Contrary [that] … many of us Resolutely opposed both ['romans' and 'bad Subjects'] while in our own Country[.] Witness the Trubles in Ireland at the Comeing in of King William of blessed memory,' McMurphy urged, when 'our Present Minister & Severall of our People [were] at the Siege of Derry & had no small share in that Glorious Defence of Our religion & Country.'⁴

In 1740 London finally confirmed New Hampshire's ownership of the upper Merrimac valley. Meanwhile, despite the troubles with Haverhill, Londonderry had flourished. By 1740 it was the second-largest settlement in the province: by 1767 it had 2,400 inhabitants, and its growing population, augmented by modest but steady migration from Ulster, had spawned other

Pennsylvania was called a 'township'. Londonderry had no urban center and, although it contained storekeepers, millers, weavers, and other full- or part-time craftsmen, it was an overwhelmingly rural community dominated by farmers.   4 McMurphy's petition, dated 17 March 1730, is catalogued as CO5/871 ff. 186–87 in the New England correspondence of the papers of the Board of Trade and Secretaries of State (America and West Indies) in the Public Record Office, Kew, England.

communities in the Merrimac and Connecticut valleys. Although London-derry's farms produced goods primarily for local exchange and consumption, as in Ulster its townspeople also developed a regionally-unique and thriving industry in the household manufacture of linen yarn and cloth that were mar-keted throughout New England.

After the Revolution, new Ulster immigration to New Hampshire virtu-ally ceased, and by the late 1700s observers sometimes claimed, albeit wrongly, that save for unusual emphases on flax cultivation and linen production, little distinguished the farmers of Londonderry and its satellite towns from neigh-boring Congregationalists. However, in the early and mid-1800s the descen-dants of New Hampshire's Ulster Presbyterian settlers formally emerged as a distinct ethnic group, particularly in a series of centennial celebrations and authorized town histories whose orators and authors, usually clergymen, staked their ancestors' claims to 'founding father' status. Most important, they argued vehemently that their forbears had not been 'Irish' – although that had been the term most commonly applied to, and acknowledged by, Ulster Presby-terians in late eighteenth-century America. Instead, their eulogists contended, the founders of Londonderry and all other Ulster Presbyterian immigrants had been members of the 'Scotch-Irish race,' a group distinct in its Scottish origins and Protestant faith, and consequently superior in habits and morals to the 'native Irish' Catholics against whom their ancestors had struggled in Ireland.

Since then, the controversy between the celebrants and the critics of what the latter often called the 'Scotch-Irish myth' has been unceasing and often acrimonious. Of importance here is the fact that 'Scotch-Irish' spokesmen such as the Reverend Edward L. Parker, the author of Londonderry's first town history, almost invariably buttressed their arguments by drawing on early statements such as those in the foregoing petitions, particularly on the Reverend James McGregor's strenuous objection to the application of the 'Irish' label to his people.[5] Hence, an analysis of the precise content and con-text of these petitions may be useful.

It is important to note that neither McGregor nor McMurphy identified their countrymen as 'Scotch-Irish.' Indeed, the petitioners essayed no posi-tive ethnic identifications, but focused on statements of what their people were *not*, thus illustrating an uncertainty or fluidity in their early ethnic iden-tity that later generations, in an era of nationalist fervor, would find unac-ceptable. There were several specific reasons why McGregor, in his 1719–20 message to Boston, took pains to deny that his parishioners were 'Irish.' Of

5 Rev. E.L. Parker, *The history of Londonderry* (Boston, 1851). The importance of Parker and his peers in asserting 'Scotch-Irishness' was first argued by R.S. Wallace, 'The Scotch-Irish of provincial New Hampshire' (PhD Diss., University of New Hampshire, 1984).

course, he desired to draw a sharp distinction between the Nutfield settlers and the native Irish, a few of whom had already come to New England as poor indentured servants and who were associated with a Catholicism that was abhorred ideologically and feared practically—especially in the danger it posed from French Québec—throughout England's colonies. However, even McGregor's supporters in the New Hampshire government referred favorably to his flock as 'a company of Irish at Nutfield,' so it was already clear that disinterested or sympathetic observers would *not* confuse Irish Presbyterian and Catholic immigrants.[6] Thus, there may have been additional reasons for McGregor's statements.

First was the fact that many, perhaps most, of McGregor's followers had migrated from Scotland to Ulster only during the reigns of James II (1685–8) and William III (1688–1702), and in the Bann valley allegedly 'they had kept together in church relations, as well as in residence, more closely than most of the Scotch settlers' in northern Ireland. If true, it would be natural if they had little identification with Ireland, even as a place, when they remigrated to New England scarcely twenty or thirty years later. In length of residence, then, the Nutfield colonists were certainly far less 'Irish' than other Scots Presbyterians whose ancestors had come to Ireland in the Ulster Plantation, the Cromwellian era, or even the reign of Charles II. Likewise, their identification with Ireland as homeland was far less secure than for the great majority of Ulster Presbyterians who would emigrate to America in the mid- and late 1700s – often three, four, or more generations after their ancestors had left Scotland.

Ironically, one of the truly 'Irish' characteristics of the New Hampshire colony was its eventual name, Londonderry. Indeed, one wonders why, if the first settlers wished to clearly distinguish themselves as non-Irish, they did not name their community, say, 'Argyle' or 'Ayrshire,' after their most common Scottish places of origin, or 'Glasgow' in honor of Scottish Presbyterianism's ecclesiastical and educational center? Or why they did not name their settlement after one of the Bann valley congregations, whence most of them had emigrated? The traditional explanation is that Nutfield's settlers 'naturally' renamed their township to commemorate the walled Irish city in which many of them had fought and suffered during the siege of 1689. Allegedly the Reverend McGregor himself had fought on Derry's walls, although but a boy of twelve years old, and supposedly others had done so as well. True or not, there is no doubt that the siege already had assumed mythic proportions and become a symbol with which all Ulster Presbyterians wished to associate – per-

---

6 Likewise, Rev. James McSparran, an Ulster-born clergyman of Scottish parentage and the author of the first Irish emigrants' guide, *America dissected* (Dublin, 1752), referred to Londonderry's inhabitants – indeed, to all Ulster Presbyterian settlers in the New World – as 'Irish.'

haps especially in view of Irish Anglicans' denial of their prominence in Derry's defence. Yet given Londonderry's totemic significance, why did Nutfield's first colonists not rename their community at once, rather than four years after its initial settlement and a year after its incorporation?

Perhaps there were very pragmatic reasons for McGregor's and his people's choice of name and for their precise timing. As McGregor probably – and Wentworth certainly – were aware (and as Boston and London authorities were not), the Nutfield settlers' hold on their New Hampshire lands was extremely tenuous, not only because of Haverhill's competing claims, but because the old 1629 Wheelright patent that McGregor's followers purchased in 1719, and which he defended in his 1719–20 petition, was a *forgery*, cleverly executed only a dozen or so years earlier by Portsmouth politicians. Hence, to reinforce their shaky title, Nutfield's leaders promulgated what became the traditional (albeit fallacious) explanation of their grant – namely, that it had been a 'free gift of King William,' promised to the 'faithful champions of his throne in the siege and defense of Londonderry.' Thus, the renaming of Nutfield not only symbolized its inhabitants' loyal Protestantism, but also implied and justified an 'ancient' title to their new possessions. The name 'Londonderry' signified a northern fortress, not only against the Catholic French and their Indian allies above, but also against counterclaims from Haverhill and Boston below, as even after its incorporation in 1722, the new community remained as besieged by 'outsiders' as its settlers had formerly been threatened – first by Irish Catholics and then by contemptuous Anglicans – in Ulster itself.

It may also be significant that, in his early petition from 'Nutfield,' the Reverend McGregor did *not* specifically evoke the siege of Derry or 'King William of Blessed memory.' Not until after the township's rechristening, McGregor's death in 1729, and his replacement as Londonderry's parson by the elderly Reverend Matthew Clarke, a recent arrival whose scarred face clearly demonstrated *his* military service on Derry's walls, did those themes emerge and become prominent, as in John McMurphy's petition of 1730. Likewise, it may be illuminating that McMurphy did not repeat McGregor's denial that the Nutfield-Londonderry settlers were 'Irish.' (Indeed, one wonders whether the date of McMurphy's petition, St Patrick's Day, was merely an ironic coincidence.) Instead, he stated only that they were not 'romans,' apparently assuming that the distinction between 'Irish' Protestants and Catholics would be clearly understood. In his tactical shift, McMurphy may have presumed for his intended audience a greater sophistication than McGregor had credited, or the change may have reflected the sentiments of later settlers whose families had lived for generations in Ulster and who therefore regarded themselves as 'Irish' at least in geographical origin.[7]

7 During the 1700s the populations of Londonderry and its satellite towns became more

Nevertheless, the religious distinction and political loyalism that McMurphy emphasized were crucial, and not only because of the virulent anti-Catholicism prevailing in the colonies, but for another reason peculiar to Londonderry. During all the French and Indian wars that ravaged the northern frontiers from 1722 to 1760, Londonderry was never attacked, allegedly – as the townspeople believed – because McGregor and the Marquis de Vaudreuil, governor of Québec in the 1720s, had been schoolmates and friends in the Netherlands and maintained a cordial correspondence in America, and so the marquis persuaded the Jesuits in Canada 'to charge the Indians not to injure' McGregor's people, 'as they were different from the English.' If true, this was a remarkably fortuitous circumstance for Londonderry's inhabitants. However, it was also a coincidence which, if widely known outside the community, would have provoked intense suspicion and hostility at a time when Anglo-American colonists, and especially New England Congregationalists, regularly confused or conflated Protestants and Catholics from Ireland and often charged that 'Irish papist' traders in the backcountry were inciting the Indians to war 'in the French Interest.'

Yet it is equally revealing that neither McGregor nor McMurphy described their people as 'Scotch-Irish,' for that term's origins and associations – both in the British Isles and in America – were highly problematic. In the late 1500s and the 1600s, apparently its most common British and Irish usage was pejorative, as both Irish Anglicans and Lowland Scots Presbyterians labeled as 'Scotch-Irish' the Catholic, Gaelic-speaking McDonnells and other Highlanders who migrated back and forth between Argyll, the Western Isles, and the north Antrim glens, causing political and military problems for Protestant officials in Edinburgh and Dublin alike. By contrast, Scots Presbyterian settlers in Ireland were then and well into the early 1700s more commonly described as 'Ulster-' or 'northern Scots,' as the 'Scottish Interest' or 'Nation' in Ireland, or occasionally as 'British' – not in the later, inclusive sense, but to distinguish them from the 'English.'

To be sure, Ulster Presbyterian students at the universities of Glasgow and Edinburgh were individually registered as 'Scottus Hibernicus,' and some scholars have suggested this was the origin of the modern term, 'Scotch-Irish,' with its exclusively Protestant and positive connotations. In fact, however, Scottish university officials, faculty, and local magistrates almost invariably referred to such students as 'Irish' – and often linked their 'Irishness' to negative attributes (stupidity, drunkenness, insubordination) traditionally associated with their 'papist' countrymen.[8] Moreover, by the mid-1700s Presbyterian

diversely 'Irish'. For example, nearby Bedford's Revolutionary War casualties included John Callahan and Valentine Sullivan – 'native Irish,' whatever their religion.   8 Indeed, Professor Thomas Reid, Scotland's famous 'common sense' philosopher, scorned Ulster Presbyterian students at his Glasgow University as 'stupid Irish teagues'!

spokesmen in Ulster itself were referring increasingly to their people as 'Irish' – a development that reflected longer residence in Ireland, feelings of greater security from Catholic rebellion, and, as among Irish Anglicans, a growing 'national' identification with the economic and political interests of 'Ireland' *versus* 'England.'

Spurring the latter development was the steady divergence between Scottish and Ulster-Presbyterian political conditions that began after the Glorious Revolution and widened after the Act of Union between England and Scotland. In Scotland after 1690 Presbyterianism was the legally established religion, and after the Union of 1707 the upper and middling ranks of Scottish Lowlands society rushed to seize the economic benefits of full membership in the Empire, strove to emulate the alleged superiority of English 'civilization,' and gloried in a new 'North British' identity that obscured the realities of English contempt and their country's economic and political subordination to its larger, wealthier, and more powerful partner. By contrast, Ireland's Presbyterians endured and bitterly resented their legal inferiority, and, ignored politically by their Scottish co-religionists (and unable, for religious reasons, to sympathize with Catholic-Jacobite opponents to the new Scots establishment), many became increasingly receptive to the rhetoric of Dublin's 'patriot' politicians who promoted a vague but inclusively 'Irish' colonial nationalism that subsumed denominational differences and promised economic and political reform. Consequently, Ulster Presbyterians' political interests and identities were increasingly oriented to Ireland's capital rather than to Edinburgh or London. Thus, although eighteenth-century Scottish and Ulster Presbyterians shared similar political *cultures* – both based heavily on the works of Ulster-born Francis Hutcheson, the 'father of the Scottish Enlightenment' – the very different contexts in which Scottish and Ulster Presbyterians' political ideas operated determined equally distinct applications and conclusions.

In eighteenth-century America, Ulster Presbyterian identities appear to have developed along lines somewhat parallel to those in Ireland. From the early 1700s Anglo-American colonists normally described Ulster Presbyterian immigrants as 'Irish' – as New Hampshire officials had labeled Londonderry's settlers. By contrast, the term 'Scotch-Irish' was less common and often had profoundly negative socio-cultural and political connotations. Thus, in 1767 the Anglican missionary Charles Woodmason described backcountry South Carolina's inhabitants as 'a Sett of the most lowest vilest Crew breathing – Scotch-Irish Presbyterians from North of Ireland,' and during the Revolution the American general Charles Lee condemned the people of the Shenandoah Valley as 'a Banditti of Scotch-Irish Servants or their immediate descendants.'

By contrast, to be 'Irish' in a broad, ecumenical sense was meanwhile becoming useful, even fashionable, among wealthy or ambitious Irish Protest-

ant immigrants. From the early mid-1700s, for example, Ulster Presbyterian
merchants and professionals in New York, Philadelphia, and other American
seaports had joined with Anglican and even Catholic compatriots in celebrating
St Patrick's Day and in organizing specifically 'Irish' or 'Hibernian' associations. (Conversely, Scottish-born Presbyterians congregated separately in St
Andrew's societies.) Moreover, the American Revolution appears to have accelerated Ulster Presbyterian immigrants' tendency to embrace – and of Anglo-
Americans to perceive – a generic and positive 'Irish' identity. Both native-
and Irish-Americans, whether rebels or loyalists, commonly viewed 'Ireland's'
proverbial discontent with English rule – now identified with the Protestant-
led Patriot movement – as virtually synonymous with the American struggle
for self-government. Correctly or not, the 'Irish' in America were associated
with wholehearted support for the Revolution, whereas Scottish immigrants
were perceived as obsequiously loyal to the crown, as well as selfish and avari-
cious.[9] Thus, perhaps it was not surprising that, for a while after the Revolution, the 'Scotch-Irish' designation, already infrequent, almost disappeared from
public print. It is surprising, therefore, that in the nineteenth century the term
'Scotch-Irish' reappeared and soon became commonplace, and in the eyes of
Protestant native- and Ulster-Americans, it now enjoyed associations that were
much more unambiguously favorable than in previous centuries.

For scholars 'Scotch-Irish' *could* be a useful label, reflecting valid dis-
tinctions between Ulster Presbyterian immigrants (and their descendants) of
Scottish origin and other Irish Protestants (Anglicans, Quakers, etc.) of largely
English ancestry and Irish Catholics (and Protestants) of Gaelic, Hiberno-
Norman, and other backgrounds. During the nineteenth century, however,
the term broadened to embrace *all* Americans of Irish birth or descent who
were not *currently* Catholic, regardless of their religious or ethnic antecedents.
Among Irish-American Catholics, 'Scotch-Irishness' became a source of grievance and resentment – primarily because the term allegedly re-emerged from
obscurity during the Great Famine of 1845-52, when Ulster Americans rushed
to distinguish themselves as 'Scotch-Irish' Protestants and, hence, as different from and superior to the overwhelmingly Catholic, impoverished, and
often Irish-speaking Famine refugees.

However, the modern meanings of 'Scotch-Irish' – its 'Protestant' and
positive connotations, its strident reassertion of an impermeable, quasi-racial
division between its members and the now once more exclusively Catholic
'Irish' – began to take shape much earlier, in the 1790–1820 period, long
before Irish Catholics or their church became significant factors in American
society. Hence, it is likely that the new 'Scotch-Irish' ethnicity had other,
subtler origins – that initially it was generated, not by an external threat (real

9 See Miller et al., *Land of Canaan*, chap. 58.

or perceived) from Irish Catholic immigration, but rather by Ulster-American society's internal dynamics and by its relationship to native America's socio-economic, cultural, and political hierarchies. Specifically, it is arguable that modernized 'Scotch-Irishness' was largely the product of an *intra*-communal contest for political and cultural hegemony – a contest led in New England (as elsewhere) by Ulster-America's politically conservative clergy and 'respectable' laymen. And although this was an *American* contest, it mirrored a parallel struggle in contemporary Ulster, between Presbyterians who embraced or rejected the ultra-democratic and ecumenical ideals of the United Irishmen.

Genteel Ulster-Americans, eager for acceptance and influence in an Anglo-American 'society' that in New England was dominated by Federalist merchants and Congregational ministers, needed to expunge from their own communities the radical political tendencies and the 'backward' socio-cultural traits that both offended genteel American sensibilities *and* were embarrassingly similar to those traditionally associated with the Catholic 'Irish.' In the 1790s Federalist polemicists applied the term 'wild Irish' – laden with historic connotations of *Catholic* Irish barbarism, treachery, and rebellion, as in the 1641 Ulster rising – to *all* Irish-Americans who opposed the Washington and Adams administrations, sympathized with the French Revolution, and supported the Jeffersonian Republicans. Federalists knew well that the overwhelming majority of their 'wild Irish' adversaries were *not* Catholics but Ulster Presbyterian farmers, weavers, and radical journalists. However, the message was clear: if Ulster Presbyterians wished to avoid 'wild Irish' associations, their putative leaders should follow and expand on the Reverend McGregor's precedent and identify themselves and 'their people' as the "Scotch-Irish' antitheses of the proverbially uncivilized, drunken, and rebellious 'Irish.' Not coincidentally, it was New Englander Jeremy Belknap – Congregational clergyman, staunch Federalist pamphleteer, and future Harvard president – who, by discovering and publishing McGregor's old petition in his *History of New Hampshire* (1784–92), first pointed those leaders toward a 'Scotch-Irish' resolution of their political and cultural dilemmas.

Their problem was that ordinary Ulster Presbyterians in New England (and elsewhere) often behaved in ways that seemed suspiciously 'Irish.' From the start, Londonderry's settlers were confused with Irish 'papists' and embroiled in violent conflicts over land titles with colonial officials and Anglo-American elites – as were their countrymen on the Maine and Pennsylvania frontiers. Although the Revolution forged a political alliance between New England's Scots-Irish farmers and Anglo-Congregational leadership, in the 1780s that disintegrated rapidly as the region's Presbyterian clergy joined the Federalists in espousing law and order, deference and hierarchy, whereas most of their parishioners vociferously demanded greater democracy and fairer taxes. In winter 1786–7 the inhabitants of Pelham and other Scots-Irish set-

tlements in western Massachusetts supported Daniel Shays's rebellion against
the Boston government. In 1787–8 most Ulster Presbyterian farmers in
Londonderry and elsewhere opposed ratification of the U.S. Constitution. In
1794, the year of the largely Scots-Irish 'Whiskey Insurrection' in western
Pennsylvania, New England's Ulster Presbyterians staged their own protests
against Hamilton's excise. Afterwards, most enlisted in the Republican Party,
and by 1797 Vermont's Irish-born congressman, Matthew Lyon, a former
indentured servant, epitomized everything New England's Federalists feared
and hated about Jefferson's 'wild Irish' adherents.[10] In the 1820s most of New
England's Scots-Irish were *still* voting for Republican candidates – and in the
1830s for Jacksonian Democrats.

New England's genteel Presbyterians were alarmed as well by the apparent
cultural similarities between 'their people' and Irish Catholic peasants. Given
their recent origins in parts of western Scotland where Scots Gaelic was
common, it is likely that many of Londonderry's first settlers were linguistically alien from New England's Congregationalists, provoking the latter's suspicion and contempt. Well into the late 1700s the immigrants' offspring – and
more recent arrivals – still spoke Ulster Scots (the language of commoners in
the Scots Lowlands and much of rural Ulster) or at least English in a 'broad
Scotch' accent that Yankees found almost unintelligible. Likewise, in the late
1700s the inhabitants of Londonderry and other Ulster settlements remained
notorious among their Anglo-American neighbors for their alleged uncleanli-
ness, aversion to bathing bodies or clothes, indifference to sanitary facilities,
and slovenly farmsteads. They also had a notorious reputation as heavy drinkers,
and their marriages, wakes, and funerals were proverbially sodden, boisterous
affairs that scandalized polite contemporaries. Finally, by virtue of
Londonderry's 1722 charter its farmers enjoyed a uniquely 'Irish' institution, a
semi-annual fair which, like Catholic Ireland's Donnybrook, had by the
mid–1700s become infamous for its 'scenes of vice and folly.' Even the fair's
dates were suspiciously akin to those of two ancient and pagan Celtic festivals.

Perhaps it was little wonder, then, that McGregor and McMurphy had
been so defensive – especially the former, given his own intemperate record.
Or that one hundred years later the Reverend Parker and other 'Scotch-Irish'
eulogists would blame what they described as their people's temporary devi-
ations from Scots-Protestant virtue, order, and sobriety on their ancestors'
brief but contaminating exposure to Ulster's Catholics. Inadvertently, however, their argument revealed that modern 'Scotch-Irish' ethnicity was rooted
ultimately in neither ancestral origin nor even religion, but instead was based

10 In 1797 Lyons, a Protestant, outraged opponents by spitting on a Connecticut Federalist,
during a Congressional debate; in 1798 a Federalist judge sentenced Lyon to a $1000 fine and
four months' imprisonment for libeling President John Adams under the newly-passed Sedition
Act.

on relatively new 'middle-class' behavioral standards. The thrifty, law-abiding, sober, respectable 'Scotch-Irish' that Parker and his peers invented and celebrated had been common in neither seventeenth-century Scotland nor eighteenth-century Ulster. Nor were they representative of the great majority of Ulster Presbyterian immigrants or even their descendants in eighteenth and early nineteenth-century America. Rather, their new image reflected the hegemonic imperatives of an emergent Ulster-American *bourgeoisie* whose goals and ascendancy remained woefully incomplete even in the early 1800s.

Not coincidentally, the local clergy's first attempt to tame Londonderry's raucous fairs occurred in 1798, the year of the Federalists' Alien and Sedition Acts in America as well as the United Irishmen's rebellion in east Ulster. However, not until 1839, in the midst of a region-wide temperance crusade, would they finally suppress what had long been an integral expression of their ancestors' traditional culture. Yet between those dates the poems of Robert Dinsmoor (1756–1836), grandson and great-grandson of two of Londonderry's first settlers, from Ballywattick, County Antrim, heralded the changes that commercialization, evangelicalism, and the urge for gentility eventually wrought among New England's Ulster Presbyterians. The few scholars who have studied New Hampshire's self-styled "Rustic Bard" have portrayed him as an American analogue to the 'Rhyming Weavers' of late eighteenth and early nineteenth-century Ulster. Linguistic similarities aside, however, in fact they were strikingly different.

Like their Scottish hero Robert Burns, many – perhaps most – of Ulster's Rhyming Weavers were liberal or sceptical in religion, radical in politics, and defiant of genteel conventions. Because they wrote in the vernacular of Lowland Scotland and Presbyterian Ulster, some scholars in Northern Ireland have claimed them as cultural markers of a unique 'Ulster Scots' cultural and political identity – distinctly non-'Irish' and hence the equivalent of 'Scotch-Irish' ethnicity in America. In fact, many of the Rhyming Weavers' compositions evince strong Irish nationalist sentiments, and more than a few of these plebeian poets, such as James Orr of Ballycarry, joined or sympathized with the United Irishmen and the 1798 rebellion. By contrast, and despite his humble persona, Dinsmoor was an orthodox Calvinist and a fiercely conservative Federalist for whom the French Revolution and Jeffersonian Republicanism, as well as Roman Catholicism, literally represented the many faces of the Anti-Christ. In his poems, published in New England newspapers, Dinsmoor linked American religious and political conservatism to both his Presbyterian heritage and his Scottish ancestry. 'The highest pedigree I plead,' he wrote, is a 'Yankee born' of 'true Scotch breed.'[11]

11 Robert Dinsmoor ['The Rustic Bard'], *Incidental poems ... and sketch of the author's life* (Haverhill, Mass., 1828).

Thus, McGregor's and McMurphy's early eighteenth-century search for a definition – and for Anglo-American recognition – of their followers' non-'Irish' identity was realized in New England, a century later, in part through the poetry, hagiography, and sermons of Ulster-stock Presbyterians such as Robert Dinsmoor and the Reveerend Edward L. Parker. Indeed, so successful were the latter's efforts, and those of their counterparts in Pennsylvania[12] and elsewhere, that soon their people's ambiguous origins and embarrassing 'Irish' interludes were all but forgotten in the subsequent scramble for a purportedly timeless and respectable 'Scotch-Irish' ancestry that eventually nearly all non-Catholic Americans of Irish descent would eagerly claim.

12 On parallel developments in Pennsylvania, 1780s–1820s, see Miller et al., *Land of Canaan*, chaps. 62–4 and 67

III. LANGUAGE AND LITERATURE

Ulster Scots: lost or submerged?

MICHAEL MONTGOMERY

Ulster and Scotland lie on the periphery of Europe, but an abiding consequence of their proximity has been the frequent movement of peoples across
the north channel of the Irish Sea.[1] Since pre-historic times many have passed
along this sea-bridge, carrying with them their languages if not always much
else. Just as the Celtic language Gaelic crossed to the Western Isles around
AD 500 and developed in Scotland a separate character through the experiences and contacts of its speakers there, so speakers of the Germanic tongue
Scots more than a millennium later retraced this route in extending its linguistic territory to the north of Ireland. In these two migrations and other
comings and goings before and since, the narrowness of the channel (11 miles
from northeast Antrim to the Mull of Kintyre, 22 from the Ards Peninsula to
the Mull of Galloway) has made, according to one historian, this 'connexion
between West Scotland and North-east Ireland ... a constant factor in history'.[2] This closeness was pivotal in producing what are known today as
'Scottish Gaelic' and 'Ulster Scots' and in bringing about a multilingual landscape on each side of the bridge.

The history and identity of Scottish Gaelic and Irish Gaelic are well
researched and well known, though their status at present is not always secure
in real-world terms.[3] However, to listen to and read recent discourse in
Ireland, one cannot be blamed for believing that the opposite is true for Ulster
Scots. Few issues regarding it do not remain open to debate or exploration.
This situation reflects in part the cultural politics that have entangled Ulster

1 I am is grateful to Dr William Kelly and Dr Philip Robinson for help in presenting the oral
version of this paper at the Common Ground conference held at Magee College, University of
Ulster, in June 2001. In this essay I use 'Ulster' to refer to the historic, nine-county territory,
an important usage because Ulster Scots is spoken in County Donegal in the Republic of Ireland
in addition to parts of Northern Ireland.   2 G.M. Trevelyan, *A shortened history of England*
(Baltimore, 1959), p. 60.   3 However, the accepted view of the chronology of Scottish Gaelic
has recently been challenged by Campbell, who finds no archaeological evidence to support the
migration of Irish Gaels to Scotland in the fifth century and argues that Gaelic speakers 'had
always lived in Scotland and ... had shared a common language with their [Irish] Gaelic neighbours'. See E. Campbell, *Saints and sea-kings: the first kingdom of the Scots* (Edinburgh, 1999),
p. 15.

Scots, but also other factors, especially insufficient research and inadequate dissemination and use of the research that exists. The Scots language arrived in Ulster, it is conventionally stated, with the phalanx of Scottish Lowlanders who came under the plantation scheme launched by James I in 1610,[4] but this arrival in fact happened slowly and gradually, not once and for all. Speakers of Scots had begun to filter into Antrim and northeast Down in the previous generation.[5] Not only did many return to Scotland in the 1640s, but the largest group arrived in the 1690s, indicating that the planting of Scots-speakers in Ireland was less a datable incursion of language than a century-long process, one of the many chapters produced by the afore-mentioned proximity of Scotland and Ulster.[6]

What happened to the Scots language in Ulster after the seventeenth century relates directly to issues of the present day. Was it lost, eroding at the expense of English and merging with it, after diffusing some of its elements into regional English? This is the thesis of one scholar recently for Scots in both Lowland Scotland and in Ulster.[7] Or did Scots merely disappear from writing, go underground, and change its trajectory over time? I will argue not only that the latter is an accurate characterization, but that this has specific implications for the present day. With the recent launching of the Institute of Ulster-Scots Studies at Magee College of the University of Ulster, I will sketch four perspectives that enlarge and refine our understanding of what Ulster Scots is and will propose a foundation for future thinking and work. These perspectives are the historical, the geographic, the European, and the community. In many ways they intersect and reinforce one another.

Fundamental to all four are the culture and language of Lowland Scotland. In Ulster a variety of cultural activities, such as Scottish country dancing and pipe and drum bands, indicate popular awareness of common ground with Scotland. In recent years the importance of the Scottish connection has reached academia in the form of the Irish-Scottish Academic Initiative, a consortium of four universities, but it remains largely unrealized in wider spheres, including in Scotland and the south of Ireland.[8] Linguistic scholars in Ireland have for so long preoccupied themselves with

---

4 A typical account can be found in B. Kay, *Scots the mither tongue* (Darvel, 1992). 5 See G. Hill, *Historical account of the plantation in Ulster, 1608–1620* (Belfast, 1873). The earliest known document in Scots written in Ulster is a 1571 letter to Elizabeth I from Agnes Campbell, a member of the house of Argyll, on behalf of her husband Turlough O Neil. 6 See especially W.A. Macafee, 'The movement of British settlers into Ulster in the seventeenth century' *Familia*, 2 (1992), 94–111. 7 J.M. Kirk, 'Ulster Scots: realities and myths' *Ulster Folklife*, 44 (1998), 69–93. 8 Headquartered at the Research Institute of Irish Scottish Studies at Aberdeen University, the consortium also includes the University of Strathclyde, Queen's University Belfast, and Trinity College, Dublin.

relations between the English and Irish languages and literary scholars the literatures of the two countries in English that writing in Scots has rarely merited a note, much less recognition for making a substantial contribution.[9] it is even more conspicuously absent from works on Scottish writing; for example, the four-volume *History of Scottish Literature* has nothing on Ulster Scots,[10] but has at least passing reference to literature in Irish Gaelic). Literature in Ulster Scots apparently presents a problem of classification for established taxonomies. Nor have historians in Scotland taken notice of the migration of Lowland Scots language and people to Ulster.[11] In fact, more is written about Scots who migrated to Panama in the 17th century than about those who went to Ulster.[12] Scottish historiography has an almost completely blind eye to the latter.

In this paper I strive to avoid the terminology that has strait-jacketed much discussion of Ulster Scots. I am referring to the 'language' vs. 'dialect' issue. Each of these terms has multiple senses and applications.[13] Suffice it to say that for linguists they form a multidimensional continuum and not a simple dichotomy, and they are based upon a variety of internal (mainly structural) and external (mainly socio-political) criteria that relate more easily to some real-world cases than others. Among prominent criteria used to identify a language are its structural distinctiveness and its use by a historic community. It is not clear how well conventional linguistic criteria apply to regional and minority forms of speech in modern Europe such as Ulster Scots. But it is clear that Ulster Scots today has communities that use it as a spoken idiom daily in the home and the countryside, if never in the educational system and arenas of public life. At the same time Ulster Scots is for younger generations less marked and less distinctive. Many are choosing not to learn or use it.

9 Of a dozen volumes surveying Irish literature in English examined by this writer in his institution's library, only three had any mention or inclusion of them. Samuel Thomson's 'To a Hedgehog' is reprinted in J. Montague (ed.), *The Faber book of Irish verse* (London, 1974). Norman Jeffares has one rather puzzling comment on James Orr, stating that 'Northern dialect was aimed at by' him; see A.N. Jeffares (ed.), *Anglo-Irish literature* (Dublin, 1982), p. 109. Loreto Todd has commentary and excerpts from Orr and Thomson; see L. Todd, *The language of Irish literature* (Savage, 1989). None of these works refers to the Weaver Poets as a group.   10 See C. Craig (ed.), *The history of Scottish literature*, 4 vols (Aberdeen, 1987).   11 For example, Michael Lynch (1991) in a 500-page history of Scotland makes no mention of James' plantation or the migration of Scots to Ulster in the seventeenth century; see M. Lynch, *Scotland: a new history* (London, 1991). Nor does the exhibit on emigration ('Scotland and the World') in the newly opened National Museum of Scotland.   12 See, among other studies of the Darien colonization scheme by J. Prebble, *The Darien disaster* (Edinburgh, 1978).   13 I deal with the relevant issues extensively elsewhere; see M. Montgomery, 'The position of Ulster Scots' *Ulster Folklife*, 45, pp. 86–104.

HISTORICAL PERSPECTIVE

One answer to the language vs. dialect question is that Ulster Scots is a dialect of Lowland Scots. The latter is a Germanic tongue, a close sibling to English. It is the historic language of Lowland Scotland. Having a common source with English in the Anglo-Saxon of more than a millennium ago, Scots developed along separate lines in north Britain and in some respects has remained closer to its roots than its modern-day southern relative. Like English, Scots became an all-purpose, national language in Renaissance times, proceeding very far down the road toward standardization as Scotland's medium for commerce, literature, law, and the court. It replaced Latin as the language of government records, for example, in the fifteenth century. By the late sixteenth century, Scots had been the 'vehicle of a considerable and distinguished literature'[14] for more than two centuries, including for epic poetry, historical narrative, and other genres, and its sound system, grammar, vocabulary, and orthography had come to differ markedly from English. About all this there is no dispute.

The primary historic affinities that link modern Ulster Scots to its parent across the channel involve structural features of pronunciation and grammar that distinguish it from Ulster English and are easily traceable to Lowland Scotland. These include such pronunciations as *richt* and *round* for 'right' and 'round' and such grammatical patterns as negatives formed with *-nae* (*dinnae* and *cannae*). These connections were established in detail by Robert J. Gregg, a native of Larne who began writing about Ulster Scots more than forty years ago and was the seminal academic figure in the field of Ulster Scots studies.[15] However, as early as 1931 William Grant, founding editor of the *Scottish National Dictionary*, stated that 'Ulster Scots is in the main a variant of w[est]m[id] Scots' from Ayrshire and Renfrewshire.[16] The evidence used by Gregg, Grant, and others to identify Scots and to distinguish its varieties has usually come from informal speech, the everyday spoken language on the ground. The existence of a written form is conspicuous by its absence in the linguistic literature as a criterion for distinguishing a language from a dialect.

Nonetheless, it is useful to identify and examine four stages of writing in Ulster Scots. Collectively these indicate that Ulster Scots has had a constant

14 See D. Murison, 'The future of Scots' in D. Glen (ed.), *Whither Scotland?: a prejudiced look at the future of a nation* (London, 1971), p. 172.   15 See especially R.L. Gregg, 'Scotch-Irish urban speech in Ulster' in G.B. Adams (ed.), *Ulster dialects: an introductory symposium* (Cultra, 1964), pp. 163–92; R.L. Gregg, 'The Scotch-Irish dialect boundaries in Ulster' in M. Wakelin *Patterns in the folk speech of the British Isles* (London, 1972), pp. 109–39; and R.L. Gregg, *The Scotch-Irish dialect boundaries in the province of Ulster* (Ottawa, 1985). In his published work Gregg employed the term 'Scotch-Irish' but in his later life shifted to 'Ulster Scots' for the traditional speech about which he wrote.   16 W. Grant (ed.), *The Scottish national dictionary* (Edinburgh, 1931), p. xli.

livelihood as a spoken form and has from time to time surfaced in print. These stages represent sometimes-overlapping but independent manifestations of Ulster Scots in writing. They do not constitute a typical European literary tradition, do not involve epic poetry or high prose, and have often been over-shadowed by developments in Scotland. If an assessment of Ulster Scots rests on its character as a living spoken form, the linguist faces the seeming para-dox that historic details of speech can be surmised only from surviving writ-ten records that may not represent speech well. Even so, this is less a prob-lem for Ulster Scots than for many other regional language varieties because whenever Ulster Scots has been written in the past three centuries, it was employed deliberately to reflect a spoken register. The four stages constitute a useful outline for tracking the development of Ulster Scots and glimpsing its community of speakers. They have consistently shown that the Ulster Scots speech from which they draw maintains conservative, Scottish features.[17]

Stage 1 (1600–1630) The Documentary Period. Scottish Lowlanders who came to Ulster in the 17th century were, with few exceptions, speakers of neither Gaelic nor English, but of Scots.[18] In Scots they left behind personal correspondence, legal documents, and other texts.[19] For instance, extract 1 comes from an assignment of land from Robert McClelland to David Cunningham that dates from the second decade of the century.

Extract 1

I Sir Robert McClellane of Bomby knight be thir presentis does faith-fullie promeiss to my gud freynd David Cunynghame of Heurt his airis and assignayis to set to thame ane sufficient Laice of twell scoir aikeris of land that I haif of the Happerdaschers portion of Londary and that for the space of one and fiftie yeirs lyand within the Countie of Culraine in ony pairt of the said Happerdaschers proportioun now perteyning to me exceptand and reservand the stone hous and mannis … (Robert McClellan of Bomby Legal Documents, Public Record Office of Northern Ireland, 1614)[20]

17 Much more discussion of these periods can be found in M. Montgomery and R. Gregg, 'The Scots language in Ulster' in C. Jones (ed.), *The history of Scots* (Edinburgh, 1997), pp. 569–622. 18 The evidence that Scottish Gaelic persisted in southwestern Scotland into the seventeenth century suggests that the language was at best moribund and did not function except as an auxiliary language to Scots; see W.T. Lorimer, 'The persistence of Gaelic in Galloway and Carrick', *Scottish Gaelic Studies*, 6 (1949), 114–36; 7 (1950), 26–46. Blaney's esti-mate that a quarter of Scottish Lowlanders who migrated to Ulster during the Plantation period were Gaelic-speaking is unsubstantiatable, but improbable; see R. Blaney, *Presbyterians and the Irish language* (Belfast, 1996). 19 See P. Robinson, 'The Scots language in seventeenth-century Ulster' *Ulster Folklife*, 35 (1989), 86–99. 20 This document is on deposit at the Public Record Office of Northern Ireland, collection T640.

In this short passage we find numerous Scottish forms, including the plural demonstrative adjective *thir* 'these', the indefinite article *ane* 'a', and the present-participle *lyand* 'lying', among many others. After this early period Scots disappeared as a language of literacy in both Ulster and Scotland, and by the end of the seventeenth century Scots was detectible in writing only in occasional spellings such as *quh-* for *wh-*.[21] From the eighteenth century on, Ulster Scots is found only in self-conscious renditions of prose and poetry that speech. This could hardly have been otherwise. As English became the language of literacy in the Ulster plantation community and people no longer read Scots regularly, it required a deliberate decision to write in Scots, even if that were one's native speech. That the formal, written register of Scots 'merged' or 'converged' with English has been documented in much detail[22], but the distinctiveness of folk speech was a largely unrelated matter, as later stages of Ulster Scots writing show. From the loss of its written form we can presume little if anything about the vigor or character of spoken Scots at the time.

Stage 2 (1780–1860) Development of Vernacular Poetry. The many versifiers known collectively as the 'Rhyming Weavers'[23] because they were usually weavers of linen by trade represented a genuine social movement that flourished for the better part of a century.[24] They were influenced by Robert Burns less than by the Scottish predecessors they shared with him, especially Ramsay and Fergusson. Many assumed the stance of community spokesmen, signified by their nicknames. For example, James Orr (1770–1816) was the 'Bard of Ballycarry' (see extract 2). Ivan Herbison has chronicled the demise of this literature in the mid-nineteenth century (Herbison 1997).

Extract 2

(from James Orr's 'The Dying Mason' *c.*1790)[25]
Nae mair shall I gang, while in this side o' time …
Nae mair, while ilk mouth's clos'd, an' fast the door bar'd,

---

21 For a study of the erosion of Scots in Ulster and its replacement by English, see M. Montgomery, 'The anglicization of Scots in Early seventeenth century Ulster' in G.R. Roy and P. Scott (eds), *The language and literature of early Scotland*, Studies in Scottish Literature 26, pp. 50–64. 22 For commentary and analysis of the Anglicization of Scots in Scotland, see A.J. Aitken, 'The pioneers of anglicized speech in Scotland: a second Look', *Scottish Language*, 16 (1997), 1–36; A. Devitt, *Standardizing written English: diffusion in the case of Scotland, 1520–1659* (Cambridge, 1989); L. MacQueen, 'The last stages of the older literary language of Scotland: a study of the surviving Scottish elements in Scottish prose, 1700–1750' (Edinburgh, 1957); A. Meurman-Solin, 'Differentiation and standardisation in Early Scots' in C. Jones (ed.), *The Edinburgh history of the Scots language* (Edinburgh, 1997), pp. 3–23. 23 See J. Hewitt, *The rhyming weavers and other country poets of Antrim and Down* (Belfast, 1974). 24 For a mapping of these poets, see P. Robinson, *Ulster Scots: a grammar of the traditional written and spoken language* (Newtownards, 1997), p. 17. 25 Reprinted in P. Robinson (ed.), *The country rhymes of James Orr, the bard of Ballycarry* (Bangor, 1992), p. 96.

Initiate the novice, baith curious and scaur'd;
Nae mair join wi' scores in the grand chorus saft,
Nor fandly toast 'Airlan' – and peace to the craft';
I aye cud been wi' ye, but now I maun stay
Confin'd in my lang hame – the cauld house o' clay.

Stage 3 (1850–2004) Rise of Ulster-Scots Prose. A prose tradition in Ulster Scots began in the 1850s and consisted of popular sketches, commentaries, serialized novels, and similar items that appeared most often in local newspapers in Antrim and Down (extract 3 is an example by W.G. Lyttle, editor of the *Newtownards Chronicle* in the 1880s and 1890s).

Extract 3

Newtownards Chronicle, 18 November 1882
AN ECHT-DAYS RETROSPECK O CUMMER DOINS.
To the editur o the 'Newtoun Chronickel'.
SUR–You wull nae doot wunner at my lang silonse, but the awfu things that hae hapened ye ken gies me a terble time o truble, gest to think that ony thief can gang intil yer back yeard and steel pig troughs, and make three-legged pots rin awa wi hachets is enuff to mack yen's hair stan on thar heed; and day a this, mind ye, an get off scot frae. It ocurs to my mind that the star wi the lang tale has sumthin to day wi these miricals, but mebbe the aturney wha sayed sich quare things ti the fella that the pot and ither things rin awa frae hes som nollege o astronmy, and caused the lang tailed comit to dezzel the eyes o folk a could name, wha think it no crime to day the like ... (W. G. Lyttle, 1882).

Typically these texts were written in a folksy, first-person style, and often they dealt with local social and political issues. Like the poetry of the Weavers, this literature saw itself as a voice of the people and was strikingly paralleled in Scotland in the Victorian period.[26]
Stage 4 (1990–) Contemporary Writing. The past decade has seen much new writing in Ulster Scots of both prose and poetry. Much of this has been published in *Ullans*, the magazine of the Ulster-Scots Language Society. Ulster Scots has become the vehicle for full=length works of prose (as with Philip Robinson's 2000 novel *The Back Streets o the Claw* and Hugh Robinson's 1999 memoir *Across the Fields of Yesterday*).[27] Its most widely known poetic exponent today is the James Fenton (extract 4, from his book *Thonner and Thon*).

---

26 See W. Donaldson, *The language of the people: Scots prose from the Victorian revival* (Aberdeen, 1989). **27** See H. Robinson, *Across the fields of yesterday: memories of an Ulster*

Extract 4

Dailygon[28]
An noo the lichts ower Brochanor
mak blak the brae behin;
The sallies, hoovin saft an grey
com getherin, cloodin in;
The watter, glancin ower its dark
babs lippin, whusperin by;
The boag's dark-sweelin quait, aroon
the tummock whar A lie.

The peats' quait low, the week's saft licht
mak blak the ootby noo;
The prootas plowt; the neeps' sweet steam
cloods roon hir sweetin broo;
Bae qua an boag, ower queelrod wa,
thon licht's a gleekin ee
Frae what A come an whar Ah'll gae
tae nether stie nor lee.

    The foregoing sketch of four stages is open to refinement and revision
because linguists have hardly begun to exploit the documentary record to
reconstruct the development of Ulster Scots. The archival work remaining
to be done, especially to find and analyze newspapers and other local publications in stages two and three, should greatly enlarge our view of this spoken
regional tongue that came to the surface in local literature from time to time.
Ulster Scots literature is important for what it reveals of everyday life and
society of former times and the creative skills of individual writers, but its
greater significance lies in its indication that spoken Ulster Scots has had a
distinctive character and thriving, continuous existence in the countryside for
centuries. The contention that Scots in Scotland and Ulster Scots in Ulster
have converged steadily with English since 1600 pertains to written language
(orthography, grammar, and idiom) and undoubtedly to formal registers of
the spoken language and is uncontroversial, a well-established finding of
research. But in taking scant account of the evidence from the three centuries
of literature in Ulster Scots surveyed here, the thesis that Ulster Scots 'converged' quickly with English is open to serious doubt in the more important
realm of vernacular speech.

Scots childhood in the Ards (Belfast, 1999), and P. Robinson, *Ulster Scots: a grammar of the traditional written and spoken language* (Newtownards, 1997).   28 J. Fenton, *Thonner and Thon*
(Belfast, 2000), p. 1.

GEOGRAPHICAL PERSPECTIVE

Robert Gregg provided a geographical perspective on Ulster Scots by interviewing 125 native speakers to determine its maximal extent on the ground in the early 1960s. He found systematic distinctions in pronunciation and grammar between Ulster Scots and Ulster English in parts of four Ulster counties: Down, Antrim (London)Derry, and Donegal. Gregg's work on the core Ulster-Scots territory produced one of the most carefully mapped speech areas in the British Isles. In both Gregg's day and ours Ulster-Scots speakers within this region usually shift toward standard English in towns or when speaking with outsiders, but the geographic character of Ulster Scots is shown that in its territory both Protestants and Catholics use it.[29] Precursors to Gregg's mapping work are not hard to find. In seeking the boundaries of Ulster Scots, he relied on a tradition of ethnological and historical scholarship dating back to Abraham Hume, who first outlined the Scottish parts of Antrim and Down in the *Ulster Journal of Archaeology*.[30]

EUROPEAN PERSPECTIVE

A European perspective is important for many reasons. The European Bureau of Lesser-Used Languages (EBLUL), an autonomous body representing speakers of 'minority' and 'regional' languages within the European Union, designated 2001 as the European Year of Languages. In the process it brought to Europe-wide attention several dozen historic tongues, including ones spoken in their own neighborhoods that many Europeans heard about for the first time. The year-long observance culminated a decade of work by EBLUL to expand the focus from the 'national' languages of western and central Europe to other, often closely related ones lacking official recognition and public awareness. Here we are not talking about languages that have communities of speakers resulting from displacement or emigration in the twentieth century (e.g. Turkish), but communities that have been on the European landscape for centuries (Catalan in Spain, Frisian in the Netherlands, etc.) In most cases it is impossible to say when, if ever, they 'arrived'. Some have not had a name until recently and are now in the process of labeling themselves. Many have long been considered only an illegitimate form of a national language, a rural or regional 'dialect' believed to deserve being left behind.

29 See L. Todd, 'Ulster Scots'. in T. McArthur (ed.), *The Oxford companion to the English language* (Oxford, 1992), pp. 1087–88; J. Fenton, *The Hamely tongue: a personal record of Ulster-Scots in County Antrim*, revised edition (Belfast, 2000).   30. See A. Hume, 'Ethnology of the Counties of Down and Antrim', *Ulster Journal of Archaeology*, Series 1, vol. 4 (1856), 154–63; and 'The elements of population in Down and Antrim, illustrated by the statistics of religious belief', *Ulster Journal of Archaeology*, Series 1, vol. 7 (1859), 116–30.

Other recent developments in the British Isles increase the prospect that the history of these traditional varieties of speech will be seen in a new light. EBLUL now recognizes forty-one of them, including six in the British Isles (Irish Gaelic, Scots Gaelic, Welsh, Cornish, Scots, and Ulster Scots). In 1992 the Council of Europe formulated the European Charter for Regional or Minority Languages. This was formally signed by the United Kingdom in March 2001 (but to date not by the Republic of Ireland). In countless ways developments with Ulster Scots over the past four centuries have mirrored those of comparable language varieties in Spain, Italy, Austria, and elsewhere in mainland Europe. EBLUL's designation of them as regional or minority languages offers a way to recognize the influence of national ideology on the classification of languages in modern Europe and a way to supersede this ideology and thereby reduce the distortions created by national boundaries.

Caught in a terminological and political web like many European minority languages, Ulster Scots must be seen within the larger European context for us to understand that what may seem to be local dynamics are quite typical European ones. The European frame helps address the limits of terminology limited to 'language' and 'dialect'. Two fundamental realities that affect the status of Ulster Scots are that it has never been identified with a state and has never existed apart from English, with which it shares much structurally if often little socially. As long as writing is viewed as the primary manifestation of language, and this is a profound tendency in the western world outside the academy, this keeps languages like Ulster Scots in a second- if not third-class position.

Scots and Ulster Scots are merely two of many European languages that went underground in the sixteenth and seventeenth century. The erosion and loss of the written form of Scots reflected the triumph of the idea of a national language. As modern European nation-states arose, one of the constant features was the extension, aided mightily by the printing press, of a single, more-or-less uniform language or language variety throughout the realm as a tool of government and bureaucracy. This process facilitated mass literacy, but at the same time it marginalized traditional forms of language that were often spoken by hundreds of thousands of people. The long-term result is that minority languages like Ulster Scots have an image problem today and their status, at least in the public eye, is often ambiguous, if not dubious.

COMMUNITY PERSPECTIVE

Implicit in the recognition of minority and regional languages is the right of historic communities to name, preserve, and claim identity for their traditional speech. This community perspective on Ulster Scots, like the European perspective, removes issues of language status from the hands of academics and public officials alone and shares them with speakers themselves. This perspective acknowledges that what speakers think of their minority or regional language is paramount. Within the last generation many who were once told that Ulster Scots was nothing more than 'bad English' are now claiming it as something quite different from what outsiders have designated it, including outsiders who have sought to apply 'standard terminology'. And why not?

To approach the language vs. dialect issue from another direction, let me present an analogy. A few years ago I was driving in north County Tyrone with a colleague. When he asked me what I thought of the Sperrin Mountains and I replied, 'When are we going to see them?', he said, 'We're in them'. 'Surely', I protested, 'these are not mountains,' and I imagine that natives of south Down, with the Mournes out their window, would agree and say, 'Well, the Mournes are real mountains. People in Tyrone don't know what a mountain is.' Highland Scots might look up at Ben Nevis and say, 'Now that's a real mountain. It has snow in June. Folks in Tyrone and Down don't know the meaning of "mountain".' No doubt people from many other parts of the world would look at Scotland and say something similar. A rise in land may be called a mountain rather than a hill on the basis of any of several criteria that are not necessarily related – its height, its steepness, its rockiness, its difficulty to climb, and so on.

The usual view one has of a mountain is from below. By the same token, the dimensions of a mountain are relative and a matter of perspective. From there mountains look much more alike than from above. Likewise, issues of language vs. dialect can be debated in academia, political circles, and many other contexts. But at some point it is people on the ground who define who they are, what they speak, and what they are going to call it. What may not be a mountain or a language to you may be one to me.

If mountains and hills, along with other sets of natural and physical phenomena, do not form a dichotomy, but a relative and even fluid distinction, why shouldn't languages and dialects do the same? Once we open this question we begin to think unlike so many Europeans who conventionally associate 'language' with a nation-state and any related variety that is not connected with a nation-state a 'dialect'.

CONCLUSIONS

Ulster Scots as a subject matter and as a language faces many difficulties, among which are inattention from scholars, its almost-inevitable ensnarement in cultural politics, and a severely handicapped public image because of its unequal relations with English. This paper hopes to have furthered a broader, more dispassionate, and more realistic discussion of these difficulties and to have brought forth a more-informed understanding of what Ulster Scots is and what it is not.

The written record of Ulster Scots is invaluable in many ways, but we cannot rely on it simplistically, as it presents only a partial view and is conventionalized in ways that have often been influenced by its Scottish counterparts. It is the spoken language that provides the moorings for Ulster Scots both in historical periods and today. From the available evidence we conclude that Ulster Scots has often been out of sight or submerged, but not out of hearing, and it was never lost. The extent of its decay is questionable, given that Gregg found that its speech area closely corresponded to settlement patterns laid down in the seventeenth century.

The act of silently reading Ulster Scots (and Lowland Scots for that matter) inevitably compares it to English, which is the language of literacy in the British Isles. For this reason scholars – perhaps all of us – need to hear more of Ulster Scots. This will enable us better to consider Ulster Scots in its own terms and to identify more clearly the Scottish input into Ulster speech. More broadly, greater understanding of Ulster Scots will enable us to overcome the presumption that anything that is not Standard English in Ulster speech is ipso facto of Irish provenance or, as is sometimes claimed, from Shakespearean-era English. Indeed, because Ulster Scots has much to teach us about the linguistic and cultural pluralism of the island, we all have a stake in learning about it.

Gaelic, Scots and English: the politics of language in inter-war Scotland

RICHARD FINLAY

> It's possible that Scotland yet
> May hear its ain voice speak
> If only we can silence
> This endless-vatterin beak ...
> For the puir bird needs its rest
> Wha else'll be the waur o't?
> And its lang past the time
> The claith was owre the parrot?
>
> *To Circumjack Cencrastus*, Hugh MacDiarmid 1930

On the eve of the Second World War, the literary critic, William Power, stated that there were two ways to know a nation. The first was to visit a country and the second was to study its literature and he noted with some satisfaction that a younger generation of writers had breathed new life into Scottish writing. Power concluded that the state of Scottish literature was at its most healthy since the eighteenth century:

> In history and biography there has been real progress. The old Ultra-Protestant and anti-Celtic prejudices have been overcome, social and economic history is being given its due place, and, for the first time, we are beholding Scotland's past as it really was. The revaluations of Burns and Scott have increased our real appreciation of these writers, and have helped to clear the way for modern literature. Fiction and general literature have definitely improved in quality, and they have become truer to the realities of life. From Scots literature of last century, it is almost impossible to obtain a clear and reliable picture of Scots life at that time. But the Scotland of the post-War years is faithfully and graphically mirrored in contemporary Scots literature. That of itself constitutes a real 'literary renaissance.[1]

His judgment was not universally accepted at the time, but it would find much support among today's literary scholars. The Scottish renaissance of

---

1 G.R. Allen (ed.), *Scotland, 1938* (Edinburgh, 1939), p. 160.

the inter-war years is rightly seen as a cultural flowering that followed the
arid and sterile era of the Kailyard, which can best be described as a sentimental and inward-looking period in Scottish cultural history. Inspired by
the international phenomenon of modernism, a new generation of Scottish
writers sought to break the pawky and complacent hold of Kailyardism on
the nation's culture by challenging coothy aesthetic standards and denounc-
ing the artistic and intellectual laziness of prevailing attitudes. For cultural
historians and literary critics, the renaissance is a rewarding and challenging
artistic vein running through the nation's history, which is seen as vital to
restoring Scottish cultural health in the twentieth century.

Yet, artistic appreciation of the output of the renaissance has meant that
its political dimension has received less scholarly attention, in spite of the fact
that most of its leading luminaries believed that politics was an essential element of their creative endeavours. Although biographies of leading individuals do discuss their subject's political outlook and involvement, there has
been no real attempt to examine the renaissance as a socio-political movement. Indeed, this might be regarded as an odd state of affairs as politics was
a central aspect of the cultural aspirations of most of the leading figures of
the renaissance, even though the movement did not encompass either a coherent or united political outlook. In the aftermath of the First World War and
with the rise of mass political ideologies revolving around nationalism and
socialism, writers of the renaissance sought to engage culture with politics.
This was in stark contrast to the couthy, sentimental and politically neutered
writings of the Kailyard. If there was one consensus that writers of the renaissance shared, it was to shake things up and relate Scottish culture to the wider
international world and relate it to the dynamic of the changing world at
home. Culture was an important arena, and many of them would say the most
important, for political combat.

In essence, the politics of the renaissance can be divided into two camps;
in one corner stood nationalism, in the other international socialism. Cultural
nationalists were profoundly effected by the rise of nationalism in Europe
during the nineteenth century and central to the 'nationalist project' was the
role of language. Iceland and Norway had reinvented their languages and in
Ireland, a Gaelic cultural revival was underway and had been a key component of the nationalist agenda. Herder's dictum that a nation lives through
its language was one that had widespread currency and was believed by many
to be the ultimate form of national authentication. The period after 1919, far
from settling the issue of national self-determination in Europe probably created as many problems as it attempted to solve. The existence in Central and
Eastern Europe of linguistic minorities helped to further fuel the idea of irri-
dentist nationalism, i.e. that the nation should be whole in the sense that
nationals outside the nation state should be reconnected or the non-nation-

als within the nation state should be expelled.[2] Ideas of linguistic and ethnic nationality were part of the mainstay of European though after 1919 and the discussion of Scottish nationalism in this period must be understood in this context. It is the objective of this essay to examine the issue of language as a badge of national authenticity in the period of the Scottish cultural renaissance and address its significance in nationalist politics.

Nationalism could exist without linguistic homogeneity, as is demonstrated by the case of Switzerland, and it did not need original ownership of language, as is demonstrated by the United States. Yet, in inter-war Europe, the intellectual assumption was that linguistic and national purity went hand in hand. Ireland was the most commonly cited example of national regeneration in the Scottish nationalist pantheon. A number of features made it so. The idea of a common Celtic racial stock was one, the 'imperial' relationship with 'Saxon' England another. The Scots had three languages to choose from: Gaelic, Scots and English. Not surprisingly, those nationalists most heavily influenced by the Irish example plumped for the Gaelic language. The Scots National League (SNL) was formed in 1920 to promote Scottish nation self-determination.[3] Its members had connections with the Highland Land League, which likewise had been closely associated with Irish issues before the First World War and a large number were Gaelic speakers, although many of them were now London exiles. The League was imbued with racial ideas and believed that Scotland's culture was Celtic, but, like Ireland, had been subverted by Saxon imperialism.

> We in Scotland have much to learn from Ireland; in this respect, we are more than ten years behind her. First we must build up our national conscience, and blushing from its discovery, we must set ourselves to build up our nationality from its foundation. The foundation – the bedrock of our Celtic origin – is already there awaiting the builders, and the cornerstone – our Gaelic language; the only national language of Scotland, is already in the hands of the hewers. (*Liberty*, July 1920)

Independence, it was argued, would only come once the Scots had reconnected with their Celtic cultural inheritance. For the SNL, culture was a political weapon. Needless to say, such a limited political agenda would attract few converts in the political climate of post-war Scotland where class inter-

---

2 For an up-to-date discussion of these issues see Oliver Zimmer, *Nationalism in Europe, 1890–1940* (Basingstoke, 2003).   3 The following is based on Richard J. Finlay, *Independent and free: Scottish politics and the origins of the Scottish National Party, 1918–1945* (Edinburgh, 1994), pp. 29–71.

est had become the dominant issue in politics. The cultural purists in the
League were gradually isolated by the late twenties as the pragmatists began
to form more bread and butter policies and strategies, and increasingly became
absorbed into negotiations with other nationalist organizations, which would
pave the way for the formation of the National Party of Scotland in 1928.

Nationalist politics would largely be dominated by questions of electoral
strategy and political objectives throughout the inter-war period. Issues of
culture were largely abrogated from the political agenda, but were, nevertheless, pursued more explicitly in designated cultural arenas. One figure who
towered above most in the debate on Scottish culture was Christopher Murray
Grieve (Hugh MacDiarmid) and it was he who most actively pursued the
issue of language and its relation to culture and politics. An initial Gaelic
enthusiast, MacDiarmid came to believe that there was insufficient scope for
making it the language that of the nation. It was an enormous task and
instead, he plumped for the recreation of the Scots language. In many
respects, this was a more realistic prospect. The Scots language, or its historical residue, was omnipresent in Scottish society and although existing in
many regional forms, there was arguably a sufficient base for its reconstruc-
tion into a working national language. The popularity of the work of Robert
Burns was testament to the appeal that Scots still held in Scottish society and
in many respects would have been an ideal template for its reinvention. It
was distinctive and different from the everyday speech of Scottish society in
the inter-war period, but not so different that it was possible to be understood and spoken with a little effort.

Yet, Burnsian Scots was problematic for most of the leading figures in
the Scottish renaissance, even those who did not work to the nationalist
agenda. It is an important issue to examine why neither the socialists, or the
nationalists, harnessed Robert Burns to their camp. As a cultural icon, Burns
was omnipresent in Scottish society and as with other political movements
elsewhere, ideologues engaged in projects designed to reinvent figures of historical and cultural authority in a light which legitimized their aspirations.
Reinvented tradition was a powerful way in which to lend credibility and
authority to new ideas. Paradoxically, while Burns was used by mainstream
nationalists and socialists to propagate their message during the inter-war
period, it was the self-appointed new creators of Scottish culture which stead-
fastly refused to engage with him.

One of the key reasons why Burns disappears from the renaissance project is the difficulty in disentangling the Bard from the cult that grew up
around his reputation in the nineteenth and early twentieth centuries. The
Burns cult attracted special opprobrium from all sides of the renaissance
because it was emblematic of the cultural morass into which the nation had
sunk. 'The Scots are incapable of appreciating their writers unless they are

the occasion for a sermon or an excuse for a dram', was the caustic remark of George Malcolm Thomson. Marion MacNeil in a review of Catharine Carswell's biography of Burns, which upset the purists, likewise poured scorn on the uncritical admiration for the Bard:

> If any additional argument were needed for the re-establishment of a cultural centre in Scotland, it is provided by the spate of letter that followed the publication in the 'Daily Record' of parts of Mrs Carswell's 'Life of Robert Burns'. Here we have the inevitable chorus of the 'bodies', who provide a running commentary on Scottish life and letters, in the manner of a Greek chorus – but with what a difference! For whereas one speaks in the accent of ancient Athens, the other speaks in the accent of Drumtochty and Thrums. Well so long as we continue to export our aristocracy and intelligentsia en bloc, and to drive from the land, slumwards, shipwards, that sturdy population whose very proximity to the soil keeps their judgement sound, so long must we thole the ascendancy of the 'petite bourgeois' or parish-pump mentality. (*Scots Independent*, December 1930)

The opinion of the Scottish literary establishment was that Burns could not be surpassed in terms of his use of the Scots language: 'the work of Burns is not the beginning of a period, but its climax and close. The Scottish muse has many things to her credit in the century and more since Burns died, but singly they are slight and innovate little upon the past'.[4] Burns almost became the dead hand of history on the artistic endeavour of the renaissance project in that none were allowed to escape his shadow. Edwin Muir was equally as scathing about the uncritical admiration heaped upon the bard and even went as far as to call for the destruction of Burns's cottage which had become a commercial totem for his cult following:

> It was so unlike my expectation of a visit to Burns's cottage that I could hardly believe in it, and only when I was out again and had time to compose myself did I see that this was exactly what the cult of Burns worship was bound to turn into in a commercialized, newspaper-reading, bus-driven, cinema-educated age. It is difficult to see what makes it so ridiculous, for the whole business is excellently organized. But one wonders how the management will deal with this enormous traffic in another fifty years time, presuming that it goes on increasing. The cottage will certainly have to be enlarged, or else the price of admission raised until

4 George Gordon, 'Scottish literature' in the Duke of Atholl (ed.), *A Scotsman's heritage* (London, 1932), p. 210.

only the well-to-do can get in. There seems no third alternative except demolition. (*Scottish Journey*, 1980 edition, 88)

'Sham bards for a sham nation' was how Muir described the uncritical admiration for Burns and Scott in his poem 'Scotland 1941'. MacDiarmid was especially incensed by the fad for collecting as many details and minutia of Burns's life as it showed little thought or appreciation for his work. Indeed, it acted as a way to avoid discussing his literary output. In his apocryphal tale, 'the last great Burns discovery', MacDiarmid poked fun at the Burns Cult by inventing a story that they had discovered the bard's toilet and at as such was a national treasure which ought to be preserved as part of the nation's heritage.

Although the renaissance critics were careful to state that it was the Burns Cult and not the man himself who was the object of their wrath, it is hard to see how this did not spill over. After all established literary critics claimed that the language used by Burns could not be surpassed and that there was little point in this new generation in trying. Burns was a cultural albatross hanging around the neck of every new Scottish writer or poet whose work would always be found wanting when compared to the great man. The *Scots Magazine* described MacDiarmid's efforts to reinvent the language as a sort of artificial respiration and implied that it was pointless because the language was already dead.[5] Furthermore, many claimed that it could not be used to convey complex or intellectual meaning and worst for MacDiarmid, this was a point endorsed by Edwin Muir in *Scott and Scotland*. Burns and his veneration had led to cultural ossification. If that was not bad enough, Burns was used to push a Kailyard vision of Scotland and Scottish identity that was sentimental, pawky and romantic. Burns was also used to give credence to establishment values. In other words, Burns was seen as an ally of bourgeois Scotland. The reason for this state of affairs was that Burns was venerated in an unthinking way. The Burns cult represented the worse in a sterile and unimaginative culture. As part of the objectives of the renaissance it was necessary to sweep away the Kailyard and reconnect with the European mainstream. It should come as no surprise, therefore to find that the Burns cult came under sustained and ferocious intellectual fire as the most visible symbol of Scotland's degenerate culture. Yet, one important question remained, what to do with Burns himself and how to ensure that he was not a victim of the cultural cross-fire.

In a review of recent writing on Burns, MacDiarmid complained that the Scots were incapable of reinventing or adapting the bard in line with contemporary events:

5 *Scots Magazine*, May 1926; April, 1927.

It would seem that most of the people who write essays or books dealing with Burns first of all cut themselves away from all literary standards and deal with their material in a hopelessly demoded manner.
Why is this? If Burns is the great world poet he is acclaimed to be,
his life and poems ought to be susceptible to re-presentation and re-
interpretation in terms of current modes of biographical art and literary criticism. But some fatality seems to dog almost every writer on
Burns, forcing him to write in a fashion that prevents his book taking,
in and for itself, any reputable place in the class of studies to which it
belongs ... What this comes to in the long run is that interest in Burns
is confined to inferior minds, and the poet's reputation is not being
continually renewed and readjusted to modern consciousness as it ought
to be. (*Scots Independent*, February, 1929)

Yet, in spite of his exhortations, MacDiarmid did little to engage with
Burns nor did he adapt and reshape the image of the bard to suite contemporary cultural aspirations. The reasons behind MacDiarmid's reluctance to
engage with Burns can be found within his programme for a nationalist regeneration of Scottish culture. MacDiarmid's idea of nationalism and the role of
culture in promoting a nationalist programme was strongly influenced by
events in Europe. Central to his philosophy of cultural nationalism was the
fundamental importance of language. Language was regarded by him and
other European nationalists as the bedrock of national identity. To be a separate nation required a separate language and the more distinctive and unique
the language the more distinctive and unique the nation. MacDiarmid was
strongly influenced by the example of Irish nationalists and believed that a
degree of cultural separation was an essential pre-requisite for political separation. He outlined some of these ideas in an article projecting his vision of
the future of Scotland:

This was part of a wider movement, shifting the interest in the civilised
world away from economics and sociology, which had too long monop-
olized attention, to spiritual values. The younger people, who had never
been subject to the demoralizing influence of the old Anglo-Scottish
party political system, speedily repudiated the methods and ideology
of organized – and English controlled – democracy then in vogue; and
no longer confining themselves to English precedents, availed themselves readily of the examples of Italy and Ireland, and, powerfully re-
enforcing the transitional organization of the Scottish Nationalist Party
(up till then still deplorably liberal and Anglophile) with their mili-
taristic neo-Fascist auxiliary, 'Clann Albann', carried the movement to
the successful conclusion we know of by 1965, and re-established the

ancient Gaelic Commonwealth in Scotland on a modern basis. (*Scots Independent*, June 1929)

As with other European nationalists, MacDiarmid believed in a form of linguistic purity, hence his call for Scottish literature and language to go back to Dunbar and the medieval makars. By using medieval Scots as a linguistic template for the revival of the Scots language, MacDiarmid believed that a new national literature could be created which was historically unsullied by British unionism. Indeed, it ought to be remembered that MacDiarmid flirted with the idea of using Gaelic as the medium for a cultural regeneration for precisely the same reason that it was linguistically unassociated with English or Britishness. The idea of using Gaelic was boyed up by racial notions concerning the ethnic identity of Scotland which he argued was Celtic and that this Celticism meant that the Scots were racially different from the English and therefore, should have no part in the Union. Such ideas concerning racial identity and literature were not confined to MacDiarmid and were echoed elsewhere. William Power urged writers to look to folklore for inspiration and cited the example of Germany where Wagner had turned to the mythic past to form the basis of national culture.[6] MacDiarmid was an ardent supporter of Yeats's Greenshirt movement in Ireland and called for Scottish nationalists to endorse Fascism. He briefly flirted with the idea of setting up his own militarist organization, Clann Albann, which collapsed due to lack of organization and interest.

While MacDiarmid did set himself as an intellectual agent provocateur and many critics have questioned the degree of commitment he had in propounding such extreme views, his lack of ideological consistency, as Chris Harvie, puts it, belies a number of features which remained constant in MacDiarmid's ideas during the inter-war period. Such themes would impact on his perspective not only of Burns but previous Scottish writers. Firstly, national culture had to be created in a new form and Burns was not new. Secondly, national culture had to be created from 'pure' material and Burns was not pure Scottish. Thirdly, MacDiarmid believed that the bourgeois contaminated culture and Burns was contaminated by his absorption into the bourgeois. Finally, language, folklore and myths were more important in the construction of national culture than the literary canon. In spite of his exhortations for fellow writers and critics to engage with Burns and recast him in a new light, MacDiarmid did not. This was left to rank and file nationalists who utilized Burns's statements on the Union and his neo-Jacobitism to recast him as a nationalist.

For Edwin Muir capitalism and the social consequences which followed in its wake was more important than questions of national identity. The same

6 *My Scotland* (Edinburgh, 1934), p. 302.

can be said about Lewis Grassic Gibbon. This is not to say that they were hostile to national identity, rather it just never made it to the top of their list of priorities. According to Muir, the Burns cult was the epitome of a washed out, bourgeois, commercial culture. In appreciating Burns's literary talents, the cult turned the Bard's genius into something common place and every-day. Although Muir and MacDiarmid did not share the same political agenda, they both agreed that there were difficulties in reconstructing the nation's culture from contaminated material. Whereas MacDiarmid's poison was England, for Muir it was the Reformation, but the Reformation as the har-binger of capitalism. Like MacDiarmid, Muir believed that the best of Scottish culture was contained in the medieval period. Whereas MacDiarmid was to start rebuilding from the medieval base, Muir believed this to be point-less because the same capitalist system which had corrupted Scottish culture in the first place was still intact and would do the same to any reconstituted culture. In part, this effected Muir's opinion of Burns. After all, Burns's God was Protestant, and he lent credibility to bourgeois Scotland. Muir believed that the past was done and nothing could change it, the future lay with inter-national socialism and nationalism could only get in the way.

Paradoxically, MacDiarmid's vision of nationalism which he hoped would wipe away anglicized, bourgeois Scotland was very close to classic nineteenth century bourgeois nationalism with its emphasis on race, national myths, cul-tural and linguistic purity. Indeed, it probably had more chance of catching on in the Scotland of 1848 than in the 1920s and 30s where the political agenda was dominated by the grim social and economic realities of the age and where politics meant appealing to the masses rather than the middle-class elite. As a political programme, MacDiarmid's appeal for nationalist culture had little chance of success. The politics of language failed to mobilise public sympathy. In part, the quest for linguistic purity put the Scots language beyond many of its potential users. It was an elitist project, ill sited to the demands of a growing democracy.

The political identity of the Scots-speaking community in Scotland and Ulster, 1545–1760

DAVID HORSBURGH

THE POLITICS OF SCOTS LANGUAGE HISTORY

To date there have been no attempts to introduce into the Scottish or Northern Irish education curricula a systematic introduction to the origins, development and history of the Scots-speaking community. Therefore, it is small wonder that much of the comment made on the past and recent history of Scots is ill-informed, and often tainted with pejorative, politically-loaded, or openly prejudiced opinion.

During the past twenty-five years increasing study has been made of the history of the Irish and Scottish Gaelic-speaking communities – both of which have traditionally been neglected by the state – and, as a result, a better understanding of the past and present culture and politics of the *Gaidhealtachd* has been arrived at. However, the linguistic history currently being written is still incomplete and is anachronistic. In one recently revised work, *The Atlas of Scottish History to 1707*, a few pages have been devoted to the history and extent of Gaelic in Scotland, thanks mainly to the work of the innovative historical geographer Charles Withers. But one looks in vain for any corresponding account of Scots, the language of the Lowland community, and instead the *Atlas* speaks only of the retreat of Gaelic in the face of 'English', that imprecise and politically-loaded term.[1] How has it come to pass that a speech form, once the language of state, possessed of a notable literature, and enjoying an undeniable political identity, is almost forgotten outside linguistic journals?

The Scots language finds itself squeezed between born-again Celticness – which has placed a new emphasis on the history of Gaelic in Scotland – and anglicized historians, who, like most of us, have been trained to believe that Scots is at best the rustic dialect of farming and fishing folk, or, at worst, a contemporary and worthless slang on which the inhabitants of our *schemes* are suckled.[2] The neglect of our (Lowland) linguistic history is largely governed

---

1 P.G.B. McNeill & H.L. MacQueen (eds), *Atlas of Scottish history to 1707* (Edinburgh, 1996), pp. 427–9. See also C.W.J. Withers, *Gaelic in Scotland, 1698–1981: the geographical history of a language* (Edinburgh, 1984); idem, *Gaelic Scotland: the transformation of a culture region* (London, 1988). 2 'Scheme', in this context, is the Scots equivalent of English 'local author-

by *contemporary* attitudes which in turn greatly affect the shape of history currently being written in Scotland and Ulster. For example, in a recent work on the reign of James VI, language in Scotland is described in the following terms:

> two main languages were spoken in Scotland: Middle Scots, one of the dialects of English, in the south and north-east, and Scots Gaelic, a Celtic language related to Irish, in the west.[3]

Why is Scots here described as a dialect, quite apart from the fact it comprised five main dialects, while Scottish Gaelic is described as a separate language? This does not accord well with the historical record since, if anything, in the reign of James VI the common perception *vis-à-vis* Gaelic and Scots was that Gaelic was *Earse* ('Irish'), while Scots was a distinct language closely related to English. Scots Gaelic was only beginning to be perceived as a distinct entity *in the minds of men* with the break down of the wider Irish-Scottish *Gaidhealtachd* in the wake of the Nine Years War (1594–1603). There are, so far as I am aware, no references to such a thing as *Scottish* Gaelic, prior to an entry in the Annals of the Four Masters compiled in the 1620s. There is little doubt, of course, that such a thing as Scottish Gaelic was a linguistic reality by 1600, but what matters most is the perception contemporary with that period, not the revival of interest in the late twentieth century.

In their account of Scotland under James VI, Goodare and Lynch are basing their assessment of Scots in the seventeenth century on their own contemporary attitudes which are partly shaped by the current interest in Gaelic and the almost total disregard for Scots which the authorities in Scotland have so far shown. Both are consequently being anachronistic in their approach to the linguistic history of Scotland.[4] Others, such as John Morrill and Jane Dawson, make quite sweeping statements in relation to the language of the Lowlands in order to uphold the progress of Anglo-Scottish Union. It can be argued that their interpretation is flawed because they confuse the willingness of Scots to use English for a British audience – including an anglicized printing press – with an abandonment of Scots at home.[5]

ity housing estate' (or American *project*).   3 J. Goodare & M. Lynch, 'The Scottish state and its borderlands, 1567–1625', in idem, *The reign of James VI* (East Linton, 2000), p. 197.   4 Such an attitude is echoed elsewhere. In *Medieval Scotland: the making of an identity* (London, 1997), Bruce Webster comments, 'Southern English has now largely replaced Scots', p. 3. Mark Nicholls in *A history of the modern British Isles, 1529–1603* (Oxford, 1999) states that the Lowlanders spoke English and footnotes it 'the jury remains out on whether we have here a once-distinct tongue gradually merging with English, or simply a strong regional variant', pp. 80, 127. Nevertheless, Scots, at that time, was the language of state, and was commonly acknowledged as a language. Why not describe Scots in terms of its role and status during the period under discussion rather than questioning it on the basis of (modern) contemporary attitudes? 5 John Morrill, 'Three Stuart kingdoms, 1603–1689', in John Morrill (ed.), *The Oxford history*

As a result of the political situation in Ulster today, a new emphasis is being placed on the Scots language in the past history of the province, and Scots there certainly enjoys a profile – and public funding – which speakers of Scots in Scotland can only dream of. This is, of course, intended to reflect some parity with the support given to Irish in the island of Ireland by both the Irish and UK governments.[6] Commentators are generally polarized between supporters of English and Irish, who both regard Scots as having less legitimacy, and supporters of Scots in Ulster who have overcompensated in trying to better establish the credentials of Scots.[7] Such debate raises two main questions in relation to Scots in the period 1545 to 1760; what were the roles and status of Scots, both before and during the dual-monarchy, and are there historical reasons for considering the Scots spoken in Ulster to possess a separate status from the Scots of Scotland?

THE STATUS OF SCOTS IN THE BRITISH ISLES, 1545–1707

What constituted a Scots-speaking political identity? It is partly administrative, partly ethnic, and partly religious. Geographically the speakers of Scots were identified with the east and south of Scotland – the *Lawlands* – and this term carried an ethnic meaning. A *Lawland paroch* ('Lowland parish'), a *Lawland man* ('Lowland man'), these were synonymous with Scots-speaking. In this sense those parts of Ulster settled by Scots were also *Lawland*. From the point of view of administration, the organs of central government lay in the *Lawlands* and were conducted through the medium of Scots which also gave the language an identity at national level before 1707. The vast majority of *Lawland* people were also Presbyterian, and, as I shall outline, Scots was the preferred language of Presbyterian preachers. The Englishman Edward Burt was struck by the way in which language was an important ethnic marker in Scotland, and also by the influence which the Church of Scotland exerted in this respect. During the 1720s he commented:

> This Rule wherby to denominate themselves, they borrow from the Kirk, which, in all its Acts and Ordinances distinguishes the Lowlands from the Highlands by the Language generally spoken by

of Tudor and Stuart Britain (Oxford and New York, 1996), pp. 74–89. See also Jane Dawson, 'Anglo-Scottish Protestant culture and integration in sixteenth century Britain', in Steven G. Ellis and Sarah Barber (eds), *Conquest and union: fashioning a British state, 1485–1725* (London and New York, 1995), pp. 87–114.   6 Under the terms of the Good Friday Agreement and Council of Europe Charter for Regional or Minority Languages.   7 These questions include the manufacture of Scots prose to look as different from English as possible, but which also looks alien to genuine speakers of the language.

the Inhabitants, whether the Parish or District lies in the High or Low Country.[8]

It is also noteworthy that Scots was the medium of anti-union and pro-Jacobite writings in the eighteenth century which in itself is a political statement considering that English was an option by that time. Such writing served to reinforce the link between Scots speaking and Scottish national and political identity. Therefore, Scots speakers, identified with a fixed geographical area, an administration, and espousing their own religion – often quite militantly – stood out as a distinct polity within the British Isles and Europe. Their involvement in Ireland represented the expansion of this polity.

When James VI added England and Ireland to his inheritance in 1603, Scots was the undoubted language of state in Scotland. Yet, in two articles on the Scots language in Ulster, Kevin McCafferty has claimed that the heyday of *written* Scots was over by that time.[9] Manifestly, of course, that was not so. What *is* true is that by 1603 it was apparent that the language of England was exerting a growing influence on the *written* language of the Lowlands, through the medium of printing. However, Scots – both spoken and written – continued as an administrative and official language as long as Scotland existed as a separate kingdom with its own institutions. This was so in 1650 and substantially so in 1707. For example, there are references to the appointment of different secretaries for business in the Scots, Latin and French languages in the Scottish government.[10] By the early 1700s spoken Scots was giving way, among the nobility, to a language which approximated the language of England. By 1760, the language of all classes below the nobility was still ordinarily Scots, in public, in the courts, in the kirk session[11] and elsewhere. This would not begin to be seriously undermined until the nineteenth century with the introduction of centralized education which insisted on spoken as well as written English.

Then, as now, people debated the status of their forms of speech. Questions of possible Anglo-Scottish Union naturally concentrated the minds

8 R. Jamieson (ed.), *Burt's letters from the North of Scotland with an introduction*, i (Edinburgh, 1876), p. 35. Burt was employed by General Wade in Scotland during the years 1724–28.   9 Kevin McCafferty, 'Frae "wile norn aksints" tae oor ain national leid?', *Causeway* (spring and summer 1996), 453–83. McCafferty asserts that James VI 'stopped writing the language as soon as he took himself and his court to London' (ibid., 63). James continued to use Scots – on occasions – but it should come as no surprise that a king living in England should primarily employ the language of the country he resided in. His son Charles I sometimes had documents issued in his name written in Scots when dealing with Scottish affairs; undoubtedly this depended on those secretaries who were available at the time.   10 See John Spotswood, *The history of the Church of Scotland, beginning the year of our Lord 203, and continued to the end of the reign of King James the VI of ever blessed memory*, ed. Robert Peters (London 1655; 1972), p. 379 for appointments in 1589.   11 The English equivalent of the 'kirk session' is 'parish council'.

of men on the two languages of state. It was common then to refer to Scots
and English as either two dialects or two languages, depending on the argument of the individual, but it is important to remember that the concept of
the language of England as the standard and the language of Lowland
Scotland as a variant, had not yet been born. It is also worth noting, by way
of comparison, that contemporary Norwegian was classed as a Danish dialect
because of the Kalmar Union, and the language of the Netherlands was known
interchangeably as *Dietch* ('German') or *Nederlands* just as Scots was variously called *Inglis* or *Scottis*. Therefore, if the identity of Scots was not always
clear cut, Scots speakers were not alone in Europe.

The Englishman Henry Saville, in discussing possible union in 1604,
referred to the Scots and northern English as speaking a less corrupted language than the southern English and described Scots and English as dialects
of *Germane*.[12] The same writer regarded Scots and English as differing as
much as Castillian and Portuguese,[13] while Thomas Chamberlayne, an
Englishman who had served in Russia, wrote in 1631 that the Polish and
Russians were "not so much more divident in Language then the English and
the Scotts is".[14] In the introduction to his *Etymological English Dictionary* of
1730 Nathan Bailey described *English*, *Scotch* and *Frizian* as distinct branches
of *Saxon* comprising one dialect of *Teutonick*. This example should also alert
us to the fact that the word *dialect* did not carry the negative non-standard
connotations of today.[15] There was also an awareness of a clear distinction
between the two traditions as is illustrated by a letter of Sir Thomas Lake to
William Cecil in 1605 concerning the works of King James VI which were
being printed as a *Collection*. Lake informed Cecil that

> The language his Majesty doth also excuse, being neither good Scottish
> nor English, but lays that to the transcriber's fault.[16]

When Edward Burt first arrived in Edinburgh, in 1724, he found the
spoken language very different from English, and was sometimes at a loss.
Indeed, he was once given directions in the city but declared 'This Direction
in a Language I hardly understood ...'; this was not merely a different accent,
but a whole range of constructions, idioms and vocabulary which he con-

12 Bruce R. Galloway & Brian P. Leveck (eds), *The Jacobean union: six tracts of 1604* (Scottish
History Society, Edinburgh, 1985), p. 213. 13 Ibid., p. 230. 14 S. Konovalov, 'Thomas
Chamberlyne's Description of Russia, 1631', *Oxford Slavonic Papers*, 1954, p. 115. 15 John
Algeo (ed.), *Problems in the origins and development of the English language* (New York, 1993),
pp. 226–7. 16 G.P.V. Akrigg (ed.), *Letters of James VI and I* (California, 1984), p. 259.
Historical Manuscripts Commission [HMC], *Calendar of the manuscripts of the most honourable
the marquess of Salisbury, preserved at Hatfield House, Hertfordshire, Part XVII*, ed. M.S. Giuseppi
(London, 1938), pp. 17, 298.

stantly cited in his letters back home to England. It is evident that, as an Englishman, Burt found the language of Lowland Scotland *alien*.[17] I have also discussed elsewhere the use and recognition of Scots as a language of diplomacy in the Netherlands, North Germany and Scandinavia, where official translators for the Scots language were employed by the respective governments.[18] The significant difference between Scots as employed in Scotland and Scots as employed in Ulster was one of status. In Scotland it was official, but in Ulster it was not. As John Kirk explains:

> As it developed in Ulster from the seventeenth century onwards, Scots never enjoyed the reinforcement of political autonomy which had given mainland Scots its earlier status as a language; it never performed in Ulster any of the legal, legislative or other institutional, formal or performative functions it had in Scotland.[19]

Though broadly speaking this is true, strictly-speaking it is not, for in the seventeenth century Scots was recognised out of necessity by the royal council sitting in Dublin. In a now well-known reference, dated June 1624, the council decided to appoint a clerk to deal with Scottish petitions since those 'written in the Scotch hand are either not read or understood.' The Scottish settlers petitioned that Mr Patrick Hannby should be appointed, 'he well knowing the customs of the Scots and English, having been servant to the late earl of Dunbar ...' It is also evident that letters and petitions written in Scots formed part of the correspondence with Irish officialdom between *c.*1545 and *c.*1640.[20]

TWO COMMUNITIES OR ONE?

Today it is common to speak of an Ulster-Scots community, but did such a concept exist in the minds of men within this period? Was 'Ulsterness' a separate identity at once related to but distinct from Scottishness, and did the Scots-descended people of Ulster regard their speech as a separate language? It can be argued that they regarded Scotland as the mother country and as speaking one and the same language. Certainly, the vocabulary used to describe the language of Lowland Scotland and Ulster is identical. Yet, at one time, the memory of this seventeenth century expansion seems to have

---

17 Jamieson, *Burt's Letters*, p. 23.   18 See Dauvit Horsbroch, 'Nostra Vulgari Lingua: Scots as a European language, 1500–1700', *Scottish Language*, 18 (1999), 1–16.   19 John M. Kirk, 'Ulster Scots: realities and myths', *Ulster Folklife*, 44 (1998), 69–93; see p. 75.   20 Charles W. Russell and John P. Prendergast (eds), *Calendar of the state papers relating to Ireland, of the Reign of James I, 1615–1625* (London, 1880), p. 502

been virtually forgotten. Writing in 1836, Sir Samuel Ferguson, an Ulster poet, wrote: 'It is remarkable that the recollection of the mother country is scarcely if at all cherished; yet there is a perfect similarity of habits and disposition.'[21] However, it was not this Protestant seventeenth-century expansion which first brought the Scots language to Ulster.

GAELS, PLANTERS, AND ULSTER-SCOTCH, 1545–1760

It is perhaps an irony of history, at least from a nationalist, Irish-speaking point of view, that it was Gaelic speakers who first brought the Scots language to Ulster, by 1545, and possibly before. This is an important point which has been largely forgotten in the polarization of the pro-Irish language and pro-Scots language communities within Ulster. The earliest surviving documents written in Scots and relating to Ireland all belong within a Gaelic context. This should not be regarded as strange but merely reflects the status of Scots as a language of the Scottish court and administration; it was natural that Scottish Gaels should employ Scots, the sister tongue of English, when dealing with representatives of the English crown in Ireland. The earliest of such documents of which I am aware is a letter addressed to the English privy council by Donald of the Isles and dated 5 August 1545 at Carrickfergus.[22] The same lord and his followers swore an oath to Henry VIII – in Scots – at the castle of Carrickfergus on the same day.[23] On 24 January 1546/7 James Macdonell of Antrim and the Glens and Ewen Allan of Locheil both addressed letters in Scots – dated at Ardnamurchan and Inverlochy – to the privy council sitting at Kilmaynan near Dublin.[24] When Alasdair Og Macdonnell, a Scottish Gaelic Redshank, wrote to Captain Piers, governor of Carrickfergus, in December 1566, it was in a full-blooded Scots.[25] A letter of Shane O'Neill, written to Cormac O'Conner, then in Scotland, in March 1567/8, was translated from Irish Gaelic into both contemporary English and Scots, and the differences between the two are striking.[26] Similarly, Agnes

21 Linde Lunney, 'Ulster attitudes to Scottishness: the eighteenth century and after', in Ian S. Wood (ed.), *Scotland and Ulster* (Edinburgh, 1994), p. 57.   22 The surviving copy contains some English forms in Scots spelling – such as *moir* (more) – but it is undoubtedly Scots. See *State papers of King Henry VIII Part IV continued: Correspondence relative to Scotland and the borders, 1534–1546* (London, 1836), pp. 483–4. In Scots Carrickfergus is known as *Craigfergus*. 23 Ibid., pp. 484–5. There are also other examples on pp. 501–5.   24 *State papers King Henry VIII Part II continued: Correspondence between the governments of England and Ireland 1538–1546* (London, 1834), pp. 548–50. There is, in addition, a letter of 13 May 1546 from Rory Ranaldson and Patrick MacLean addressed from 'Deblin' to Henry VIII in a curious mixture of English and Scots forms. See ibid., pp. 567–8.   25 For the text of this see *Ulster Journal of Archaeology*, VII (Belfast, 1859), p. 61.   26 For the three versions see Roland M. Smith, 'Shane O'Neill's last letter', *Journal of Celtic Studies*, 2 (1958), 131–3.

Campbell, wife of Turlough O'Neill, addressed a letter in Scots from County Tyrone to Elizabeth I of England in 1571.[27] The strong connection between Scots-speaking and Scottish identity is illustrated in a chronicle entry for the year 1594 which described James MacConell's visit to Edinburgh when he was knighted by James VI:

> This Sir James wes ane Scottis man of bluid, albeit his landis lyis in Yrland. He wes ane braw man of persone and behaviour, bot had nocht the Scottis tong, nor na language bot Eirse.'[28]

By descent Sir James was regarded as a Scot even though he was technically subject to the English crown, and even though he did not have the *Scottis tong*, which the author has emphasized. Clearly, at that period, it was expected that a knowledge of Scots would not necessarily be alien to a Gael, as the documentary record demonstrates. The Plantation of Ulster in 1610 – from a linguistic perspective – built upon the previous forty years' use of Scots by settling Lowland Scots in the province. North Down and East Antrim were not included in the Plantation since they were already settled by Scots anyway, a fact which had presented a security threat to the English crown. Now Scots began to emerge as a recognizable speech community in Ulster consolidated in part upon the written tradition already established by Scottish Gaels. Indeed, the seventeenth century may be regarded as the period of the greatest geographical expansion of the Scots language within the British Isles moving into Ulster, Orkney and Shetland.

But were the Scots speakers in Ulster regarded as a distinct political community in this period? The answer is yes and no. Yes, they were looked on as forming a group distinct from the Gaels and from the Anglo-Irish – and also from the new Protestant English – but, no, they were not a *Scotch-Irish* polity which later American history would distinguish. They were regarded in most respects as an extension of Scotland in general, and Lowland Scotland in particular. When first offered land in Ulster in 1609 some Scots were worried that they would be dispersed among the English but the Secretary Alexander Hay wrote to the privy council of Scotland informing them although the Scots would not be planted *en masse* 'some nowmer of Scottismen wilbe ever togither'.[29] Therefore the Scots, from the start, were concerned that they should

---

27 See Michael B. Montgomery & Robert J. Gregg, 'The Scots language in Ulster' in Charles Jones (ed.), *The Edinburgh history of the Scots language* (Edinburgh, 1997), p. 586. In this connection it is interesting to note that Scots is among those languages which Elizabeth I is stated to have spoken in 1578: see *Florio His First Fruites: a perfect introduction to the Italian and English tongues*, Imprinted for Thomas Dawson for Thomas Woodcocke, at London, 1578.   28 J.W. MacKenzie (ed.), *A chronicle of the kings of Scotland from Fergus the First to James the Sixth, in the year MDCCCXXX* (Edinburgh, 1830), p. 157.   29 *The register of the privy council of Scotland, [RPCS], volume VIII, 1607–10*, ed. D. Masson (Edinburgh, 1887), p. 793.

form a distinct Scottish community in Ireland. In other words, Lowland
Scotland in Ulster. In May 1638 the Venetian ambassador to the Stuart court,
Francesco Zonca, wrote the following illuminative letter to the Doge and
Senate on the subject of the National Covenant:

> They have sent the proposals to Scotland, whence news has lately come
> that those registered in the union number over 400,000, to which are
> added the inhabitants of the northern part of Ireland, who profess the
> same faith, and are Scots by origin, settled there and only separated
> by a short stretch of water.[30]

In the aftermath of the Irish uprising of 1641 the Scots in Scotland
regarded the settlers as fellow countrymen in danger. On 1 February 1642
the privy council of Scotland referred to 'our countrey men thair'[31] while the
governor and mayor of Derry, along with the English inhabitants, complained
James Butler, first marquis of Ormonde, in 1644 that the Covenanters there
were interfering with the liberties of the kingdom stirred up by 'ministers
sent out of Scotland.'[32] John Wilson, recorder of Derry, wrote to Ormonde
in June 1668 about two distinct interests in the town, one *Scotch* and the
other English, and in 1679, writing to Michael Boyle the chancellor, Wilson
described the Presbyterians as integral to the doings of their '... brethren in
Scotland.'.[33] The Reverend Patrick Adair, who ministered in Ulster for 48
years, writing in the 1670s, spoke of the 'Scotch nation in Ireland' and of the
sufferings of the 'Scotch nation' in Tyrone and Derry during the 1640s.[34]
Individuals born and bred in Ireland continued to define themselves as Scots.
One such was Colonel Hugh Hamilton whose parents were Scottish settlers.
In 1653 he appeared before the Swedish *Riksråd* (royal council) during which
the stenographer recorded that Hamilton held a discussion in the council with
another Scot, Robert Buchan, in the Scots language.[35] As an illustration of
the modern attitude towards Scots, a transcription of a letter by Hamilton,
dated January 1662 is described as written in 'bad English' by the transcriber
in *Calendar of State Papers Ireland*. Evidently the English or Irish transcriber
did not allow for Hamilton's first language being Scots.[36] One other reference is illustrative of attitudes towards the identity of Ulster folk. In 1654,
during Middleton's rising in Scotland, Sir James Turner, then in command

30 *Calendar of state papers Venetian, volume XXIV, 1636–1639*, ed. A.B. Hinds (London, 1923),
p. 407.   31 *RPCS, vii, 1638–1643*, ed. P.H Brown (Edinburgh, 1906), p. 189.   32 *HMC, 14th
Report, Appendix, Part VII, The manuscripts of the marquis of Ormonde, preserved at the castle,
Kilkenny*, i (London, 1895), p. 91.   33 *HMC*, ibid., pp. 100, 101.   34 Charles A. Hanna, *The
Scotch Irish*, i (New York and London, 1902), pp. 353, 354.   35 S. Bergh, *Svenska Riksrådets
Protokoll*, 15 (Stockholm, 1920) p. 425.   36 *Calendar of state papers Ireland, 1660–1662* (London,
1905), p. 186.

of a detachment captured 'Johnston, a Scot, bot born in Ireland' to whom he gave quarter, but who was later killed. Regardless of birth, such men could be, and were, regarded as ethnic Scots and not as separate *Ulster-Scotch*.[37]

The terms *Scotch-Irish*, and Ulster Scots, are both relatively recent. The first is an eighteenth-century American term referring to those ethnic Scots who crossed from Ulster to the American colonies. The second – as a term embracing the whole of Ulster – is decidedly twentieth century and represents the search by those of a Unionist persuasion for a uniting identity and language in distinction from Irish language and identity. As post-eighteenth-century terms they are valid enough, but are inappropriate to a period in which Scots in Ulster regarded Scotland as the mother country.

Between 1690 and 1697 some 50,000 Scots settled in Ireland which ensured that close links were not only renewed but Scottish identity was strengthened.[38] But the Scots-speaking Presbyterians of Ulster laboured under a disadvantage unknown in Scotland; in 1704 the Test Act, approved by Queen Anne, required all public officers to take communion according to the rites of the Episcopal Church. All Presbyterians resigned their offices and were effectively excluded from parliament and public office. This came at the same time as the Alien Act, passed in England, and directed against Scotland. England, at war with Louis XIV, and on bad terms with Scotland, was fearful of Scottish intentions, which included the Scottish population in Ulster so recently increased. One result of this exclusion was emigration to the American colonies. By 1728 emigration by Nonconformists from Ulster to America – mostly Presbyterians – was significant, and the government tried unsuccessfully to stem it hoping to retain Protestants as a buffer against the majority Catholic population. Nonetheless, significant migration to the American colonies now paved the way for the emergence of a new group in history, the *Scotch-Irish*.

It was at this time that letters and pamphlets – written in Scots – were directed back home from the colonies. While their purpose is not altogether apparent, they do represent a reinforcement of the Scots-speaking identity of Ulstermen in common with Lowland Scots.[39] For example, the Scots language in Ulster continued to stand distinct from English. As late as 1756 the *Belfast Newsletter*, a newspaper of the period, printed a notice regarding an apprentice from Newtonards in North Down who had absconded and could be recognized outside the area on account of the fact he 'speaks the Scotch tongue'.[40] Something which would, of course, have been unremarkable in Scotland.

---

37 *Memoirs of his life and times by Sir James Turner, 1632–1670 from the original manuscript* (Edinburgh, 1829), p. 111. 38 *Ulster Journal of Archaeology*, VI (1858). 39 Montgomery & Gregg, 'The Scots language in Ulster', pp. 592–3. 40 Philip Robinson, *Ulster-Scots: a grammar of the traditional written and spoken language* (hereafter *Grammar*) (Belfast, 1997), p. 13.

WRITTEN AND SPOKEN IDENTITIES

During the seventeenth century the trend towards adopting spelling conventions more usual to writing in English was accelerated. Keith Williamson has summed up this change in the written language in the following terms:

> The process might very broadly be described as a shift from a fairly full Scots through an anglicized Scots to a Scotticized English.[41]

As outlined above, the early Scots settlers in Ulster naturally brought their language with them, building on the use of Scots by Gaels over the previous sixty years. For example, the letters of Archibald Edmonstone of Duntreath, who settled in Ballycarry, Antrim in 1609, and dated between 1609 and 1631, demonstrate that the writers were used to conducting all kinds of business through Scots.[42] Scots in high office within the Irish administration also employed the language in the early days. For example, Malcolm Hamilton, archbishop of Cashel, and primate of Ireland, issued certificates in a language mixing Scots and English forms together.[43] The general transformation of the written language happened in Ulster much more rapidly, presumably because the administration was already established in English. However, written English could be, and was, pronounced as Scots which perhaps explains why there was no great dissatisfaction; when Scots speakers did complain, it was about particular vocabulary, rather than spelling. After a relative period of dearth in the late seventeenth century, written Scots underwent a revival, principally for poetry. Writers such as Allan Ramsay in Scotland, and William Starrat in Ulster, are, arguably, representative of an alternative view of language – beginning around 1715 – which regarded Scots as an important expression of Scottish identity in the aftermath of Union. In Ulster men such as Francis Boyle from County Down followed in the footsteps of Starrat and wrote poetry in Scots from about 1730.[44] And these writers were conscious of each others' work, corresponded, and wrote in a common language which they universally called *Scotch*, and, on occasions, *Doric*.[45] Their work and the popular songs of the period were distributed far and wide and consumed by an eager public. William Donaldson explains the process:

41 Keith Williamson, 'Lowland Scots in education: an historical survey, Part I', *Scottish Language* (autumn 1983), no. 1, p. 57.   42 Montgomery and Gregg, *The Scots language in Ulster*, pp. 587–8; and HMC, *Report on manuscripts in various collections*, v (London, 1909), pp. 112–140.   43 HMC, *14th Report, Appendix Part III, The manuscripts of the duke of Roxburghe; Sir HH Campbell, Bart; the earl of Strathmore; and the countess dowager of Seafield* (London, 1894), pp. 79–80.   44 Billy Kay, 'The Scots ower the sheuch', *Scotland and Ulster* (Edinburgh, 1994), p. 90.   45 Ramsay was the first to use the name *Doric* in relation to Scots.

> Broadsides were the main vehicle of commercial popular song during
> the first half of the eighteenth century. They were printed, usually
> fairly crudely, in double columns on large sheets with decorated bor-
> ders and woodcut designs ... They were sold in urban areas by pro-
> fessional street-singers and distributed throughout the country by pack-
> men and pedlers of the lower sort.[46]

The broadsheets were now written according to the spelling conventions of
England, and with some English grammatical constructions, but it is clear from
the rhyming schemes that words were intended to be pronounced a Scots way.
As Philip Robinson has commented, poets writing in Scots in Ulster,

> since the 1700s, have consciously written verse with a fuller Ulster-
> Scots vocabulary than later writers, while at the same time preferring
> English rules of grammar and sentence construction.[47]

One of the reasons for the continuing support of literary Scots in the eighteenth century was the fact that schooling was conducted through the medium
of the language in both Scotland and Ulster. One Ulsterman, Morgan Jellett,
from the end of this period recalled in his memoirs 'My early education was
one which a country school master, who spoke broad Scotch, could be
expected to impart'.[48] Only from the second half of the nineteenth century
with the advent of centralized education – which increasingly demanded abil-
ity in spoken English – can we chart in detail the gradual divorce between
the written and spoken forms of Scots which has resulted in the mistaken
idea that Scots equals illiteracy.[49]

'ANE GODLIE EXHORTATIOUN': PREACHING IN SCOTS

In 1996 the Reverend Andrew Herron, a former moderator of the General
Assembly of the Church of Scotland, wrote:

> 'braid Scots' was not at any time the language in which Scots folk
> offered their worship. When the Scot of yester-year prepared himself

46 William Donaldson, *The Jacobite song: political myth and national identity* (Aberdeen, 1988),
p. 25.   47 Robinson, *Grammar* pp. 5–6.   48 The Public Record Office, Northern Ireland (D
2777/1a–b), *Extracts from the anecdotal recollections of Morgan Jellett*. Morgan Jellett was born
in Moira, County Down, in 1769 and wrote his *Recollections c.*1830.   49 For an outline history of Scots as a medium of education in Scotland, the story of which is beyond the scope of
this present article, see previously cited Keith Williamson, 'Lowland Scots In education: an
historical survey', in *Scottish Language: An Annual Review*, 1 (autumn 1982), pp. 54–77; 2
(autumn 1983), pp. 52–87 (Edinburgh, 1982, 1983).

for the kirk, he laid aside his workin' claes in favour of his Sunday best, and by the same token he turned his back on the language of the stack-yard and the stable ...[50]

The problem with this statement is the annoying habit of historical fact to get in the way of pejorative and anachronistic opinions. What is striking about the period under discussion – striking because we are not used to it today – is how commonly Scots was employed as a medium of preaching and worship. As well as surviving texts of sermons,[51] there are many references to preaching in Scots even as late as the nineteenth century.[52] Due to the fact that the Bible was never fully translated into Scots, and because sermons were often 'Englished' (to use the *parlance* of the time) for publication, in order to appeal to the wider English readership, it has simply been assumed that services were conducted in English.[53] Such an assumption springs from interpreting only *written* (largely *printed*) evidence, to the exclusion of contemporary descriptions. It is clear that Presbyterianism was inseparable from Lowland political identity at this time, and, indeed, contemporary commentators often testify to the close relationship between the established Church of Scotland and preaching in Scots. There are many instances. About the year 1615 an Englishman visiting Orkney – where Norse was giving way to Scots – noted the style of a Scottish service:

tis nothing strange to here them in the churches leave their text and raile in person against this or that man and speake plaine Scots wordes against those who set in their stoole of repentance.'[54]

In the 1692 pamphlet entitled *The Scotch Presbyterian Eloquence* ministers are ridiculed by Episcopalians for preaching in Scots. The reply to this – *An Answer* – defended the use of what was called 'our dialect' since it was better

50 *Life and work*, August 1996, p. 5.   51 See, for example, the recently discovered sermons (1623–50) of David Lindsay, minister of Belhelvie in Aberdeenshire, held in the National Archives of Scotland, Edinburgh, of which the present author intends to make further study. 52 For example, the eminent Dr Chalmers – later first moderator of the Free Church of Scotland – preached in the language of the 'stack-yard and stable' in 1817. In that year T.H. Wightman heard him preach in Glasgow and commented: 'A stranger who had never heard of his fame, did he happen to hear him commencing the service, with a broad Scotch dialect ... would not be disposed to form the most flattering opinion of him': The Public Record Office, Northern Ireland: serial 9006049, 26 Dec. 1817. 53 Certainly there were Scots preachers noted for their use of English within this period. For example, Zachary Boyd, minister of Barony parish in Glasgow, 1623–1653, comes into this category, but even his printed works are sprinkled throughout with Scots vocabulary. It was precisely their use of English which arguably set them apart as unusual. See David W. Aitken (ed.), *Selected sermons of Zachary Boyd* (Aberdeen, 1989). 54 Keith Williamson, 'Lowland Scots In Education', p. 57.

understood by the people of Scotland than the English text.[55] An English visitor to Edinburgh in 1705 was struck by the language and commented:

> The Minister made such a prodigious noise in broad Scotch, and beat his Pulpit so violently, that he seem'd better qualified for a Drummer than a Parson.[56]

That this was substantially the case among the older clergy in the eighteenth century is alluded to by Edward Burt in the 1720s who commented that 'the young Ministers are introducing a Manner more decent and reasonable, which irritates the old stagers against them',[57] while James Buchanan in 1757 commented of the Scots in general:

> Their acquiring a proper accent and graceful pronunciation, would embellish and set off to far greater advantage the many excellent and rhetorical speeches delivered by the learned both from the pulpit and at the bar.[58]

It was the rise of the so-called Moderate Party, within the kirk of Scotland, from the 1750s onwards, which led directly to the decline of preaching through Scots, though, undoubtedly, the pattern varied from region to region. The flavour of one of these sermons can be sampled from that preached in the cathedral church of St Giles, at Edinburgh in 1638, and subsequently famed as the *Pockmanty Sermon* because it was taken for reading material during journeys. In its day (and into the eighteenth century) it was a best-seller precisely because it was in Scots. The minister, Row, declared:

> First, the Kirk of Scotland is wounded in her head, shee has gotten sik a clash in her head as has gart all her harns japp, and her senses … The Kirk of Scotland was a bony Naig, but then shee trotted sae hard, that never a man durst ryd her; but the Bishops wha after they had gotten on her back corce langled her, and hopshaikled her, and when shee becam a bony paceing beast they tooke great pleasure to ryde on her.'[59]

Undoubtedly, forms such as *head*, *was* and *after* were pronounced as *heid*, *wes* and *efter*. According to the Reverend Herron this text should not exist. It is

55 Ibid.   56 *A journey to Edenborough in Scotland by Joseph Taylor, late of the Inner Temple, esq.* (Edinburgh, 1903), p. 137.   57 Jamieson, *Burt's letters* p. 185.   58 Charles Jones, *A language suppressed: the pronunciation of the Scots language in the 18th century* (Edinburgh, 1995), p. 13.   59 James Maidment (ed.), *Memorials of the family of Row* (Edinburgh, 1828), pp. 21, 23. A version printed at London in 1642 is far more anglicized.

also clear that paraphrasing of English texts was common in order for the congregation to better understand. One of the complaints at the time Charles I tried to introduce his new Prayer Book in the 1630s was the importation of vocabulary from England which was unknown in Scotland. Objections were made against the new metaphrase of the psalms because

> ... the people must be first taught to vnderstand these and the lyk French, Latine, and hard Englisch tearmes, and harsh phrases ... Our awin metaphrase hath non bot such may be understood, except tuo or three that war wele knowin to that tyme when the psalms war translated in meeter, and may be easilie changed. Bot to bring in a number of words which have need of a dictionarie in the end of the metaphrase, is to mak worse and not better.[60]

Among the words included as unknown to the ordinary Lowland Scot were *regall, opposites, various, gratefullie, divulge, exorbitant, impetuous* and *emulate*.[61] That the ordinary people did have problems with English-derived vocabulary can be illustrated in one instance. In the 1660s Sir John Lauder of Fountainhall commented on catechising:

> Mr J. Smith, Minister of the Colledge Kirk, examining a bonnet maker, of whilk theirs a great number in his parish, he speared at him what was effectual calling; the fellow clawing his head, replied, the feeklesest calling I keen, Sir, is my oune.[62]

Evidently the bonnet maker confused the word *effectual* with the Scots *feckless* meaning 'lifeless' or 'poor'. In other words, he thought the minister was asking him what was the poorest occupation. Even in the early eighteenth century such confusion was still an issue among some Lowland Scots. In 1703 the Reverend James Kirkwood, in the course of writing about the difficulties of employing an Irish Bible for Scottish Gaelic speakers, made the observation:

> Does not everybody know that in our English Bibles there are severall hundred words and phrases not vulgarly used nor understood by a great many in Scotland who have no other Translation.[63]

The fact that there is no torrent of comment on Scots preaching from within Scotland is perhaps evidence in itself that it was everyday and unre-

60 Sir W. Scott, D. Laing & T. Thomson (eds), *The Bannatyne miscellany: containing original papers and tracts, chiefly relating to the history and literature of Scotland*, i (Edinburgh, 1827), pp. 240–1. 61 Ibid. 62 Donald Crawford (ed.), *Journals of Sir John Lauder Lord Fountainhall with his observations on public affairs and other memoranda, 1665–1676* (Edinburgh, 1900), p. 127. 63 Victor Edward Durkacz, *The decline of the Celtic languages* (Edinburgh, 1983), p. 23.

markable. It was visitors to Scotland, only used to reading English versions of Calvinist sermons, who were struck by the significant differences between the printed and spoken word in Scotland.

The first Presbyterian preacher to settle in Ulster was Edward Bryce, from Drymen near Loch Lomond, who took up the charge at Ballycarry (or Broadisland) in Antrim and served from 1613 until 1636. He was soon followed by a trickle of Presbyterians fleeing the imposition of bishops and the ratification of the Articles of Perth by the Scottish Estates in 1621. But it was not until the arrival of the Covenanting army under Robert Monro in 1642 that Presbytery began to be formally organized in Ulster, and, at that point, it was an extension of Scottish Calvinism in Ireland. Much of the details of this, and the progress of the war in Ulster, is based on Patrick Adair's *Narrative*. Adair is perhaps the best known of the early Presbyterian ministers in Ulster. He served as minister at Cairncastle near Larne from 1646–1674 and then of Belfast from 1674 until he died in 1694. In common with ministers in Scotland, some of those in Ulster also appear to have preached in Scots, despite the English texts which were ordinarily issued for publication. It has been commented that:

> Ulster Scots may have been replaced by English in the writing of clergymen, but did not necessarily disappear from their sermons; Patrick Adair (d.1694) is said to have been accustomed to preaching in it ...[64]

That this was indeed the case – that preaching in Scots or an approximate of Scots was common – may be inferred from broadsheets of the early eighteenth century. For example, the *North-Country Man's Description*, a pamphlet from 1733 which describes two Ulster seamen in search of a Presbyterian kirk in Dublin, but who find only an Anglican church:

> When first I ged in, I ged doon a great place that a' the Floor was cover'd we bread Stens, and a Warld o ' Foke gaing up and doon thro' yen another. We cam tell twa great Stairs, and ged under them, whar was a Door gaing in. This place was amest foo o' Foke; as well aboon as whar I was, this they cad the Kirk ...[65]

Another example, the *Baptist Boyd Letter*, printed in the *Virginia Gazette* and the *Pennsylvania Gazette* in 1737, purports to be addressed to the Reverend Baptist Boyd in Aughnacloy, Tyrone, and is full of Scots.[66] These,

---

64 Montgomery and Gregg, 'The Scots language in Ulster', p. 590. See W.D. Killen (ed.), *A true narrative of the rise and progress of the Presbyterian Church in Ireland by the Reverend Patrick Adair* (Belfast, 1866).   65 Montgomery and Gregg, 'The Scots language in Ulster', p. 593.   66 Ibid., pp. 592–3.

and other examples, poked fun at Presbyterians but are good evidence of the close relationship between that religion, Scottish identity, and preaching in the Scots language.

A LANGUAGE RECLASSIFIED

What is significant about the abortive negotiations for Anglo-Scottish political Union during 1604–7, in distinction to the successful incorporating union negotiations of 1706–7, is that language formed part of the debate. It is interesting to note, for example, that prior to 1603 James VI was quite supportive of the integrity of the Scots language. In the 1580s he described Scots and English as related but separate languages which followed different rules, at least in the realm of poetry, and at the Burntisland Assembly of 1601 was in favour of a new (presumably Scotticized) translation of the Bible and revision of the psalms.[67] His advice to his heir, Prince Henry, also touched upon language and it is clear that James had Scots as his model in the 1590s. He advised Henry that:

> in your langage be plaine, honest naturall, cumlie, clene shorte + sententiouse escheuing baith the extremities alsueill in not using a rusticall corrupt leid, nor yett booke langage + penn + inkorne terms ... I ualde also aduyse you to uritte in youre awin langage for thaire is nathing left to be said in græke + latin ...[68]

However, this commitment to Henry's 'awin langage' faltered after 1603. On becoming 'his imperial majesty' of Britain James had new political objectives which included the merging of the Scots and English languages, and, indeed, emphasising similarity. During his speech to the English parliament of 19 March 1603/4 he declared: 'Hath not God first vnited these two kingdomes both in Language, Religion, and Similitude of maners? Yea, hath hee not made vs all in one Island ...'[69] Manifestly this argument ignored the fact that many of his subjects spoke one or other of the Celtic languages – or even Norwegian in the Northern Isles – but James had English and Scots in mind precisely because they were *both* the languages of political power. Developing this line of argument further Sir Thomas Craig in 1604 wrote:

> In connection with the present union it is unneccessary to discuss identity of language, seeing that both peoples use the same speech; though,

67 James Craigie (ed.), *The poems of King James VI of Scotland*, i (Edinburgh and London, 1955), p. lxxvii. 68 James Craigie (ed.), *The Basilikon Doron of King James VI*, i (Edinburgh and London, 1955), pp. 178–9. 69 *James I The Workes* (1616), facsimile (New York, 1971), p. 486.

if our neighbours will allow me to say so, the Scottish vernacular is more akin to Old English than is the language spoken in England to-day. For the English, admitting new words from neighbouring languages, Latin, French, and Italian, with the object of strengthening it, have corrupted their own.[70]

Craig was at pains to emphasize similarity in order to further a political purpose (*in connection with the present union*) but all the same had to qualify what he was saying. Evidently something which set the vernaculars of Scotland and England apart, at least as a perception, was Scots holding true to the 'ancient' language while English imported foreign terms; Scots was increasingly seen as conservative.

It is clear from the comparisons being cited, that Scots and English were commonly considered on equal terms; there is no suggestion that the language of England is standard and the language of Lowland Scotland a variant. By the late seventeenth century, however, the idea was present that Scots was better fitted to some areas of life and English to others. In 1673 Sir George MacKenzie of Rosehaugh, a Scottish lawyer and future lord advocate, echoing the idea that Scots and English were sister tongues, described 'the Scottish idiom of the British tongue' as better suited to using in legal courts than English, and speaking of the English in general, commented 'their language is invented by courtiers, and may be softer, but ours by learned men and men of business'. The implication is clear; Scots was still the language of business and learning, but English had triumphed at the royal court because it was now based in England; English was increasingly seen as innovative.[71]

The removal of the Scottish parliament and privy council meant there were no longer *political* bodies in which Scots could be the *lingua franca*. Scots sitting at Westminster rapidly conformed to the language of England. Between the Union of 1707 and the mid-eighteenth century Scots was reclassified as a provincial dialect: there could not be two languages of state in the new kingdom of Great Britain. This is an eighteenth-century ideology which manifested as a logical outcome of the political Union, at least to its supporters. As one linguist has commented:

> The linguistic concerns so typical of the Enlightenment had important political, as well as social ramifications. Political events in Scotland throughout the 18th century had contributed to movements embracing both linguistic and cultural uniformity and diversity.[72]

70 C. Sanford Terry (ed.), *De Unione Regnorum Britanniae Tractatus by Sir Thomas Craig* (Edinburgh, 1909), p. 288. Translated from Latin the original describes the Lowland language as 'nostra hodie vernacula Lingua ...' p. 61.   71 Billy Kay, *Scots the mither tongue* (Alloway Publishing, 1993), p. 82.   72 Jones, *A Language suppresse*, p. 7.

As a result of this reclassification of Scots, and the erosion of its national status, some Scots speakers fell back on their own regional dialects which further helped to classify Scots as 'provincial'. Indeed, Alexander Ross, writing in the mid-eighteenth century, was among the earliest to articulate an explicit identification with region when he wrote 'Speak my ain leed, 'tis gueed auld Scots I mean/ Your Southern gnaps I count not worth a preen.'[73] Scots would cease to be a political language in the eighteenth century – at least in formal situations – but the language remained, spoken by the majority, in both Lowland Scotland, and Scottish Ulster, and would continue to be a defining factor of Lowland identity, if not of Scotland as a whole.

CONCLUSION

English, Irish and Scottish historians need to look more objectively at the social and political history of the Scots language and compare and contrast it with the positions of both Irish and Scottish Gaelic on the one hand, and English on the other, in terms of the standing which it enjoyed in this period. To date few works which describe identity and language have devoted space to Scots simply because the language enjoys little status today. This is in marked contrast to the acknowledgement which other ethnic and linguistic identities now receive as a result of changing political circumstances. The processes which led to marginalization and assimilation in the British Isles were not confined to Celtic-speaking peoples alone but also affected the Germanic speakers of the Lowlands, Ulster and the Northern Isles. The Lowlanders were certainly a distinct ethnic group, with a distinct speech form, but to assume that they simply saw their world in terms of 'Anglo-Saxon' *versus* 'Celtic', is facile. I hope that my own endeavours will encourage historians to dig more deeply into the role and perceptions of the Scots language and perhaps go some way to according it a proper recognition in historiography.[74]

73 Alexander Ross (1699–1784) was a North-East Scot and lived most of his life in the county of Forfarshire (now Angus). He was writing in opposition to the school of Scots as favoured by Ramsay and others. See David Hewitt, 'The ballad world and Alexander Ross', in David Hewitt and Michael Spiller (eds), *Literature of the North* (Aberdeen, 1983), pp. 42–54. 74 Scots is now recognized officially by the UK government under Part II of the European Charter for Regional or Minority Languages, ratified by the UK in 2001; in addition, the Scottish parliament, and Scottish Office, both recognize Scots as one of the older indigenous languages of Scotland, and the language has (since 1996) been permitted as a study option within the 5–14 school curriculum in Scotland.

'Ravelling narratives': Irish and Scottish Gaelic life stories compared

ALAN TITLEY

The Irish rural autobiography has been central to literature in Ireland for nearly a hundred years. In fact, for all the woolly tourist talk about the imaginative Celt and his harking after the otherworld and the misty high brazils of the past, the greatest chunk of popular literature from Charles J. Kickham's *Knocknagow* (1879) to the latest emanation from the happy-clappy bestselling uncomplicated narratives of Alice Taylor has been rooted and rooting in a rural life which certainly existed for some as an idyllic time and clime, but which for others was the pits of rottenness and despair. Whatever these narratives were, they were not imaginative. They were not infused with imagination no matter how many lies they told. They were documentary to the deep. Even Frank McCourt's awful, but determinedly not aweful, *Angela's Ashes* for all its attempts at the imaginative recreation of the horrors of Limerick in the mid-twentieth century can never approach the reality of piss poor depravity that was rural Ireland at that time. Whatever the depravity of life was as he described, the reality must have been a great deal worse, especially of living in Limerick.

Autobiographies in Irish faced the same difficulties. They were caught between the necessity of documenting a life which had ne'er been expressed before, and recreating an idyllic society which might serve as a blueprint for a new Ireland. Commentators, otherwise known as literary critics, have struggled between the silly of documentary and the carapace of language.

The one big thing that these personal histories have in common is they are the stories of the common people, rather than apologetics for those who lived and lorded it in the big house. Those who delved and spun and fished and ploughed opened their throats and shouted their piece of history, more or less for the first time. They also have in common the fact that they were written, or composed, or narrated by Irish and Gaelic[1] speakers living on the western shores of their respective countries. They also shared a similar way of life and a mental furniture well-stocked with mutually recognizable points of reference.

---

1 In this essay I refer to the language in Ireland as Irish, and that in Scotland as Gaelic. This is the accepted nomenclature and is more historically accurate. Although the Gaelic language of Scotland was also known as 'Irish', or 'Scottish', or even 'Erse', Gaelic has been the most

There is no need here to belabour the common heritage of poets, scribes and musicians that travelled between the two realms up to the great rupture of the sixteenth and seventeenth centuries. Nor their similar political loyalties in following the dubious Stuarts in song, in battle and in mutual destruction. A new nationalism grew in Ireland which in turn took sectarian, Catholic separatist and republican twists, while Gaelic Scotland was slowly drawn into the entire British project. A lingering memory remained in the nineteenth century of some kind of shared past, but receded as the old bog road led to some kind of independence for most of Ireland, and the mist rolled in from the sea over the Mull of Kintyre dampening the landscape and burying the tradition. It is true that a Scottish poet such as Uilliam Mac Dhuinnshléibhe or William Livingston composed a poem on Ireland entitled 'Eirinn a' Gul' ('Ireland Weeping') treating of the destruction of the country before and after the famine, and that Màire Mòr nan Oran gained some measure of strength from the Irish struggle for the land. But these were isolated examples and not representative at all of the gap that had opened between the two countries.

In 1977 RTE broadcast a series of lectures with the engaging title of 'The Pleasures of Gaelic Literature', where 'Gaelic', of course, meant Irish. It was later published in book form.[2] It consisted of ten essays by people not always known for their professional or artistic engagement with literature in Irish. They were asked to choose and to comment on their favourite prose work. Seven out of the ten chose an autobiography, or in one case, a novel which commented on them. This seems an extraordinary number when we realize the wealth of novels and short stories and other creative fiction which has been published in Irish in the twentieth century. It would be difficult to call to mind any other western literature where a group of educated and literary people chose biographies as seventy per cent of their best literature. In fact, it would be quite bizarre.

The question therefore pops up as to why biography, or some kind of personal history was central to Irish literature for so long. The answer can only be that the 'Gaeltacht' was 'discovered' by the new philosophy of the Gaelic revival, which was part of the general 'great stir of thought' which happened in the country from the 1880s onwards. This 'discovery' of the Gaeltacht was paradoxically both modernist and romantically backward-looking: it was modernist in so far as it was trying to recreate a new country out of the shards of the old; and backward-looking in as much as there always was the temptation to view the rural population as inhabiting a more innocent and more beautiful world. For where else could a new Ireland begin

accepted form for a long period. The language has never really been called 'Gaelic' in Ireland, except by people who like to see it as not being fully Irish, and merely one strand in the entire tradition.   **2** John Jordan (ed.), *The pleasures of Gaelic literature* (Cork and Dublin, 1977).

except in a place that had never succumbed to rampant Anglicization, and where would you find a place unsullied by the 'filthy modern tide'?

The Irish language was seen as a defence against this wash upon our shores, 'a balm for this suffering society of ours, a salt for the corruption and crass materialism of our age, a refreshing breeze for the wearied and disgusted heart of the modern world' as one activist put it, and even as 'a language unpolluted with the very names of monstrosities of sin which are among the commonplaces of life in English-speaking countries'.3 The writer had obviously never spent too much time eavesdropping on ditches beyond the dance-hall on a Saturday night in a Gaeltacht area.

Even Yeats himself when he wasn't widening gyres and being haunted by spirits out of Anima Mundi had time to proffer that 'the civilisation that existed in the Irish language ... was an older and better civilisation which had been reeling under the shocks given to it by modern vulgarity everywhere' and that we had a 'duty to preserve (it) until the deluge had gone by'.4 Just because Yeats said it does not mean that it is not a load of old cobblers. Living in fancy hotels doesn't always get you to wear the spiritual flannels of the poor.

It is not too surprising, therefore, that we get a conflation between the language itself and the way of life of its most remote and destitute speakers. In the Irish autobiography we get the idea of both an unbesmirched language and an unbesmirched arcadia.

The most famous of the Irish autobiographies are well-known inside the country and not unknown outside. Many have been translated into English, and other world languages. Tomás Ó Criomhthain's *An tOileánach* ('The Islandman'), Muiris Ó Súilleabháin's *Fiche Blian ag Fás*, and Peig Sayers *Peig* all come from the Great Blasket island off the coast of Kerry, and although they are filtered through contrasting personalities, were composed or written in entirely different ways, and are charged with separate styles or energies, they appear to delineate a common way of life which was on the verge of passing away. We have not dissimilar personal stories from every other Gaeltacht, particularly from Donegal. These Ulster autobiographies only differ to the extent that the generation that wrote them commonly spent years or seasons working as cheap farm labourers in the fatlands of east Donegal or in the tougher scrapings of lowland Scotland.

There is a sense in which we can almost reconstruct a composite Gaeltacht autobiography which might include the tough circumstances in which the writer was born, his (or more rarely, her) going to school without a word of English and suffering for it, a description of work on land or on sea, a few storms thrown in to relieve the boredom, a shipwreck or two, a local tragedy, no, or little, mention of husband or wife, old age, and a longing look back.5

---

3 Quoted by Philip O'Leary in *The literature of the Gaelic revival*, p. 21.   4 Ibid. p. 32n.   5

On the surface, at least, Scottish Gaelic autobiographies seem to present
a very different case. There was no 'national' revival in Scotland which put
their language in the centre of things. The Gàidhealtachd was never seen in
any widespread way as being a treasure house of cultural revival, or a repos-
itory of aphoristic wisdom. The sense of the Scottish Gael still living in his
fastnesses and gasping to hough the cultural cattle down below still clings
unspokenly to the metropolitan life of Caledonia.

On a merely reductive quantitative and measurable count the differences
are also huge. Publishing in Gaelic was much more healthy during the nineteenth century than it was in Irish, it was 'the golden age of Gaelic printing'[6]
but unfortunately for our purposes it was largely composed of religious books
and works of poetry. In Irish, however, there was a massive growth in publishing from the 1890s onwards and most of these were of a secular nature.
We have, since then, maybe three score or more works in Irish that we may
call personal histories of the 'native' Gaeltacht kind, whereas in Scotland we
may lucky if we can drag that number up to ten. This is recognizing that the
definition, description, or account of what an autobiography or memoir or
personal history may me can be watery fluid and leaking all over. Put with
that, that the Irish works, as already mentioned, are seen as classics of their
kind, whereas the Scottish ones are largely unknown and mostly ignored.
Only one, to my knowledge, has been translated into English, or into any
other language.[7] Irish autobiography of this nature has a much longer pedigree whether we begin with An tAthair Peadar Ó Laoghaire's *Mo Sgéal Féin*
in 1915, or Tomás Ó Criomhthain's *An tOileánach* in 1929. Scottish Gaelic
autobiography does not really commence until Aonghus Mac'ill Fhialain's
(Angus McLellan) *Saoghal an Treobhaiche* in 1972. This is prescinding from
and shifting to one side Dúghall Bochannan's (Dugald Buchanan) spiritual
autobiography of 1834, which belongs to a different *genre*, and is much more
a mental than a physical or social journey.[8]

Despite this, there are striking similarities with the Irish biographies, particularly with regard to social life and customs. A similar poor life in bad circumstances with comparative power relations will throw up a likewisely syn-
onymity of reciprocation. MacLellan's description of their food could be
unmouthwateringly plucked from several Irish autobiographies:

This kind of autobiography was lovingly parodied by Myles na gCopaleen in *An béal bocht*
('The Poor Mouth') (Dublin, 1941). 6 Magnus Maclean, *The literature of the Celts* (London,
1902) p. 331. 7 Angus MacLellan, *The furrow behind me: the autobiography of a Hebridean
crofter* translated by John Lorne Campbell (1962, 1997). This is a translation of *Saoghal an
Treobhaiche* by Aonghus Mac'ill Fhialain (Aonghus Beag) 'ar a recòrdadh 's air a sgriobhadh le
Fear Chanaidh'. It was first published in the Celtic Studies journal *Lochlann 4* (1972). This
short translation is by the present author. 8 Dùghall Bochannan, *Beatha agus iompachadh
Dhùghaill Bochannan air a sgriobhadh leis fèin.* first published in 1834, but republished in 1844,
1863, 1868, 1872, 1877, 1882, 1889, 1893, 1898 and 1908.

> Agus 's e sin beatha bu mhutha a bh'aca as an amm, buntàta 's iasg. Bhìodh tì 'sa mhadaiann ann, aran is tì, buntàta is iasg air an dìnneir, brochan is bainne air an suipeir ...

> And this is how people lived at the time, potatoes and fish. Tea in the morning, bread an tea, potato and fish for dinner, porridge and milk for supper.[9]

He goes on to describe the making of home-baked bread in grinding detail, as well as other necessary rural ways of staying alive in a wild climate. Food, fishing, weather, the quotidian things of every day become the centre of the universe.

Eòs MacNìll recounts the early days at school where he only spoke Gaelic, but the system required that they must needs blabber in English:

> Nuair a bhitheamid a' cluich amuigh air feadh achadh na cluich bhitheamaid a' bruidhinn na Gàidhlig ri chèile 's cha robh dóigh air ar ceannsachadh aig an am sin idir. Dh'fheumainn-sa bruidhinn ri cuideiginn ann an Gàidhlig air neo cha bhruidhninn idir; agus dh'fheumadh cuideiginn bruidhinn rium ann an Gàidhlig air neo cha bhiodh fhios go robh iad a' bruidhinn rium fhìn ...

> When we were playing in the school yard we did used to speak Gaelic to one another, and there was no way we could be stopped at the time. I had to speak to somebody in Gaelic, or else I couldn't speak at all, and somebody had to speak to me in Gaelic or else I didn't know they were speaking to me at all.[10]

He goes on to tell of his struggles with the English language, and how even the teacher speaking to the dog in English helped him on his way. In other biographies we have the wide-eyed boys journey to the big town of Stornaway where the streets were paved with wonder,[11] not unlike the journey from the Blasket Island to Dingle, or from the Rosses to Dungloe. It is difficult to believe that these places were perceived to be both dens of iniquity and doors of opportunity for the likely local lads from the hills of the hinterland.

As in Irish, women's personal histories are more rare in Scottish Gaelic. The few that we have are not as detailed as that of Peig Sayers, but they tell

---

9 Mac'ill Fhialain, ibid., p. 10. 10 Eòs Mac Nìll (Eòs Nill Bhig), *Sgeul gu Latha, air ath-sgrìobhadh, eadartheangachadh 's a dheasachadh le Iain Seathach* (1987), p. 10. This is basically a collection of wonderful folktales, but there is a long autobiographical introduction by the author. The fact that he lived and died in Nova Scotia does not alter the similarities. The translation is by this writer. 11 Calum MacFhearghuis, *Suileabhan: sgeulachdan a eachdraidh-beatha Iain Mhic Leòid* (1983)

of a congruent life and a parallel mentality. Indeed that mentality may not be
entirely different from that of their men, as marriage and romantic love are
firmly put to one side in exchange for the call of biological necessity and the
need for getting on with normal life. Catrìona Nic Nèill's *Mo Bhrògan Ura*
('My New Shoes') tells of growing up in Barra, and working in 'menial' jobs
around Scotland and England. Suddenly and without warning she tells us:

> Aig deireadh na bliadhna 1940 bha dùil agam pòsadh fear às m'eilean
> fhèin, a bha mi eòlach air bhon bha sinn glè òg. Bha 'n soitheach air an
> robh e 'na bhòsun ri tighinn air ais mun àm sin.

> About the end of the year 1940, I felt the need to get married to a man
> from my own island, a person I knew since we were both young. The
> boat on which he was a bosun was coming back around this time.[12]

This is entirely reminiscent of Tomás Ó Criomhthain in the first edition of
An tOileánach where he meets his wife on one page, marries her on the next,
she bears him ten children on the same page, and she dies after that. Ealasaid
Chaimbeul's *Air mo Chuairt* ('On My Journey') is even more blunt: 'Sann a
thàinig e nis fainear dhomh pòsadh, oir bha mi air a dhol suas am bli-
adhnachan' / 'I noticed it was now time for me to get married, as I was getting on in years'.[13] No boxes of chocolates here, no golden shining bracelets,
no candle-lit dinners in a fancy restaurant. She is at least level with Peig and
we think that Róise Rua would have understood.[14]

Differences begin to appear in the treatment of religion, however. All of
the Irish biographies come from a Catholic community, most of the Scottish
from a Protestant, usually of the Presbyterian cast. Strangely enough, given
the virulent literature against the Catholic Church in much of Anglo-Irish
writing from Joyce, through McGahern to Dermot Bolger and beyond, very
little of this non-conformity comes through in Irish. But also, particularly in
the Gaeltacht autobiographies, religion does not loom large as a dominating
and oppressive presence. It is there in the language itself, in its prayers and
blessings, in its acceptance of *toil Dé*, the 'will of God', it is an unquestioning reality but not a threatening or coercing authority. It is a coat that is worn
with no rough edges, it is seamless with lived life. This may well have been
because of an unquestioning acceptance, as simple-minded sociologists often

12 Catrìona Nic Nèill, *Mo bhrògan ùra: Sgeulachd a beatha fhèin, ann am Barraigh, aig an ias-
gach, an Glaschù 's an Sasuinn* (1992), p. 69.   13 Ealasaid Chaimbeul, *Air mo chuairt* (Stornaway,
1982) p. 38.   14 Pádraig Mac Cnáimhsí, *Róise Rua*. This is one of the few autobiographies by
women in Irish, but in this case the hard life is lived on Aranmore Island off the coast of
Donegal, and also in Scotland. For a studied account of its genesis and accuracy, see, Breandán
Ó Conaire, 'Nótaí ar Fhaisnéis Bheatha as Árainn Mhór' in *Studia Hibernica*, 31 (2000–1), pp.
147–68.

propose, but is much more likely to be that the Catholic Church did not loom largely as an institution in their lives. Priests don't figure as much as peelers, or policemen, or excise officials, or schoolteachers, either as helpers or ogres in the Irish stories.

Scotland is different though. The Scottish church controls, destroys, excoriates and clobbers. Anybody who grew up under the oppression of institutional Catholicism in Ireland should try the Scottish experience on for size. One of the greatest Gaelic autobiographies is undoubtedly Aonghus Caimbeul's *A' suathadh ri iomadh rubha*[15] ('Struggling with many headlands'). It is written with cogency and passion, and in a high style of Gaelic that is tightly controlled in contrast with the angry expression of a life lived to the full, but with so much more to give. He is not going gentle into any good night, no way. Some of his most poetic broadsides are reserved for the church which tried to put sulphurous chains around his spirit and his culture:

> Ma bha aighear, sùgradh agus aotromas-inntinn mairsinn beò 'nar Gàidhealtachd sna làithean ud, cha b'ann a dheòin oide agus teagaisg na h-eaglaise. Cha robh càil de'n t-seann eòlas is ealain a dh'àlaich am measg ar sìnsearan a-nuas troimh na linntean, mar a bha ceòl, bàrdachd agus dannsa, nach robh air a mheas leotha truailleadh, peacadh, no mar a theireadh iad, cleasachd Shàtain.

> If there was joy, and fun and light-heartedness in the Gàidhealtachd in those days, it was despite the teachings and beliefs of the church. There wasn't one bit of the old knowledge that had grown up amongst us through the centuries, like our music, our poetry and dance that weren't seen as corrupting, sinful, or as they would say themselves, the tricks of Satan.[16]

There are more savage passages than that where he recounts the many names of the devil, only fifteen in one random passage, and he imagines that Satan must have abandoned the rest of the world entirely in order to concentrate on his own corner of Lewis. Other accounts emphasize the destruction of music, the hiding of fiddles in the corner of a room as if they were forbidden drugs, the furtiveness of fun on a Sunday.[17] One piece of folklore tells how a minister on the Isle of Skye forbade sex in case it would lead to dancing, and another said that they respected Jesus less because he allowed his followers to take an injured donkey out of a hole on the Sabbath. And yet,

---

15 Aonghus Caimbeul, *A' suathadh ri iomadh rubha: Eachdraidh a bheatha deasaichte le Iain Moireach* (1973). 16 Ibid., p. 36. English translation by the present writer. 17 James Watson, and Ellison Robertson (eds), *Sealladh gu Taobh: oral tradition and reminiscence by Cape Breton Gaels* (1987).

it was the Scottish Presbyterian Church, in all its splits and schisms, which was one of the strongest institutions in defence of the language *qua* language (forgetting about the culture bit) in the highlands and islands for most of the nineteenth and the twentieth centuries. It was certainly more active and more positive in promoting literacy and the importance of the native written word than the anglicizing Catholic Church was in Ireland.

The real cleavage between the Irish and the Scottish biographies happens in the realm of politics and travel. Whatever the reality of belief in Irish Gaeltacht areas, most personal histories were sponsored by a belief in the worth of the Irish political project. Independence was a good thing, and the dignity afforded them for the first time in hundreds of years added to their sense of themselves as Irish people and as Irish speakers. The Scottish sense of communal self takes a different shape. 'Gaels' they undoubtedly are, but they have no sense of ambiguous irony in being involved in the British imperial adventure. Ailean Friseal's lively account of the life of Sir Hector MacDonald is amazing in its uncritical depiction of the hero going out to serve some cause, without ever stopping to examine what that cause might be.[18] Hector's people were evicted from their homes in the great clearances of the highlands to make way for sheep and profits, and yet he served in an army which was doing the very same thing to 'natives' in Afghanistan, South Africa and the Sudan. Being beaten and thrashed in the political and military game at least has the possibility within it of accessing experience that is denied to the ever-conqueror. There is a massive cultural shock in reading of Cú Chulainn being summoned to the side of the imperial oppressor in Afghanistan, just because he was an icon of liberation for Irish nationalists from the self-same power. In the valleys of the Hindu Kush Hector becomes a Gaelic hero and is transformed in battle:

> 'Bha cuthach a' chath air, math dh'fhaoidte, coltach ris a' chruth a thainig air Cù Chulainn nuair a bha e ri sabaid' / 'The madness of battle possessed him, it seemed, just like the change of appearance of Cú Chulainn when he went into battle'.[19]

The difference resided also in the non-alignment of Scottish nationalism with Gaelic culture, and Scottish nationalism only ever timidly opposed the British wars. There are virtually no accounts in Irish of serving in what became known as 'The Great War', although it is never said what was great about it. Liam O'Flaherty fought for Britain in that conflict, but remained reticent enough about it throughout his life. Thousands of Irishmen did likewise, mostly for ill but maybe sometimes for good, but they also had the good sense not to flaunt their experiences. The Irish were not subtle enough to spot the difference between the German, Austro-Hungarian, British, Turkish,

18 Ailean Friseal, *Eachunn nan Cath: Eachdraidh-beatha an Ridire Eachunn MacDhomhnaill* (1979). 19 Ibid., p. 24.

or Russian greedy land grabs. A diary such as Murchadh Moireach's *Luach na Saorsa* would have been nearly unimaginable in Irish.[20] On the other hand, the bright voice of cynicism enters the conversation in Catrìona NicNèill's autobiography where she asks, 'Càite nis a robh ghlòir a bha ri tighinn leis a' bhuannachd?'/ 'Where now is the glory that was to come with victory?' and opines openly that the country that their men fought for had no time for them when they returned.[21]

The second great war receives a similar treatment. Ireland stays quiet under the blanket of the emergency, while the Scottish soldiers soldier far away and wander far away from the highland hills and the island hills and the green hills of their own. Several biographies are devoted entirely to service in the British Army. The most important of these are Dòmhnall Iain MacDhòmhnaill's *Fo Sgàil A' Swastika*[22] ('Under the shadow of the Swastika'), and Pòl Mac a'Bhreatunnaich's *Air Druim an Eich Sgiathaich*[23] ('On the back of the winged horse'). MacDhòmhnaill's is largely an account of his time in captivity in a German prisonor-of-war camp, and matches any film of such imprisonment in character and action. It is a tale of ingenuity and toughness told without any self-pity and with no small amount of humour, while Mac a'Bhreatunnaich's story is full of adventure and the comradeship of soldiery. Their experience is entirely foreign to the Irish story, unless there are personal histories of a similar nature out there still untold.

It seems, then, that the Irish and the Scottish biographies are linked together in their depiction of a 'peasant' life-style, and an analogous mentality. This derived from a shared history out of the past and of economic circumstances which pushed their speech communties to the edge of their national worlds. They also share a common heritage of language marginality in their greater societies, a marginality which ensured that they could not live their lives entirely through their mother tongue and which insisted that they should assimilate with their greaters and betters. The Irish experience began, at least, to turn some of this around and Irish Gaeltacht writers were afforded some place in a greater consciousness. In the canon of literature they may only have been grapeshot, but at least they made some impact. Scottish Gaelic writers, on the other hand, have never been seen to represent anything other than themselves. Further to that, Irish Gaeltacht autobiographies almost invariably stay at home. When they emigrate, they stay emigrated. The Scots return to their sheep after a life of adventure and tell of a world beyond the

20 Murchadh Moireach, *Luach na saorsa: leabhar latha bho àm a'chiad chogaidh.* Deasaichte le Alasdair I. MacAsgaill (1970). 21 NicNèill, op. cit. p. 25. 22 Dòmhnall Iain MacDhòmhnaill, *Fo Sgáil A' Swastika* . This was first published in 1974 by Club Leabhar, Inbhir Nis, and has recently been published with an English translation and accompanying CD of the text by Acair Teoranta, Stornaway. No date. 23 Pòl Mac a'Bhreatunnaich, *Air Druim an Eich Sgiathaich* (Stornaway, 1987).

highlands and islands. Their religion, also, seems to have had a more oppressive and meddling presence in their lives than their Irish counterparts,
although no doubt there were many for whom the brimstone of their church
was a fire of beauty in their lives. In politics, however, we see that the Scots
became part of the British system, almost without question, while the Irish
remained more stubbornly loyal to their own.

We might say that the Gaeltacht personal histories show two groups of
people united by language, economics and tradition, but divided by religion,
politics and war. The question might be asked, which of these clusters of
experience and consciousness is the more important?

Select bibliography

I. Adams & M. Somerville, *Cargoes of despair and hope: Scottish emigration to North America, 1603–1800* (Edinburgh, 1993).

I. Adamson, *The Cruthin* (Belfast, 1978).

J. Agnew, *Belfast merchant families in the seventeenth century* (Dublin, 1996).

A.J. Aitken, 'The pioneers of anglicised speech in Scotland: a second look', *Scottish Language*, 16 (1997), 1–36.

D.H. Akenson, *Half the world from home: perspectives on the Irish in New Zealand, 1860–1950* (Wellington, 1990).

—— *God's peoples* (New York, 1992).

G.R. Allen (ed.), *Scotland, 1938* (Edinburgh, 1939).

A. Aughey, 'The character of Ulster unionism', in P. Shirlow and M. McGovern (eds), *Who are 'the people'?* (London, 1997).

E.W.M. Balfour-Melville (ed.), *An account of the proceedings of the Estates of Scotland, 1689–90*, 2 vols (Edinburgh, 1954–5).

J.C. Beckett, *Protestant dissent in Ireland, 1687–1780* (London, 1946).

M. Bennett, *The Civil Wars in Britain and Ireland, 1638–1651* (Oxford, 1997).

Paul Bew, *Ideology and the Irish question* (Oxford, 1994).

E. Black (ed.), *Kings in conflict: Ireland in the 1690s* (Belfast, 1990).

G.F. Black, *Scotland's mark on America* (New York, 1921).

Roger Blaney, *Presbyterians and the Irish language* (Belfast, 1996).

P. Buckland, *Ulster unionism and the origins of Northern Ireland, 1886–1922* (Dublin, 1973).

J. Buckroyd, *Church and state in Scotland, 1660–1681* (Edinburgh, 1980).

E. Campbell, *Saints and sea-kings: the first kingdom of the Scots* (Edinburgh, 1999).

N. Canny, *Making Ireland British, 1580–1650* (Oxford, 2001).

L.E. Cochran, *Scottish trade with Ireland in the eighteenth century* (Edinburgh, 1985).

S.J. Connolly, R.A. Houston and R.J. Morris (eds), *Conflict, identity and economic development: Ireland and Scotland, 1600–1939* (Preston, 1995).

S.J. Connolly, *Religion, law and power: the making of Protestant Ireland, 1660–1760* (Oxford, 1992).

E.J. Courthope (ed.), *The journal of Thomas Cuningham of Campvere, 1640–1654* (Edinburgh, 1928).

I.B. Cowan, *The Scottish Covenanters, 1660–1688* (London, 1976).

C. Craig, *The history of Scottish literature*, 4 vols (Aberdeen, 1987).

W. Cramond (ed.), *The records of Elgin, 1234–1800* (Aberdeen, 1908).

L.M. Cullen, *An economic history of Ireland since 1660* (London, 1972).

Jane Dawson, 'Anglo-Scottish Protestant culture and integration in sixteenth century Britain', in Steven G. Ellis and Sarah Barber (eds), *Conquest and union: fashioning a British state, 1485–1725* (London and New York, 1995).

T.M. Devine, *Scotland's empire, 1600–1815* (London, 2003).

T.M. Devine (ed.), *Irish immigrants and Scottish society, 1790–1990* (Edinburgh, 1991).

T.M. Devine and D. Dickson (eds), *Ireland and Scotland, 1600–1850* (Edinburgh, 1983).

A. Devitt, *Standardizing written English: diffusion in the case of Scotland, 1520–1659* (Cambridge, 1989).

D. Dickson, *New foundations: Ireland 1660–1800* (Dublin, 2000).

—— *Arctic Ireland: the extraordinary story of the Great Frost and forgotten famine of 1740–41* (Belfast, 1997).

G. Donaldson, *Scotland. James V–James VII* (Edinburgh, various editions).

William Donaldson, *The language of the people: Scots prose from the Victorian revival* (Aberdeen, 1989).

—— *The Jacobite song: political myth and national identity* (Aberdeen, 1988).

Victor Edward Durkacz, *The decline of the Celtic languages* (Edinburgh, 1983).

J.R. Elder, *The Highland host of 1678* (Glasgow, 1914).

John Erskine and Gordon Lucy (eds), *Varieties of Scottishness: exploring the Ulster-Scottish connection* (Belfast, 1997).

James Fenton, *The hamely tongue: a personal record of Ulster-Scots in County Antrim* (Belfast, 2000).

—— *Thonner and thon* (Belfast, 2000).

Richard J. Finlay, *Independent and free: Scottish politics and the origins of the Scottish National Party, 1918–1945* (Edinburgh, 1994), pp. 29–71.

P. Fitzgerald and S. Ickringill (eds), *Atlantic crossroads: historical connections between Scotland, Ireland and North America* (Newtownards, 2001).

M. Flinn, Scottish *Population history from the seventeenth century to the 1930s* (Cambridge, 1977).

H.J. Ford, *The Scotch-Irish in America* (New York, 1941).

Lyndon Fraser, *To Tara via Hollyhead: Irish Catholic immigrants in nineteenth century Christchurch* (Auckland, 1997).

Sir W. Fraser, *The Melvilles, earls of Melville, and the Leslies, earls of Leven*, 3 vols (Edinburgh, 1890).

E. Furgol, *A regimental history of the Covenanting armies* (Edinburgh, 1990).

Alasdair Galbraith, 'The invisible Irish? Rediscovering the Irish Protestant tradition in colonial New Zealand' in Lyndon Fraser (ed.), *A distant shore: Irish migration and New Zealand settlement* (Dunedin, 2000).

Bruce R. Galloway & Brian P. Levaeck (eds), *The Jacobean Union: six tracts of 1604* (Scottish History Society, Edinburgh, 1985).

R. Gillespie, *Colonial Ulster. the settlement of East Ulster, 1600–1641* (Cork, 1985).

J. Goodare, *State and society in Early Modern Scotland* (Oxford, 1999).

—— 'The Scottish parliament of 1621', *Historical Journal*, 38 (1995), 29–51.

B. Graham (ed.), *In search of Ireland* (London, 1997).

William Grant (ed.), *The Scottish national dictionary* (Edinburgh, 1931).

Robert J. Gregg, *The Scotch-Irish dialect boundaries in the province of Ulster* (Ottawa, 1985).

—— 'Scotch-Irish urban speech in Ulster', in G.B. Adams (ed.), *Ulster Dialects: an introductory symposium* (Cultra, 1964) pp. 163–92.

—— 'The Scotch-Irish dialect boundaries in Ulster', in Martyn Wakelin (ed.), *Patterns in the folk speech of the British Isles* (London, 1972), pp. 109–39.

G. Hamilton, *A history of the house of Hamilton* (Edinburgh, 1933).

C.A. Hanna, *The Scotch-Irish or the Scot in North Britain, North Ireland, and North America* (New York, 1902).

J. Harrison, *The Scot in Ulster: sketch of the history of the Scottish population of Ulster* (Edinburgh, 1888).

I. Herbison, Ivan, "The rest is silence': some remarks on the disappearance of Ulster-Scots poetry', in John Erskine and Gordon Lucy (eds), *Varieties of Scottishness: exploring the Ulster-Scottish connection* (Belfast, 1997) pp. 129–45.

John Hewitt, *The rhyming weavers and other country poets of Antrim and Down* (Belfast, 1974).

George Hill, *Historical account of the Plantation in Ulster, 1608–1620* (Belfast, 1873).

P. Hopkins, *Glencoe and the end of the Highland War* (Edinburgh, 1998 edition).

Dauvit Horsbroch, 'Nostra Vulgari Lingua: Scots as a European language, 1500–1700', *Scottish Language*, 18 (1999), 1–16.

A. Hughes, *The causes of the English Civil War* (London, 1992).

Abraham Hume, 'Ethnology of the counties of Down and Antrim', *Ulster Journal of Archaeology*, Series 1:4 (1856), 154–63.

—— 'The elements of population in Down and Antrim, illustrated by the statistics of religious belief', *Ulster Journal of Archaeology*, Series 1:7 (1859), 116–30.

John Hume, *Personal views: politics, peace and reconciliation in Ireland* (Dublin, 1996).

A. Norman Jeffares, *Anglo-Irish literature* (Dublin, 1982).

Charles Jones, *A language suppressed: the pronunciation of the Scots language in the 18th century* (Edinburgh, 1995).

Billy Kay, *Scots the mither tongue* (Alloway, 1973).

W.P. Kelly (ed.), *The sieges of Derry* (Dublin, 2001).

J. Kenyon & J. Ohlmeyer (eds), *The Civil Wars: a military history of England, Scotland and Ireland, 1638–1660* (Oxford, 1998).

W.D. Killen (ed.), *A true narrative of the rise and progress of the Presbyterian Church in Ireland by the Reverend Patrick Adair* (Belfast, 1866).

P. Kilroy, 'Radical religion in Ireland, 1641–1660', in J. Ohlmeyer (ed.), *Ireland from independence to occupation, 1641–1660* (Cambridge, 1995).

John M. Kirk, 'Ulster Scots: realities and myths', *Ulster Folklife*, 44 (1998), 69–93.

J. Kirk (ed.), *The records of the synod of Lothian and Tweeddale: 1589–96, 1640–1649* (Edinburgh, 1977).

W.T. Latimer, *A history of the Irish Presbyterians* (Belfast, 1902).

P. Lenihan (ed.), *Conquest and resistance: war in seventeenth-century Ireland* (Leiden, 2001).

G. Leyburn, *The Scotch-Irish: a social history* (Chapel Hill, N.C., 1962).

W. Lithgow, 'Scotland's tears in his countreyes behalf, 1625', 6, in J. Maidment (ed.), *The poetical remains of William Lithgow, the Scottish traveller, 1618–1660* (Edinburgh, 1863).

W.T. Lorimer, 'The persistence of Gaelic in Galloway and Carrick', *Scottish Gaelic Studies*, 6 (1949/51), 114–36; 7: pp. 26–46.

Linde Lunney, 'Ulster attitudes to Scottishness: the eighteenth century and after', in Ian S. Wood (ed.), *Scotland and Ulster* (Edinburgh, 1994).

Michael Lynch, 'James VI and the Highland problem', in J. Goodare & M. Lynch (eds), *The reign of James VI* (East Linton, 2000).

—— *Scotland: a new history* (London, 1991).

P. Mac a'Bhreatunnaich, *Air Druim an Eich Sgiathaich* (Stornoway, 1987).

C. Macafee (ed.), *Concise Ulster dictionary* (Oxford, 1996).

W.A. Macafee, 'The movement of British settlers into Ulster in the seventeenth century', *Familia*, 2 (1992) 94–111.

Charlotte Macdonald, *A woman of good character: single women as immigrant settlers in nineteenth-century New Zealand* (Wellington, 1990).

Lilian MacQueen, 'The last stages of the older literary language of Scotland: a study of the surviving Scottish elements in Scottish prose, 1700–1750', unpublished Edinburgh University PhD thesis, 1957.

Donald M. MacRaild, *Irish immigrants in modern Britain, 1750–1922* (Basingstoke, 1999).

A.I. Macinnes, *Clanship, commerce and the house of Stuart, 1603–1788* (East Linton, 1996).

P.H.R. Mackay, 'The reception given to the Five Articles of Perth', *Records of the Scottish Church History Society*, 19 (1975–77), 185–201.

J.N.M. Maclean, *The Macleans of Sweden* (Edinburgh, 1971).

Magnus Maclean, *The literature of the Celts* (London, 1902).

Ian McBride, 'Ulster and the British Problem', in R. English and G. Walker (eds), *Unionism in modern Ireland: new perspectives on politics and culture* (Basingstoke, 1996).

—— *The Siege of Derry in Ulster Protestant mythology* (Dublin, 1997).

G. McIntosh, *The force of culture: unionist identities in twentieth century Ireland* (Cork, 1999).

P.G.B. McNeill & H.L. MacQueen (eds), *Atlas of Scottish history to 1707* (Edinburgh, 1996).

David McRoberts (ed.), *Modern Scottish Catholicism, 1878–1978* (Glasgow, 1979).

Anneli Meurman-Solin, 'Differentiation and standardization in Early Scots', in Charles Jones (ed.), *The Edinburgh history of the Scots language* (Edinburgh, 1997), pp. 3–23.

William S. Marshall, *The Billy Boys: a concise history of Orangeism in Scotland* (Edinburgh, 1996).

Kerby A. Miller, Arnold Schrier, Bruce D. Boling, and David Noel Doyle, *Irish immigrants in the land of Canaan: letters and memoirs from colonial and revolutionary America, 1675–1815* (New York, 2003).

M. Moireach, *Luach na saorsa: leabhar latha bho àm a'chiad chogaidh*, Deasaichte le Alasdair I. MacAsgaill (1970).

J. Mokyr, *Why Ireland starved: a quantitative and analytical history of the Irish economy, 1800–1850* (London, 1983).

John Montague (ed.), *The Faber book of Irish verse* (London, 1974).

M. Montgomery, 'The anglicization of Scots in early seventeenth-century Ulster', in G. Ross Roy and Patrick Scott (eds), *The language and literature of Early Scotland* (Studies in Scottish Literature 26), pp. 50–64.

—— 'The position of Ulster-Scots', in *Ulster Folklife*, 45 (1999), 86–104.

—— and Robert Gregg, 'The Scots language in Ulster', in Charles Jones (ed.), *The history of Scots* (Edinburgh, 1999) pp. 569–622.

John Morrill, 'Three Stuart kingdoms 1603–1689', in John Morrill (ed.), *The Oxford history of Tudor and Stuart Britain* (Oxford and New York, 1996).

S. Murdoch (ed.), *Scotland and the Thirty Years War, 1618–1648* (Leiden, 2001).

David Murison, 'The future of Scots', in Duncan Glen (ed.), *Whither Scotland?: a prejudiced look at the future of a nation* (London 1971), pp. 159–77.

Máiread Nic Craith, *Plural identities, singular narratives: the case of Northern Ireland* (Oxford, 2002).

J. Ohlmeyer, *Civil War and Restoration in the three Stuart kingdoms: the career of Randal MacDonnell, marquis of Antrim, 1609–1683* (Cambridge, 1993).

E.L. Parker, *The history of Londonderry* (Boston, 1851).

G.L. Pearce, *The Scots of New Zealand* (Auckland, 1976).

M. Perceval-Maxwell, *The Scottish migration to Ulster in the reign of James I* (London, 1973).

—— 'Ireland and Scotland 1638–1648', in J. Morrill (ed.), *The Scottish National Covenant in its British context 1638–1651* (Edinburgh, 1990), pp. 193–211.

T. Pitcairn (ed.), *Acts of the General Assembly of the Church of Scotland, 1638–1842* (Edinburgh, 1843).

John Prebble, *The Darien disaster* (Edinburgh, 1978).

Hugh Robinson, *Across the fields of yesterday: memories of an Ulster Scots childhood in the Ards* (Belfast, 2000).

P. Robinson, *The Ulster Plantation: British settlement in an Irish landscape, 1600–1670* (Dublin, 1984).

—— (ed.), *The country rhymes of James Orr, the bard of Ballycarry* (Folk Poets of Ulster Series, vol. 2) (Bangor, 1993).

—— *The back streets o the Claw* (Belfast, 1999).

—— *Ulster Scots: a grammar of the traditional written and spoken language* (Newtownards, 1997).

—— 'The Scots language in seventeenth-century Ulster', *Ulster Folklife*, 35 (1989), 86–99.

P. Roebuck (ed.), *Plantation to Partition: essays in Ulster history in honour of J.L. McCracken* (Belfast, 1981).

A.M. Scott, *Bonnie Dundee: John Graham of Claverhouse* (Edinburgh, 1989).

S.W. Singer (ed.), *The correspondence of Henry Hyde, earl of Clarendon and of his brother Laurence Hyde, earl of Rochester; with the diary of Lord Clarendon from 1687 to 1690, containing minute particulars of the events attending the Revolution: and the diary of Lord Rochester during his embassy to Poland in 1676*, 2 vols (London, 1828).

J.G. Simms, *The Williamite confiscation in Ireland, 1690–1703* (London, 1956).

T.C. Smout (ed.), *Scotland and Europe, 1200–1850* (Edinburgh, 1986).

T.C. Smout, N.C. Landsman and T.M. Devine, 'Scottish emigration in the seventeenth and eighteenth centuries' in N. Canny (ed.), *Europeans on the move: studies on European migration, 1500–1800* (Oxford, 1994), pp. 76–113.

D. Stevenson, 'Conventicles in the Kirk, 1619–37: the emergence of a Radical party', in D. Stevenson (ed.), *Union, revolution and religion in seventeenth-century Scotland* (Aldershot, 1997), pp. 97–114.

—— *The Scottish revolution, 1637–1644: the triumph of the Covenanters* (Newton Abbot, 1973).

—— *Highland warrior: Alasdair MacColla and the Civil Wars* (Edinburgh, 1980).

W. Stevenson (ed.), *The Presbyterie Booke of Kirkcaldie being the record of the proceedings of that presbytery from the 15th day of April 1630 to the 14th day of September 1653* (Kirkcaldy, 1900).

C.S. Terry, *John Graham of Claverhouse, viscount of Dundee, 1648–1689* (London, 1905).

—— *The Pentland Rising and Rullion Green* (Glasgow, 1905).

Loreto Todd, *Words apart: a dictionary of Northern Ireland English* (Gerrards Cross, 1990).

—— 'Ulster Scots', in Tom McArthur (ed.), *The Oxford companion to the English language* (Oxford, 1992), pp. 1087–88.

G.M. Trevelyan, *A shortened history of England* (Baltimore, 1959).

G. Walker, *Intimate strangers: political and cultural interactions between Scotland and Ulster in modern times* (Edinburgh, 1995).

Oonagh Walsh, *Ireland abroad: politics and professions in the nineteenth century* (Dublin, 2003).

J. Watson, and E. Robertson (eds), *Sealladh gu Taobh: oral tradition and reminiscence by Cape Breton Gaels* (1987).

I.D. Whyte, *Scotland before the industrial revolution: an economic & social history, c.1050–c.1750* (London, 1995).

Keith Williamson, 'Lowland Scots in education: an historical survey, Part I', *Scottish Language*, 1 (autumn 1983), p. 57.

C.W.J. Withers, *Gaelic in Scotland, 1698–1981: the geographical history of a language* (Edinburgh, 1984).

Ian S. Wood (ed.), *Scotland and Ulster* (Edinburgh, 1994).

J.R. Young, 'The Scottish response to the Siege of Londonderry, 1689–90', in W. Kelly (ed.), *The sieges of Derry* (Dublin, 2001), pp. 53–74.

—— 'The Scottish parliament and European diplomacy, 1641–1647: the Palatine, the Dutch Republic and Sweden', in S. Murdoch (ed.), *Scotland and the Thirty Years War, 1618–1648* (Leiden, 2001), pp. 77–106.

—— J.R. Young, *The Scottish parliament, 1639–1661: a political and constitutional analysis* (Edinburgh, 1996).

M. Young (ed.), *The parliaments of Scotland: burgh and shire commissioners*, vol. 1 (Edinburgh, 1992).

O. Zimmer, *Nationalism in Europe, 1890–1940* (Basingstoke, 2003).

Contributors

RICHARD FINLAY is Director of the Research Centre in Irish and Scottish History at the University of Strathclyde. His latest book is *Modern Scotland, 1914–2000* (London, 2004).

PATRICK FITZGERALD has worked at the Ulster-American Folk Park, Omagh, Northern Ireland since 1990. He held the position of Curator of Emigration History before joining the Centre for Migration Studies, on the same site, in 1998. As Lecturer and Development Officer at CMS, Dr Fitzgerald oversees an MSc programme in Irish Migration Studies which is accredited by the Queen's University Belfast. In 1994 he was awarded his PhD by the Queen's University Belfast and has published a number of articles on different aspects of Irish Migration.

DAVID HORSBURGH/Dauvit Horsbroch is currently an Honorary Research Fellow at the AHRB Centre for Irish and Scottish Studies. His research has concentrated on aspects of Scottish identity, particularly in relation to the Lowland Scots-speaking community, and he has written numerous articles in and on the Scots language. He has also focused on seventeenth/eighteenth century Scottish history and has contributed most recently to the *Oxford Companion to Scottish History* and the *New Dictionary of National Biography*. As well as being a past President (1999–2000) of the Scots Language Society, he is a contributor to the AHRB Forum for Research into the Languages of Scotland and Ulster, and is a member of the Cross-party Group on the Scots Language in the Scottish Parliament.

KERBY A. MILLER, Professor of History, University of Missouri holds a PhD from the University of California, Berkeley. He has been Senior Fellow at the Institute of Irish Studies, Queen's University Belfast, 1977–8 and Visiting Professor, QUB, 1985–6, and at Glucksman Ireland House, New York University, 2002. His most recent publication is *Irish Immigrants in the Land of Canaan: Letters and Memoirs from Colonial and Revolutionary America, 1675–1815*, co-edited with Bruce D. Boling, Arnold Schrier, and David N. Doyle (New York, 2003).

MICHAEL MONTGOMERY is Distinguished Professor Emeritus of English at the University of South Carolina. At present he serves as President of the Ulster-Scots Language Society, Honorary President of the Forum for Research on the Languages of Scotland and Ulster, and President of the American Dialect Society. He has written extensively on the English of the American South, most recently publishing a comprehensive historical dictionary of southern Appalachian speech. Since 1988 he has researched the English and Scots of Ulster and Scotland, with special emphasis on their historical development and their contribution to American English.

STEVE MURDOCH gained his PhD from Aberdeen University in 1998. He has published widely on aspects of British and Irish relations with Northern Europe and produced an online database of some 8,000 Britons and Irishmen in Scandinavia in the seventeenth century. His books include the edited collection *Scotland and the Thirty Years War, 1618–1648* (Leiden, 2001) and the monograph *Britain, Denmark-Norway and the House of Stuart, 1603–1660* (East Linton, 2003). He is currently Lecturer in Scottish History at the University of St Andrews.

MÁIRTÍN Ó CATHÁIN was awarded his doctorate in 2001 for a thesis on 'The Fenian movement in Scotland, 1858–1916'. Dr Ó Catháin is currently employed by the Institute of Ulster Scots Studies at the University of Ulster as a research assistant. His research interests are chiefly in the field of Irish labour and radical history, the Irish in Scotland, women's history, and local history.

JOCK PHILLIPS is the General Editor of Te Ara, the Online Encyclopedia of New Zealand in the Ministry for Culture and Heritage. He took up this position after serving for 13 years as New Zealand's Chief Historian. Jock Phillips has taught American and New Zealand History at Victoria University, where he founded and was the first Director of the Stout Research Centre for New Zealand Studies. He has written or edited ten books on New Zealand history, of which the best known is *A Man's Country: The Image of the Pakeha Male – A History*.

ALAN TITLEY is Head of the Irish Department, St Patrick's College, Dublin City University. Author of novels, stories, plays, film scripts and literary scholarship. He also writes a weekly column for the *Irish Times* on cultural and current affairs.

GRAHAM WALKER was born and educated in Glasgow and is currently Reader in Politics at Queen's University of Belfast. He is the author of *Intimate Strangers: Political and Cultural Interaction between Scotland and Ulster in Modern Times* (John Donald, 1995), and *A History of the Ulster Unionist Party: Protest, Pragmatism and Pessimism* (Manchester University Press, 2004).

JOHN R. YOUNG is a graduate of the University of Glasgow and is a Senior Lecturer in History at the University of Strathclyde, where he lectures in early modern Scottish History. His research interests include the pre-1707 Scottish Parliament, the Scottish Covenanters and Scotland and Ulster in the seventeenth century. He is the editor of *Scotland and Ulster c.1585–1700: Politics, Religion and Identity* (Four Courts Press, forthcoming 2005).

Index

Covenanting rebellion in Scotland,
  1679, 20, 21
Cowan, I.B., 20n, 21n
Craig, Sir Thomas, 158, 159
Crawford, John, 71
Crawford, W.H., 81n
Cullen, L.M., 78n, 82, 83n
Cunningham, Thomas, emissary to
  United Provinces, 29f, 90

da Costa, J.N., Swedish agent in
  Ireland, 96
Dalserf, Scottish place-name, 92
Danish, 146; Danish troops landing in
  Scotland, 24
Darien, Central America, expedition to,
  75, 77, 123
Daultry, S., 78n
Davis, R., 68n
Dawson, Jane, 143, 144n
de Vaudreuil, Marquis, governor of
  Québec, 112
Derry Celtic, football club, 53
Derry City Council, 8
Derry Reunion Committee in Glasgow,
  50
Devaney, Martin, AOH member, 49
Devaney, Thomas, bomber, 48f
Devine, T.M., 32n
Devitt, A., 126n
Diamond, Charles, Glasgow Irish press
  baron, 52
Diamond, William, IRB man, 52
Dickson, David, 71, 76, 78n, 82, 83n
Dickson, David, minister of Irvine, 14, 15
Dinsmoor, Robert, from Ballywattick,
  Co. Antrim, settler in New
  Hampshire, 117, 118
Donald of the Isles, 1545, 148
Donaldson, G., 13n
Donaldson, William, 127n, 152, 153n
Donegal County Library, 8
Douglas, Robert, minister, 19
Durkacz, V.E., 156n
Durrie, John, Scottish cleric, 89
Dutch Republic, 89

Edinburgh, 15, 18, 19, 26; University
  of, 112
Edmonstone, Archibald, of Duntreath,
  152
Edwards, O. Dudley, 52n
Elgin, presbytery of, 18, 19, 29
Elizabeth I, England, 149
Eriksonas, L., 87n
Erskine, Dr Robert, Jacobite at Russian
  court, 100, 102
Erskine, John, 3rd or 11th earl of Mar,
  100, 101
Espelland, A., 86n
European Bureau of Lesser-Used
  Languages (EBLUL), 129, 130
European Charter for Regional or
  Minority Languages, 160n

Fallon, J., 88n
Fedosov, D., 101n
Feeney, James, Home Ruler, 50
Fenian movement, 45, 47
Fenton, James, 127, 128n, 129n
Ferguson, Ensign Gideon, 'Danish'
  officer, 96
Ferguson, Sir Samuel, Ulster poet, 126,
  148
Fife, sheriffdom of, 19
Finlay, Richard, 8, 133–41, 135n
Fitzgerald, Patrick, 8, 27, 71–84, 86n
Fitzjames, James, duke of Berwick, 99
Fletcher, Andrew, of Saltoun, 28, 31
Flinn, M., 76n
Forbes, Arthur, lieutenant-colonel
  under Sir Frederick Hamilton, 1st
  earl of Granard, 22, 94
Ford, H.J., 84, 84n
Forrat, Margaret, 1st wife of Hugh
  Hamilton, widow of Sir James Spens,
  92, 93
Francis, Dermot, 8
Fraser, L., 65n, 66n, 68n
Fraser, Sir W., 26n, 30n
Free Church of Scotland, 35
Friseal, Ailean, 168
Frost, R., 87n